THE

TEACHER'S INSTITUTE;

OR,

FAMILIAR HINTS

TO

YOUNG TEACHERS.

BY

WILLIAM B. FOWLE.

"Not as though I had attained, or were already perfect."

FIRST NEW YORK EDITION.

A. S. BARNES AND COMPANY,
NEW YORK AND CHICAGO.

PREFACE.

SINCE the revival of education in Massachusetts, and, I may justly say, in the United States, in consequence of the establishment of our Board of Education, several valuable treatises on the important subject of Public Instruction have been published, and each in its way has done good service to the great cause; but still, it seems to me, there is room for the little volume which, perhaps, with more zeal than discretion, I am about to "cast upon the waters."

When I was invited by the Secretary of the Board of Education to take part in the instruction to be given at the Teachers' Institutes, which he proposed to hold in different parts of the State, I was not aware that my notions of the matter and manner of teaching were so different from those which prevailed. When, however, at the Institutes, some of the lessons which I had given at least a quarter of a century ago were viewed as novelties, and listened to with attention as unexpected as it was gratifying, I readily yielded to the repeated suggestion that it might aid the cause of education to publish such of my hints as could be written out, however inferior they must necessarily be to the living lessons that I had given in person.

These lessons were all given without any book, and usually without any notes; but this volume contains, I believe, a faithful sketch of them, with three of the many lectures that I delivered, and such additional remarks as occurred to me while the work was in progress. It makes no claim to be a complete treatise on education, for I had neither time nor inclination to attempt so high a task. It is no compilation, however, but a familiar record of my own experience, written in the midst of business, and with the printer at my heels,— two disadvantages which those only can fully appreciate who have been so incautious as to try a similar experiment.

Teachers' Institutes are assemblies of teachers, convened for the purpose of receiving and imparting instruction in regard to the art of teaching. They are, in fact, temporary Normal Schools, although, of course, conducted with less system and less preparation. The duty of calling them devolved upon the Secretary of the Board of Education, and he was present several days at each of the ten that were held in the autumns of 1845 and 1846, of which duty an interesting report is given in his Ninth Annual Report to the Board. The exercises consisted mainly of lessons given by some experienced teacher; of mutual instruction by the members of the Institute; of free discussions, in which the citizens, especially school-committee-men, often took part; and of lectures by gentlemen who had paid attention to the progress of public education in the State. Of course, as far as possible, teachers and lecturers on all systems, and on all educational subjects, were invited to teach and lecture, that the young teachers might see and hear all that was abroad, and be able to carry home many inventions that they would never, perhaps, have wrought out in their almost isolated districts. I spent a longer time than any other teacher at these Institutes, and probably said and did more than any other. I must, of course, have said many things about which there is a difference of opinion in this community, for I am accustomed to speak what I think, without asking whether the thought is popular or not. It is my duty, therefore, to declare, that neither the Board of Education, who honored me by the invitation, nor their Secretary, is accountable for any sentiments I uttered at the Institutes, and much less for any thing I have written in this volume. The truth of the matter is, that, until it was published, neither the Board nor its Secretary had any knowledge of the contents of this book, nor even of my intention to publish it.

THE

TEACHER'S INSTITUTE;

OR,

FAMILIAR HINTS

TO

YOUNG TEACHERS.

BY

WILLIAM B. FOWLE.

"Not as though I had attained, or were already perfect."

FIRST NEW YORK EDITION.

NEW YORK:
PUBLISHED BY A. S. BARNES & Co.,
111 & 113 WILLIAM STREET.

1866.

BLACKBOARDS.

In this volume, no set lesson on the use of blackboards is given, because the whole volume, from beginning to end, is a practical lesson on the use of this indispensable part of school apparatus.

THE TEACHERS' INSTITUTE.

READING.

THE first thing to be done is, in some way or other, to make the child acquainted with the Alphabet. Twenty years ago, there was but one way of doing this. The *names* of the letters were taught in connection with their forms, and as the teacher could only hear the child name the letters once or twice in the forenoon or afternoon, a task which occupied five or six minutes, the work was not usually accomplished in less than three months, and it not unfrequently required six.

When we consider how little amusement there is in learning the Alphabet in this way, we cannot help wondering at the patience of the little victims, and at the cruelty or awkwardness of the teacher, who cannot or does not invent some method by which the entrance to the path of knowledge may be made less painful to the little travellers.

We are by no means certain that there is a better way than to begin with teaching the *names* of the letters, but we are certain that this may be done in many ways that will engage the attention of the children, and be highly interesting to them.

We have said that six months are sometimes consumed in teaching a child the Alphabet; but this is a mistake,—*the time is consumed in idleness, and not in teaching.* If the child is allowed ten minutes a day, and this is more than the average allowance, the whole time allotted to a child in six months will be less than twenty-two hours, that is, less than one entire day. For, if the school is kept five days in a week, the number of hours devoted to the child in twenty-six weeks, or six months, will be only twenty-one hours and two thirds.

My custom was to give the child what minutes I could spare, and then to employ some older child in giving as much practice as the child desired. The consequence was, that the Alphabet was learned in a few weeks at furthest, but not, as it is usually learned, by *name* only. Let me explain my method more in detail, and illustrate it by an anecdote.

A year or two ago. I was unexpectedly detained in a village of Massachusetts, and knowing no person, I naturally wandered to the schoolhouse, where I am always sure to find a welcome. There were three schools in the building, and, by accident, I entered what was called the infant school. About sixty little children were present, and by no means idle, for it would be difficult to imagine a more busy scene. The teacher, a young lady of prepossessing appearance, was in one corner of the room, looking over the book of one of a small class, that was reading to her. The noise of the other children obliged her to place her ear close to the reader, and, of course, she could not properly overlook the rest of the school. Nothing that I had ever seen could equal the irregularities that I beheld, and had my life depended upon the effort, I could not have avoided laughing at the novel scene of fun and frolic before me. As soon as the teacher saw that a stranger was observing her, she left her class, and came forward to meet me. She blushed, and was evidently embarrassed; and I said to her, "You have a busy scene here." "Indeed I have," said she. "I never taught till yesterday, and I am so distracted that I must give up." I told her kindly that she was undertaking too much, for she should not attempt to teach until she had established something like order. "But the parents expect me to teach every child twice a day," said she, "and if I do not, I shall be censured. But," asked she, "how can I restore order amidst such confusion?" "I should introduce some general exercise," said I, "that will interest them all." "But the greater part of them do not know any thing," said she, "and how can they work together?" "I will show you," said I, "if you will excuse the liberty I take." I then tapped a few times gently on the desk, and all were silent. I kept on, and asked the children to tap as I did. They readily did so, and soon kept good time, and were highly pleased. Then said I, "Such of you as do not know the Alphabet, hold up your hands!" They did not know what I meant; but when I varied the question and said, "All who do not know the A, B, C, hold up your hands!" so many hands went up that it seemed as if some must have held up more than two. "Now," said I, "I wish all of you to go out, and stand before that large black-board." Sixteen or seventeen went out, and stood in that kind of confusion which Dr. Blair, I think, says is rather an element of the romantic than of the beautiful. I took the chalk and drew a large semi-circle in front of the board, drawing the chalk over such little feet as stood in the way, and when I told them to toe the chalk, there was such an eagerness to obey, that, for a minute or two, the whole class looked like a squad of adult recruits at their first drill. This movement attracted the attention of the rest of the pupils, and kept them still, so that the way was prepared for a lesson in the Alphabet.

I then printed a capital A on the board, and asked, " Does any one know what letter this is?" "A! A! A!" said half a dozen of them. "Yes, that is the first letter, said I, "and its name is A. Now let all say A." "A! A! A!" said they, in great confusion. "Now," said I, "say A all together, when I knock on the board." They did so ten or fifteen times. "Now," said I, "which of you can make an A like this on the board?" "I can! I can! I can!" said several. I gave the chalk to one of the largest, and she made an A thus: "Very well," said I, "but does not your A turn up its toes more than mine does?" "Yes, sir," said she, and rubbed both feet out, and tried to make them better. "Is not one leg longer than the other?" said I. "O, yes, sir!" said she, and rubbed off a portion of it. "Very well," said I; I see but one thing more. If you were sitting on that cross-bar," said I, "would not you slide down to one side?" "Yes, sir," said she, and rubbing out the bar, she made another that sloped as much to the right. When I asked if she would not slide the other way, she tried again, and made the cross-bar nearly horizontal.

"Very well, indeed!" said I. "Now, cannot some one take the chalk and make another A as good as that?" Half a dozen came forward. I selected a little boy, who had never learned a letter before, and who was the smallest child in the class. He took the chalk and made a large A, straddling over the head of the other, thus: "Bravely done!" said I; "that is a fine great A, but he is too large for the little one to carry. Can't you make him stand by the side of the other?" He gave me a knowing nod of assent, rubbed out the great one, and made another as I directed. I then called on every one of the class in turn to make an A, and not one failed to do so, and every time a new A was made, the whole class, at a signal given, called out, " A! A! A!" several times.

Then I proceeded to B; but, just then, a friend, who was travelling in company with me, entered, and seeing that the time was short, and the teacher quick to apprehend, I gave over my lesson, and asked my friend to set the whole school a singing. This exercise, of which the first line of the Multiplication Table was the subject, suited them wonderfully, and was continued several minutes. After a little familiar talk with the teacher, who by this time was relieved, and emboldened to question us, we departed. It is but justice for me to add, that, several months afterwards, as I was passing through that village, I looked in upon my young friend, and found her in the midst of an orderly school, without any fear of being disobeyed or distracted.

In teaching the alphabet, therefore, I should teach by classes, if more than one was ignorant of the letters, and I should require every letter to be made by every child. I should keep alive the interest of the child or the class by talking about the letters, as if they were things or persons, and thus I would impress upon the mind of the child, not only the general form, but the peculiarities of every letter. Children taught in this way would never do what I have seen done by many teachers; for, when I have attended Teachers' Institutes, which are conventions of teachers for mutual instruction, I have repeatedly asked each teacher to print an alphabet, and I have never failed to find some who formed the letters J, N, S, Z, thus, L , И, Ƨ, Σ. In one Institute of a hundred teachers, seven turned all these letters, and some others, the wrong way. Had they taught the alphabet as I propose, *they* would have learned as well as the children.

But I should not teach the whole alphabet before I began to use it. As soon as the child can make several letters, I keep them in a line at the top of the black-board; and, before a new letter is added, I make all the class call the name of each as I point at it. When they can make eight, and name them, or even sooner, I begin to combine them into words. Thus of A, B, C, D, E, F, G, H,—I make BAD, and pronounce it, requiring them to pronounce it after me. Then I ask them what BAD means; and, if a good instance occurs to me, I tell them of some BAD boy or BAD girl, and give them some caution or advice. Then, to teach them the sound of A, I tell them that, without the D, the word is pronounced BA; without B and D, it is A. Then I require the whole class to pronounce BAD, then BA, then A, several times, till the sound of A in BAD, and that of the B and D, are well understood. Then I write the word BAD at the top or side of the black-board, and proceed to form another word, say BED. This word must be pronounced, like the former, several times; then without the D; without B and D; and, finally, the sound of E alone must be given. Do not hurry to a new word till the old one is familiar, every sound of it.

Those who prefer to teach words before letters, or, with them, will like this method, which seems to be free from the objections that have been urged against the plan of teaching whole words, without separating them into their elementary letters and sounds.

To relieve the children, I would now give them some advice about going to BED, or rising betimes. Perhaps I should recommend a short prayer when they retire and rise, and should tell them what a prayer is, and how it should be made. A seed sown in this way may bear most precious fruit. The teacher may thus form many words. But three or four at a lesson will be enough; and at every new lesson, every word that the teacher has formed at the previous lesson must be formed by the children as a spelling lesson. The children will then see the use of letters in the formation of words, and will acquire some knowledge of what is called their *power* as well as of their *names* and *forms*.

I have sometimes even attempted to analyze the words thus formed, by spelling them by their *powers* or *sounds*, and not by their *names*. Some intelligent children very readily learn the powers in this way, and easily distinguish between the name in the alphabet and the sound in the word. To enable the teacher to do this, it may be convenient for him to have a few words of instruction in regard to the powers of the letters, and I subjoin them: —

TABLE OF VOWEL SOUNDS.

		Common School Speller.
1. A, as in Fate and in Pa-per, . . .	pp.	13, 31, 84
the same as		
AI in Aid and Rai-sin, .	"	24, 45, 148
AY in Day and Pay-ment, . . .	"	25, 47
EI in Feint and Hei-nous, . .	"	173
EY in They and Ey-ry, . .	"	25, 47
EA in Great and Steak, . .	"	82, 132

				Common School Speller.
2. A, as in Fat, and in Hab-it,		. . . . .	pp.	14, 32, 85
3. A, as in All, and in Wa-ter,		. . . . .	"	22, 44
the same as				
AU in Daub	and Cau-cus,	. .	"	24, 46, 129
AW in Dawn	and Aw-ful,	. .	"	25, 47
4. A, as in Fast, and in Pa-pa,		. . . . .	"	23, 43, 104
the same as				
AH in Ah!	and Se-lah,	. .	"	80, 113
EA in Heart	and Heark-en,	.	"	84
AU in Aunt	and Daunt-less,	.	"	174
5. A, as in Care, and in Wel-fare,		. . . .	"	46
the same as				
EA in Bear	and For-swear,	.	"	83
AI in Air	and Re-pair,	. .	"	46
1. E, as in Me, and in Sin-cere,		. . . . .	"	16, 33, 86
the same as				
EE in Beef	and A-greed,	. .	"	25, 48, 129
EA in Pea	and Ap-peal,	. .	"	26, 48, 130
IE in Field	and A-piece,	. .	"	27, 50, 130
EI in Ei-ther	and Con-ceit,	. .	"	27, 50, 139
I in Suite	and Po-lice,	. .	"	170
2. E, as in Met, and in Pro-tect,		. . . . .	"	16, 34, 86
the same as				
AI in Said	and A-gain,	. .	"	173
EA in Head	and Heav-en,	. .	"	82, 132
EI in Heif-er,	and Foreign,	. .	"	173
IE in Friend,		. . . .	"	173
1. I, as in Pine, and in Em-pire,		. . . .	"	17, 35, 87
the same as				
Y in Fly	and Re-ply,	. .	"	23, 42, 95
IE in Pie	and Be-lie,	. .	"	27
IGH in Fight	and De-light,	. .	"	56
2. I, as in Pin, and in Di-rect,		. . . . .	"	18, 37, 88
the same as				
Y in Lynx	and Sys-tem,	. .	"	42, 99, 120
EY in Val-ley	and Tur-key,	. .	"	43
AI in Vil-lain	and Cap-tain,	. .	"	174
IA in Mar-riage	and Par-lia-ment,		"	174
EI in Mul-lein	and For-feit,	. .	"	173
UI in Build	and Guilt-y,	. .	"	82

			Common School Speller.
1. O, as in No, and in Pro-mote,		pp.	19, 38, 89
the same as			
OA in Oak and Char-coal,		"	28, 52, 131
OE in Toe and Roe-buck,		"	29
OU in Soul and Poul-try,		"	29, 52
OW in Bowl and Dis-own,		"	29, 52
2. O, as in Not, and in A-dopt,		"	20, 39, 90
the same as			
A in Swan and Watch-ful,		"	45
3. O, as in Do, and in Im-prove,		"	55
the same as			
OO in Cool and Bal-loon,		"	28, 51
W in Wax and Wil-ling, (W, consonant)			
OU in You and Surtout,		"	179
4. O, as in Nor, and in For-lorn,		"	27, 50, 104
1. U, as in Cube, and in Re-buke,		"	21, 40, 90
the same as			
EW in Few and Sin-ew,		"	27, 49
EU in Feud and Neu-ter,		"	81
UE in Cue and Im-bue,		"	81
UI in Juice and Nui-sance,		"	82
2. U, as in Tub, and in A-dult,		"	21, 41, 91
the same as			
O in Monk, Li-on,	Fa-vor,	"	57, 123
OU in Touch, Coup-let,	Pi-ous,	"	58, 126
A in Vo-cal, Li-ar,	Or-gan,	"	105, 159
E in Her and	Bar-ber,	"	108
I in Sir and	Na-dir,	"	59
3. U, as in Bull, and in Pul-pit,		"	31, 55
1. OU, as in Bound, and in De-vour,		"	29, 53, 131
OW, as in Now, and in Crowd-ed,		"	30, 53, 132
2. OI, as in Oil, and in A-void,		"	30, 54, 132
OY, as in Boy, and in Em-ploy,		"	30, 54

TABLE OF CONSONANT SOUNDS

B,	in Bat	and Cab.
C, (soft)	in Cent	and Mince.
(hard)	in Cat	and Zinc.

CH,	(soft)	in Chin	and Patch.
	(hard)	in Chasm	and Conch.
	(like SH)	in Chaise	and Ma-chine.
D,		in Dot	and Bad.
F,		in Fan	and Chaff.
G,	(soft)	in Gin	and Dodge.
	(hard)	in Got	and Dog.
H,		in Hat	and Hop.
J,		in Jog	and Judge.
K,		in Kin	and Sick.
L,		in Lap	and Felt.
M		in Man	and Ham.
N,		in Nut	and Bun.
	(nasal)	in Tin-ker	and Un-cle.
P,		in Pig	and Hop.
Qu,	(as KW)	in Quit	and Quell.
	(as K)	in Ob-lique	and Li-quor.
R,	(rough)	in Rob	and Fer-ry.
	(smooth)	in Bare	and Care-ful.
S,	(hissing)	in Sun	and Lisp.
	(buzzing)	in Pins	and Was.
SH,		in Shop	and Bush.
T,		in Ten	and Flat.
TH,	(lisping)	in Thin	and Faith.
	(humming)	in This	and With.
V,		in Vest	and Give.
W,	(as OO)	in Was	and Wife.
X,	(as CS)	in Wax	and Text.
	(as GZ)	in Ex-act	and Ex-ult.
Y,	(as E long)	in Yet	and York.
Z,		in Zed	and A-maze.
	(as ZH)	in A-zure	and Bra-zier.

In using the preceding Tables, of course, there will be a great variety of methods, and a skilful teacher will hardly need any instruction. I shall content myself, therefore, with only a few general hints.

In attempting to teach the powers or sounds to mere beginners, the first column only of vowel sounds should be used, until the children are familiar with them. The teacher should first pronounce the sound, and require the class to pronounce after him; and, if any teacher is in doubt as to the precise sound of a letter, he may arrive at it by first pronouncing the word that contains the letter, say *Fate*, which consists of three sounds only, viz., F, A, T, the E being silent. Then let him drop the T, and pronounce F, A. Finally, dropping the F, let him pronounce the A alone. First drop what follows the vowel, then what precedes it, and then pronounce the bare vowel sound.

In teaching the consonants and combinations, a similar rule may be adopted. Pronounce the word Bat, for instance, then drop the T, then drop the A, and give the B, which will be found to be pronounced by the lips. Then pronounce CAB; omit the C and pronounce AB; then pronounce the B. In pronouncing the consonants, both columns of words may be used.

Some have divided these consonant sounds into sub-vowels and aspirates, the sound of the sub-vowels being heard, and that of the aspirates being only a whisper or breathing. Of this latter class are, F, H, K, P, S, T, SH, CH soft, TH sharp, and WH, which last is pronounced as if written HW, which approaches the sound of HOO. A little practice will make all these sounds very familiar. As it is very convenient to exhibit the tables to the class, and as the chalking of them on the black-board requires more time and occupies more space than the teacher can always spare, the author has caused them to be printed in large type on a sheet, to be hung up before the class.

After the pupils are familiar with the vowel and consonant sounds, the teacher may proceed to expose the unlucky richness of our alphabet, which enables us to indicate the same sound in a great variety of ways. This will lead him to notice the second column of characters in the table of vowel sounds, AI, AY, &c.

If our alphabet were what it ought to be, we should have one character or letter to represent each sound used in conversation, and but one, so that it would be impossible to spell a word with more than one set of characters; but, unfortunately, those who first wrote English, instead of inventing a new alphabet adapted to the English language, used that belonging to the Latin tongue, and did not do as well as they might have done even with that. It so happens, therefore, that several of the sounds of our language have no letter or character to represent them, and some of the characters that we have are obliged to represent more than one sound.

Thus, in the table, the character A has at least five sounds, and the first of them, viz., long A, may be represented by five other characters, viz., Ai, Ay, Ei, Ey, and Ea. Short I may be represented by six other characters, viz., Y short, Ey, Ai, Ia, Ei and Ui. The new method, called *Phonography*, if written, and *Phonotypy*, if printed, proposes to correct this evil, and to furnish one character for every sound, and to use but one. This reform has been attempted several times before, but without success ; for, besides the want of skill in forming the new characters, the educated class are reluctant to learn a new alphabet, and to have the published literature of our language become a dead letter. Whether the system of Phonotypy now offered for acceptance will succeed any better than its predecessors is doubtful; but, considering it almost certain that, for many years, it will not succeed to any considerable extent, I have prepared the tables of vowel and consonant sounds so that, while presenting no obstacle to the introduction of the new system, they will enable the teacher to make his pupils more thoroughly acquainted with the old.

It will be perceived that there are figures in the tables. These refer to pages in the Common School Speller of the author, where suitable lessons illustrating the sound may be found all prepared to the teacher's hand. In fact, his whole Spelling Book is but a practical lesson upon the tables, the classification of the words being based upon the fundamental sounds of the language, so that it is a comple system of Pronunciation as well as of Orthography. If it is used in the school, the teacher has only to direct the children to the page, and require them to spell and pronounce ; but, if the teacher alone has a copy of the Speller, he can chalk as many words as he pleases in addition to those in the tables, until the class have had sufficient practice.

After the child is acquainted with the alphabet and the elementary sounds, the question arises, "How must he be taught to read?" This is a question of some moment, and one, at first sight, might be excused for thinking it a difficult matter to answer it. I am inclined, however, to think that, with proper management, it is a very easy matter to make children read well. I should lay it down, however, as a prerequisite, essential to success, that *the teacher of reading should be a good reader himself.*

It has often been objected to this position, that children have been taught to read well by instructors who were very indifferent readers. That children have learned to read under such teachers I am willing to admit, because the fact is evident; but that they have been taught by their masters, I do not admit, for *I consider it impossible for any person to teach well what he does not understand.* If a child has sometimes learned to read or write, or cipher or sing, under an incompetent instructor, it has been, not *because* of the teacher, but *in spite* of him, and the question is, not how much has he learned, but how much more would he have learned had the instructor been fully prepared to teach him.

Before the child reads, some attention should be paid to his position. For a general rule, he should rest on the left foot, which should be a little turned out, and the right heel should be about opposite the middle of the left foot, and two or three inches from it; a position not unlike that which the dancing-masters call their second position. The book, unless very heavy, should be held in the left hand, opposite the chest, and never so high as to conceal the chin of the reader.

The reader should also be placed at a good distance from the teacher, for it is desirable that he should read so as to be heard across a common school-room, and few children will do this, if placed near the teacher, for they naturally calculate to make those whom they address hear them, and few children read aloud, if reading in a low voice is sufficient to make the teacher hear. If possible, the class should always stand while reading, and so stand that the teacher can see the entire person of every one, that he may watch their positions. At one of the Teachers' Institutes, I required every teacher to stand on a platform in full view of the others. It evidently cost many of them a great effort, and more than half of them had never been so exposed before. One young female, who had taught several summers, faltered at the first word she uttered, then trembled, dropped her book to her side, and burst into tears. She then made for her seat, but I stopped her, and encouraged her not to yield, but to do as she would advise a pupil to do in similar circumstances. She rallied, resolved, and in a minute or two read without further trouble. When called on in turn again, she came forward, and read with a sort of satisfaction at the victory she had obtained over herself. But, some children have weak voices, and cannot read so loud as their fellows. The teacher must, therefore, be careful to favor such voices, and, while he endeavors gradually to strengthen them, he must not rudely break or injure them by requiring too great an effort at first.

I am persuaded that nothing but the incompetency of teachers has led to the preparation of various series of reading books, intended, as far as possible, to help the pupil to learn independently of the master. Perhaps these books are doing a good work by calling the attention of the teacher to what he would otherwise neglect, but my experience satisfies me that, if the teacher knows how to read, those aids in which many school books abound, are worse than useless, because positively injurious.

The competent teacher needs but two rules by which to be guided in teaching his pupils to read. He must make them understand what is to be read, and then require them to read naturally. To expect a child to read what he does not understand is unreasonable, and yet nothing is more common. Until very lately, teachers were generally accustomed to pay no attention to the explanation of such pieces as are found in School Readers, and turned their attention almost entirely to the pauses and the pronunciation; important points, to be sure, but by no means the life-giving elements of good reading.

The teacher should consult all the practical works on the art of reading, but, as far as my observation goes, it is idle to put marks and rules and directions, whether by words or characters, into books intended to be read by children, for the plain reason that they seldom or never use them. The chief reading-book, when I was at school, was Scott's Lessons, and this was furnished with from fifty to a hundred pages of what were called Lessons in Elocution; but I never was required to read a word of them, and they were never explained to me, yet they cumbered the book, and increased its price one quarter at least. I am told by teachers that the same is the case with more modern books.

The child should, for a general rule, see as few things in school books, that he will not see in other books, as possible; for, when he leaves school, and the helps are withdrawn, he will be the less able to go alone, the more he has trusted to such aids. In conversation, children have no such assistance, and need none. They know what they say, and what they mean, and the pauses, emphasis, and inflections, are made without any effort, without any guide. To a great degree this would be the case in reading, if they fully understood the meaning of the piece, and the object of the writer. Not many months ago, I visited a primary school where the reading was entirely artificial. A girl, about eight years old, read a portion of a story which was chiefly dialogue, and she not only read both parts of the dialogue in a monotone, but in a monotone of the most unpleasant kind, for it was at the top of a disagreeably shrill voice. When she had done, I took the book and read a portion of it just as she had done, and when she and the whole class began to laugh, I, with the greatest gravity, asked them why they laughed. "Do I not read naturally?" said I. "No, sir," said they. "But, do I not read as that little miss did?" "Yes, sir," said they. "Well, would not the little boy and his mother in the story talk thus?" said I. "No, sir, they would laugh in each other's faces if they did." "Well," said I to the little girl who had previously read, "let me hear you read it just as the mother and boy would have spoken it." She did so, and not a pause or inflection needed correction. Here was a fault of the teacher, and not of the child. The teacher had allowed the child, and probably her whole school, to read in this unnatural manner, and the children had been led to suppose that reading and talking were different things altogether.

This fault, however, is not confined to schools. Most of our public readers, especially clergymen, early acquire one tone and manner for conversation, another for reading, especially for reading the Scriptures, and a third for prayer, without any thing of nature in either. I once made this remark to a worthy clergyman, now living, who offended beyond any man I ever knew in this respect, and his son-in-law at once said, what I had not dared to say to him, "Thou art the man." The venerable man could hardly believe it of himself, but the hint was not lost, for on the next Sabbath, he prayed and read and preached in his natural voice, and the people said he had never preached so well, though, not knowing the secret, they could not tell what the reason was, for they had heard the same sermon at least once before. I would, therefore, have the teacher a pattern worthy of imitation, in this matter of reading, and I would advise him to read much to his pupils. When I was a teacher, I had one exercise, to which more than to any other method of reading, I owed my success in this branch of instruction. I was accustomed to open school every morning with the reading of a portion of the Scriptures. At first, I read and required the pupils to listen, but this they did not always do. Then I required some one or more of them to read, but this failed to interest the rest. Then I read the verses alternately with them, but this broke up the connection of the text, and often produced a confusion of voices. At last I hit upon a plan which I pursued for fifteen years with the happiest effects. I required all the pupils to stand and read, not with me, but after me. I read as few words as the sense or the pauses allowed; and then stopping, they read the same words, all together, and, as nearly as possible, just as I had read them. For instance, in reading the Sermon on the Mount, I stopped at the bars, being careful to give the proper inflection of the voice, and to see that the whole school, which usually numbered more than a hundred, did the same.

"And seeing the multitudes, | he went up into a mountain; | and when he was set, | his disciples came unto him. | And he opened his mouth | and taught them, | saying, | Blessed are the poor in spirit, | for theirs is the kingdom of heaven. | Blessed are they that mourn, | for they shall be comforted. | Blessed are the meek, | for they shall inherit the earth," | &c.

By this method, all the pupils were engaged in reading, and all were attentive. If I stopped to correct an error of pronunciation, it was noticed by all; if I stopped to explain the meaning of any word or phrase, all were benefited; if I stopped to ask a question, every one was ready to answer; finally, if I stopped to give any moral or religious instruction, I was generally sure of a very attentive audience. By requiring every pupil to read as I did, without regard to her neighbors, the most perfect harmony was preserved, and any error produced a discord, which was as easily detected as a discord among a choir of singers.

This attention was of great advantage; but the quantity read, and well read, was a great advantage also. In the ordinary way, a school of a hundred pupils would only read a verse or two in an hour, but by the process I propose, every child reads a whole chapter in from five to ten minutes; a difference of practice that cannot but be important. Indeed, I was satisfied, after a short experiment, that, independent of the advantage of the exercise in a religious point of view, the pupils were actually advanced further by this method than by all the other practice they obtained in their classes.

Another important good resulted from this exercise. It is well known that many pious persons have a serious objection to having the Bible read as a common exercise in school, in consequence of the careless manner in which the exercise is performed, the indifference of the children to it, and the diminution of respect for the Scriptures, if not distaste for them, which is the result of familiarity.

I cannot discuss the question, "Whether it is prudent to use a part, and not the whole of the Bible in our schools?" for, although some, whom I reverence, have expressed fears lest the use of a selection of Scripture Lessons should lead the young to think that the passages not selected are less valuable and important than those taken, still it is evident that the practice of the whole Christian world is on the side of selections. What is the liturgy of the Roman Catholic Church, the liturgy and psalter of the English Church and of our Reformed Episcopal Church, but a selection? What is the custom of our dissenting clergy, not one in a thousand of whom reads the entire Scriptures in course from the pulpit, but making and using a selection? What, indeed, is the practice of using the New Testament in Sunday and secular schools, but using a part of the Bible because more convenient, as well as more generally interesting to the young? The fact is, that, whether a selection is *used* or not, a selection is uniformly *made* by all teachers that read the Scriptures in school; and who can hesitate between a selection made at leisure with great care, after much practice in the reading of Scripture, and one made on the spur of the moment, perhaps by one who neither respects the Bible, nor can read it decently?

It was my custom always to select a passage before I went to school, and to study it and read it, until I could do some measure of justice to it. Then I read it to the class as well as I could, and, by my manner, I found it very easy to impress upon the minds of the children the same respect for the sacred volume that I felt myself, and the importance of this early reverence cannot be overestimated by the parent and the instructor.

But the selection of suitable passages required much care, and much time; and, in case it was necessary to skip any portion, or turn to other passages of similar import, it was attended with many disadvantages. I contrived to do this, however, for many years, until, having gone through the Old and New Testament several times, and marked those portions that seemed to be best adapted to the instruction of children of both sexes in the presence of each other, I at last collected these passages into a small volume and printed them. As the division into chapters and verses is only useful for ready reference by students, and is of no use to children, nay, is of great disadvantage to them, in consequence of the increased difficulty of understanding the passage and reading it correctly, I followed the plan of the Paragraph Bible. The type used was better than is found in school Bibles and testaments; the punctuation was more carefully attended to, and the more emphatical words marked as usual by Italic type.

As the selection was to be used in our common schools, the text was given unaltered, with references to the chapters and verses, but without any notes or commentary. An outline of Old Testament History is given in the order of the common version, but the four evangelists are given in one connected narrative, according to Townsend's chronological arrangement. Then, as many beautiful passages are scattered over the Old and New Testament, too short of themselves for a reading lesson, but excellent for this purpose when classed with other passages of similar import, one third of the book consists of passages so selected, and arranged under various heads, such as "Reverence for God," "Love to God and Man," "Heavenly Wisdom," "Sublimity of the Scriptures," &c. This selection, called the Bible Reader, has met with much favor from teachers and clergymen, many of whom have confessed to me that it produced, in their hands, all the delightful effects that I have myself witnessed. As to the fairness with which the selection has been made, I can only say that it has met the approbation of every denomination of Christians that use the Scriptures, and this is not to be wondered at, for the manuscript was subjected to the severest scrutiny before it was put to the press.

Much has been said of the matter contained in school reading books, and a great mistake, I think, prevails on this subject. The imperfect way in which reading has been taught, in so far as little or no attempt has been made to explain the text, has led many teachers and school committees to suppose that the selections were above the comprehension of children; but I have never seen such a selection, and do not believe that any such exists.

Another mistake is made by those who suppose that a book is unfit for use because it has been in use so long. This objection, in my opinion, will lie only against such books as are brought down to the capacity of children, so that they need no study, no explanation. It seems to me that books which are to be read more than once should be so constructed that at every successive reading the master may have something new to explain, and the pupil something new to learn; and, as the old book is new to new classes, and can be more effectually taught the better it can be read and explained by the teacher, the older the book the better, if it was a good one at first. It is a favorite notion of some excellent friends of education that the reading lessons in our common schools should be mainly selected with a view to the imparting of useful knowledge, and the inculcation of virtuous sentiments. To a certain degree this plan may be adopted, but in every case in which it has been fully carried out, it has failed. We have had Peace Readers, Temperance Readers, Agricultural Readers, Scientific Readers, Religious Readers, &c., &c., and these one-idea books have contained much that is valuable; but they have always failed to make *good* readers, in the highest sense of the term *good*. Reading is an *art*, a glorious art, which can no more be learned or taught from humdrum books of science or from moral essays, than English composition can be learned by the perusal of Murray's Grammar.

In Massachusetts and New York, the legislature has provided a large supply of useful reading in the school libraries, which have been established in the districts. The books thus provided are no doubt intended to furnish the knowledge which no school Reader, made or to be made, can supply to any considerable degree, while they enable the class books to be more fully adapted to teach something more of reading than the mere pronunciation of words, and the dull monotony, which are about all that the reading of a scientific tract requires. Books of useful knowledge should be read, but not at school. The few minutes devoted each day to reading, if spent only upon the most suitable books, will hardly suffice to make good readers; and it is with reading, as with spelling, if the necessary knowledge and practice are not obtained at school, there is but little chance of their ever being obtained afterward. I think I have never known a good reader who was contented to teach from such books; and if good readers with poor tools can effect but little, what can be expected when both the teacher and the tools are bad? All the popular books with which I am acquainted contain a due proportion of moral and useful pieces, and when two essays have equal merit as reading pieces, if one contains more useful knowledge than the other, I should by all means give it the preference; but the cultivation of the taste and of the imagination is as useful and as important as the acquisition of knowledge, and any system of education that does not recognize this truth must be greatly defective.

If I were to name what I consider the great deficiency of our best school books, I should say, the want of a just proportion of dialogues. These are best understood by children, are read more naturally, and with more animation; and, as the inflections of the voice are more various than in any other class of compositions, they are peculiarly useful to the good teacher. I had a variety of such books in my school library, from which my pupils occasionally read, and in no other exercise did they seem to take so much interest, or show their power so distinctly. If possible, dialogues should be read by as many pupils as there are characters, and each should read his part without changing it, for in this way he enters better into the spirit of the piece, and makes the sentiments his own.

It is a misfortune that so few dialogues are to be found in our school books; and this deficiency, rather than any ambition to be a writer, induced the author a few years ago to publish a volume of Familiar Dialogues, that he had composed for the use of his pupils. He also published a small book for beginners, called the Primary Reader, which had the same object in view, and contains more dialogues and lively pieces than any other book intended for the same class of children. In schools where other books are used as text-books, the teacher will do well to have one or two copies of the Primary Reader and the Familiar Dialogues, in which the child can read occasionally by way of reward, or for the sake of variety.

Besides the method of Scripture Reading that I have described, I had various other methods, which I will endeavor briefly to describe.

Before requiring a class to read the paragraphs consecutively, I sometimes selected a single paragraph, or short piece, and let every member of the class read it in rotation. After the first had read, I would call on such of the class as had noticed any fault to hold up their hands. I then heard their criticisms, one at a time, and made such remarks as seemed necessary, especially such as explained the meaning of the author. The next pupil then read, and was criticised in the same manner, and so on through the class. My custom was to grant precedence to those who made important corrections, for I never saw any evil resulting from this practice that at all balanced the good produced by the earnest attention it called forth. Suppose the class to consist of A, B, C, D, E, F, G. Let A read. If D holds up his hand and points out any fault, he goes above A. B, C, and E, do not hold up their hands. F holds up his hand, but he miscorrects, and in this case goes down one. This check is necessary, or the teacher will be too much interrupted. The class then stands thus, D, A, B, C, E, G, F. D reads next, and, when called on, C and F raise their hands. C points out an important error in pronunciation and goes to the head. F detects a wrong inflection of the voice, and goes next to C. The class then stands thus, C, F, D, A, B, E, G. Then C reads, and A, B and E hold up hands. A makes a judicious correction and goes to the head. B miscorrects once, and once points out a real error, and he neither goes up nor down. E detects an error and goes next above C. Then the class stands thus, A, E, C, F, D, B, G.

It is unnecessary to go further, for the teacher must understand the process. Sometimes, instead of requiring each pupil to read the same paragraph, I required each to take a new passage. This may seem to afford the pupils a more equal chance, but I have generally found that, even when they all read the same passage, they made as many faults as we had time to correct, and before we left the paragraph, it was better read and better understood than if it had only been read once.

Another mode was to require each pupil to read the same piece, without any correction by the class or by the teacher. Then, after some general remarks upon the piece, its meaning, design, &c., I read the piece myself to the class. This method generally commands the full attention of the class, who should be called on promiscuously and not in the order in which they stand; but it is better calculated for reviewing, where the object is not so much to teach, as to ascertain the comparative ability of the readers.

A third method was to set a reading lesson, and require the pupils to be prepared to give the meaning of every difficult word, if the class were young; but, if older, they were also required to give the sense intended by the author; to point out figures of speech, and even to analyze all compound words, or words having a prefix or affix in their composition. The reading lesson affords the best opportunity for teaching the meaning of words, and the skilful teacher will improve it. The too common method of learning pages of the dictionary, is almost useless, for there is nothing to fix the definitions in the memory, and they are often various and contradictory, and more unintelligible than the word is without them; but, in the reading lesson, where the word is correctly used, it may be accurately defined, and impressed upon the memory by its association in the sentence. There is no harm in requiring the pupil to spell the difficult words as well as to define them, but the teacher must be careful not to rely upon such a spelling lesson, except for review, for the reading books will not contain half the words that the child should be taught to spell; he will never know what he has learned, and in what he is deficient; and the entire absence of system or classification will prevent him from learning what are the rules of English orthography. I have even doubted whether the selection of words, which is placed at the beginning of the lessons in some reading books, is not a positive evil, for it prevents the child, in a great measure, from using his intellect, in ascertaining the meaning, and throws him almost entirely upon his verbal memory, which will probably fail him before he has learned the next lesson.

Another method which I sometimes used had often a very good effect. I would read to the class, and occasionally mispronounce a word, place the emphasis wrong, or give a wrong inflection. I would then call on the class for corrections, and generally they would be more on the alert, than if the object were merely to discover an error of one of their companions.

But, after all, the best thing a teacher can do, for his own improvement and that of his pupils, is to read much to them, and as well as he can. He must study the lessons in the textbook, and make his pupils understand them. The Bible contains a prescription for good reading of more value than all the slides, and accents, and other contrivances to make good readers, that ever were invented. I give the passage, and commend it to the practice of teachers, even to the *opening* of the book and the *standing up*.

Nehemiah viii. 5. "And Ezra opened the Book in the sight of all the people, and when he opened it, all the people stood up. * * * * *So they read* in the Book of the Law of God *distinctly, and gave the sense, and caused [the people] to understand the reading.*"

SPELLING.

It has been shown already that I should connect spelling and reading with writing, from the very outset. As soon as the child can pronounce the alphabet, on my plan, he will be able to write it, and then, as he advances, he must continue to write all the spelling lessons, and as much of the reading lessons as time will admit. But, as this method requires a better knowledge of writing than is commonly found in our schools, especially in the lowest classes, I shall endeavor to describe my method of teaching the art of writing, by which I never failed to make my pupils write any thing they could read, and write it well too, though often less than five years of age.

On the wall, back of my desk, or in some other handy and conspicuous place, I had a long and narrow black-board, ruled in the manner described hereafter under the head of Writing. The lines were slightly cut into the board before it was painted, and though distinctly visible afterwards, they did not disfigure any writing that was executed over them. Every child had a slate ruled exactly like the black-board, and the first copies set for the pupils were written before their eyes on the board, and copied upon their slates. All my pupils could print before they could write, but the transition to writing was so easy, and done so early, that they seemed to write as fast as they learned to read and spell and print.

I believe I was the first teacher in Boston that required children of four years of age to write, and it often struck visitors with wonder to see children at five, writing a good hand, with great despatch, when it was a rare thing elsewhere to find children seven years old able to read a word of manuscript, much less to write well, without a pattern, as all my little pupils did. It is less rare to see little children writing now-a-days, but, when, within a year, I have proposed to teachers to require children of seven and eight to write their spelling lessons, I have been told either that they could not write, or that it would take them all day to write a lesson of fifty words. My pupils would write fifty words of four syllables in less than twenty minutes, and write them well too.

The despatch acquired by thus writing on the slate, and the free motion of the hand, were important points gained by this method, preparatory to using the pen.

When the object was merely to teach writing to beginners, my custom was to call the attention of the class to the black-board, and then to say, "I wish you to draw a straight but leaning line, from this line to this," suiting the action to the word. Or, "I wish you to begin an O here and end it so," describing and demonstrating every step as I advanced. If encouraged, I shall soon prepare boards, slates and books, and a manual for instruction on this plan, and, therefore, shall not be more particular, especially as my object now is to show how spelling may be taught by writing, and not how writing itself may be taught.

The author was glad to perceive that of the thousand teachers whom he has met at Teachers' Institutes, nineteen twentieths were tolerable penmen, and if those he saw are not more than a fair specimen of the teachers of our district schools, there is no reason in the world why every child, in every school, should not be a good penman at a very early age. The immense advantage of this acquisition to the children cannot be overrated, for, besides the mechanical skill, the child has a means of constant employment, which will keep him out of idleness and mischief, and the teacher can make this skill bear upon almost every exercise in other branches of instruction. In Boston, for more than half a century, writing was entirely separated from every other branch except Arithmetic, to which it administers less aid, perhaps, than to any other study; but, of late, one or two other branches have been added to those taught in the writing schools, although orthography, grammar and composition are still taught in a separate room, by other teachers, who are not required to teach penmanship. This separation of things so nearly allied, has never been attempted in the district schools out of Boston, and it is to be hoped it never will be introduced there.

But, let us return to Orthography, and describe some of the processes by which it may be connected with writing.

If the teacher is unacquainted with the use of monitors, or is not allowed to use his better pupils as assistants, he may require every class to write every word of the spelling lesson upon the slate, on the lines that correspond to those on the black-board, in which case, but few words can be written at a time. This is better, while the hand is forming, than to require the whole lesson to be written in smaller letters, on that side of the slate which is not ruled. If he cannot find time to examine every slate, the mere writing of the words will be of great service to the learners; but the active teacher will contrive some way to examine every slate, and to mark the errors. If the words are written in a large hand on the ruled lines, he can, at a signal, have all the slates held up by the pupils so that he can see them; or, if the desks are so constructed that he can pass behind the pupils, he can easily walk around and correct them. But, if the teacher is allowed to use his pupils as assistants in such matters as may safely be taught by them, all the words may be dictated, and promptly examined, without interruption to the teacher, who may be otherwise engaged.

Suppose the teacher to have heard a recitation of one class, and to have called out another, which is to recite to him. If he wishes to keep those who are at their seats employed in writing their spelling lessons, he can appoint one well-behaved scholar to dictate the words from the spelling book, and to inspect the slates, book in hand. My pupils were arranged in rows, each row perhaps forming a class. Between each row there was room for a person to pass. If there were several classes, the monitor, as the assistant pupil was called, had a mark in his spelling book at each of their lessons. He then dictated the first word of the lesson to the highest class, by spelling it distinctly. They began to write it, and he proceeded to the next row or class, and dictated a word of their lesson by spelling it aloud. They began to write, and he went to the next class, and so on. By the time he had dictated a word to the lowest class, the highest was ready for another; he gave them one, and proceeded to the next as before. As soon as they had written as many words as the lines on the slate admitted, he walked behind and examined the slates; or, he told each pupil to change slates with some neighbor, or to compare slates; or, if there was not time for this, he ordered all to clean slates at a signal given, and then prepare to write another slate full.

It is a grievous evil that so few of our common district schools have the seats so constructed that the teacher can get at his pupils so as to inspect their work; and, where this evil exists, the ingenuity of the teacher will be severely tried. But, as I have said before, if the pupil writes the words quietly from the book, or from the dictation of a monitor, he will be greatly benefited, whether his work is examined or not. In many cases, the teacher will be able to direct this exercise himself; and practice will enable him to overcome many obstacles, which, at first, may seem insurmountable.

By thus writing the word, the eye as well as the ear is trained, and a child thus taught is in little danger of exhibiting that common phenomenon of correctly spelling even the hardest words orally, and of misspelling the most common words when called upon to write them. Every teacher knows that children unaccustomed to write do this, and yet how few have applied the only remedy!

In oral spelling, or in written, of course it is important what words are spelled, and in what order they are presented to the child. A few years ago, at a convention of teachers and friends of education in Berkshire County, it was unanimously voted to be the opinion of the convention that, for twenty or more years, spelling had been retrograding in our schools. There can be no doubt of this fact; but as I have endeavored to account for it in the Lecture on Memory that forms a part of this volume, I shall not enlarge upon the subject here any further than to remark, that, in my visits to the Teachers' Institutes of New York and Massachusetts, I have uniformly found the young teachers more deficient in spelling than in any other branch of study, and I rarely found one who had been educated to write words, and to require his pupils to do so.

Very soon after I became a teacher, I felt the necessity of a spelling book that should present the words of our language so classed and arranged, that, without knowing it, the pupil should become acquainted with the rules of English orthography and pronunciation; and, by the aid of association, should have the form of words indelibly impressed upon his memory. Although oppressed with labor, I then prepared a small spelling book, called the Improved Guide, which answered my purpose better than any other, and which, a few years ago, when I had more leisure and experience, was enlarged into my "*Common School Speller.*" This Improved Spelling Book has met with a reception unexampled, I think, in this country, for the annual sale, only the third year after its publication, exceeded 40,000 copies.

In the selection of words for the Speller, great care was taken not to admit any that were unsuitable in any respect, and yet the vocabulary is intended to contain all words that a well educated young gentleman should be acquainted with, and able to spell. To explain the classification, I know not that it will be unfair to say that there is as much difference between this and other spelling books as between order and confusion. In other spelling books, to be sure, there is a sort of order, but it is rarely calculated to aid the eye or the memory of the pupil. Some definition spelling books, as they are called, place the words alphabetically, as they are placed in dictionaries, but in such books the words are no more classed than are the buildings in a long street that happen to be consecutively numbered. Such an arrangement may enable the child to find a word easily, but it affords him no aid in learning to spell.

In other spelling books, the words are arranged according to the number of syllables they contain, but such words are no more classed than the lower animals would be if arranged according to their different sizes, when the real differences of form and structure are disregarded.

In the best spelling books, those which are the most popular, the words are placed very promiscuously; but the authors seem to think they have rendered a strict classification unnecessary, because they have placed over each word some accent, figure, or other mark, referring to a key, where the pronunciation is explained. But, who does not see that words so situated and marked are no more classed than the scattered plants of a flower-garden that happen to be labelled. The difference between my spelling book and such as I have described may be illustrated by a very familiar comparison. Every one probably has seen what in Massachusetts is called a General Muster, when all the troops of a brigade are assembled on a spacious field for review and exercise. Before they are called to order, the members of the various companies, wearing different uniforms, are intermixed in such a manner that the spectators can form no idea of the number of companies, to say nothing of getting acquainted with each individual soldier. It is true that each soldier wears a knapsack on which the spectator may read the name of the company, and perhaps of the regiment, to which he belongs; but, even with this aid, he can have but a confused idea of the number and variety of the troops. Let the drum then call to order, and the line be formed, and one glance will enable the spectator to judge of every particular relating to the troops

But it has been objected to my book that where the words are so exactly classed, it is difficult to distinguish one from another of the same class, and, therefore, it seems better to have them in confusion. When they are learning to spell, it is said, if they can spell one word of the class they can spell all the rest too easily, and they will not be likely to distinguish between the words, because they look so much alike. Now, if the objection have any force, it will lie against classification in every science, as well as against the classification of words. Linnæus owes his immortality to the fact that, when the various plants and animals were running all over creation with labels on their backs, like the words in a "promiscuously arranged" spelling book, he discovered their points of resemblance, classed them, and enabled his successors to learn in one year what before was the work of a life. Because two varieties of the helix, or snail, very nearly resemble each other, shall we put an oyster between them to set them off? Or, because two roses resemble each other very nearly, shall we place a sunflower between them? We shall, if this objection has any force. It must be a mistake, then, to suppose that it is not safer to examine words that resemble each other side by side, where only the point of difference needs to be noticed, than to examine them apart from each other, independently, in which case it is necessary to observe every peculiarity of every word,—those in which they agree as well as those in which they differ.

In the year 1841, the Secretary of the Massachusetts Board of Education delivered a lecture on the subject of spelling books, and having fallen accidentally upon my old one, "*The Improved Guide*," he made the following remarks which are entitled to more weight than common notices of books, because I had not sent him the book, and had never spoken to him, or seen him.

"When," says Mr. Mann, "reading has become easy, and it is expedient to carry forward the orthography of the language faster than it is possible to comprehend the meaning of all its words, a spelling book, constructed according to the law of association, should be put into the hands of the pupil. Although this idea has been acted upon to some extent before, yet the only spelling book with which I am acquainted that carries it out fully is one prepared by Mr. Fowle, of Boston. A few specimens from the book will give an intelligible view of its plan." After giving the specimens, Mr. Mann adds

"Now, it would seem to need no argument to prove that a *child will master twenty pages of words arranged in this way more easily than he will a single page of words classed* according to the number of syllables, and the place of the accent, *irrespective of their formation; — where a and eigh, e* and *eo*, *i* and *igh*, *o* and *eau*, *u* and *ew*, with countless other combinations, have respectively the same sound, and are jumbled together after the similitude of chaos. On such lessons as these, scholars will very rarely spell wrong. They can go through the book twenty times while they would go through a common spelling book once; and each time will rivet the association; that is, it will make an ally of the most unconquerable force of habit. A connection will be established between the general idea of the word and its component letters, which it will be nearly impossible to dissolve." After more remarks in the same strain, this sagacious observer, as if anticipating the objection under consideration, says, after having recommended the frequent spelling and *writing* also of the words thus classed, "It will be well, as a testing or experimental exercise, to put out words from the different tables promiscuously, in order to determine whether or not it may be necessary to drill the pupils longer upon it." And what is this but saying, that spelling should be taught by the well classed spelling book, and all the chaotic ones should be used only by way of review?

To show that this matter is not overstated, let us take a fair example from one of our popular spelling books, and it is hoped that this will not be deemed invidious, since the object is only to show the operation of the two plans. In one of them, then, I find the following column of words, printed just as I give them.

The child has been told in the introduction that letters in Italic are not to be sounded, and the figures refer the child to the key which is printed over the lesson. Let it be recollected that the child always studies the lesson before he hears the words pronounced by the teacher; and with no other aid than the figures, and the Italic letters, how will he succeed in finding the pronunciation of the several words? and how much will the *variety* aid him in remembering how to spell them?

1 2 3 4 5 — 1 4 8 9 — 1 4 8 10 — 1 3 5
late far fall hat wad — mete met her they — time tin sir pique — tone for not

6 7 8 — 1 4 7 — 1 — 1 4
do look love — mute cut full — new — dry hymn.

1	4	1	4	1	6
fu*s*e	melt	stra*i*n	stretch	twa*i*n	t*w*o
free	frank	te*a*l	duck	1	oi
go*a*d	prick	te*a*t	lug	fa*y*	join
grade	rank	tra*i*l	track	po*a*ch	boil
gross	thick	tro*w*	think	2	1
gyre	ring	type	stamp	barm	ye*a*st
haze	mist	1	5	blanch	ble*a*ch
heave	swell	bla*i*n	blotch	blast	bli*gh*t
ju*i*ce	sap	chore	job	charg*e*	lo*a*d
le*a*p	spring	ce*a*se	stop	clasp	hold
le*a*se	let	fleer	mock	gant	le*a*n
le*a*ve	quit	jeer	scoff	grant	y*i*eld
l*i*eu	ste*a*d	ode	song	grasp	se*i*ze
pli*gh*t	pled*ge*	queer	odd	lanc*e*	spe*a*r
prune	trim	score	notch	rasp	file
qua*i*l	sink	sta*i*n	spot	slant	slope
ru*e*	plant	1	6	staff	cane
spru*e*	thrush	brog*ue*	sho*e*	vast	gre*a*t

This lesson contains one hundred words, and in the Common School Speller, instead of being together, they are distributed into at least twenty-seven classes thus :

Class 1, p. 13.
grade
haze
—

Class 2, p. 14.
track
stamp
rank
frank
plant
sap
—

Class 4, p. 15.
pledge
swell
melt
let
stretch

Class 5, p. 17.
file
—

Class 6, p. 18.
prick
thick
trim
ring
spring
sink
think
mist
quit
—

Class 7, p. 19.
ode
hold
slope
chore
store
gross
—

Class 8, p. 20.
job
mock
odd
scoff
song
stop
spot
blotch
notch
—

Class 9, p. 21
fuse
—

Class 10, p. 21.
duck
dug
thrush
—
Class 11, p. 23.
type
gyre*
—
Class 13, p. 23.
barm*
charge
. . . .
staff
lance
blanch
gant*
slant
grant
clasp
rasp
grasp
blast
vast
—
Class 15, p. 24.
trail
quail
blain
strain
stain
twain

Class 18, p. 25.
fay
—
Class 19, p. 25.
jeer
fleer
free
queer
—
Class 20, p. 26.
bleach
teal
lean
leap
spear
cease
lease
yeast
heave
leave
teat*
—
Class 22, p. 27.
yield
. . . .
seize
—
Class 27, p. 28.
goad
load
poach
—
Class 28, p. 29.
trow

Class 33, p. 30.
boil
join
—
Class 35, p. 31.
prune
—
Class 39, p. 56.
blight
plight
—
Class 53, p. 81.
rue
sprue*
—
Class 54, p. 82.
juice
—
Class 55, p. 82.
stead
. . . .
great
—
Class 82, p. 175.
brogue
—
Class 85, p. 183.
lieu
—
Class 86, p. 188.
cane
two
shoe

Gant, *barm*, *gyre*, *teat*, and *sprue*, and one or two others, are not admitted into the Common School Speller; and *Rue* is not placed, as here, under long *u*. The other words are classed by their chief characteristics, and numbered and paged according to the classes of the C. S. Speller, in which they may be found, with all the other words that resemble them and have the same characteristics.

Now, in classing the 14,000 words of the Common School

Speller, it was only necessary to form 87 classes; and yet the above lesson of only a hundred words contains nearly one third of all the classes needed, and, of course, the hundred words must be as well mixed up as any child of chaos can desire.

I have already provided for the writing of every word in the spelling book, in the order of the spelling book; but there is another exercise in orthography, to which I would now ask attention. After writing the words of the book, detached from all definitions, the children must be taught to use the words in sentences, and for this purpose I have prepared a book, called, "*The Companion to Spelling Books, in which the Orthography and Meaning of many thousand words, most liable to be misspelled and misused, are impressed upon the memory by a series of exercises to be written by the pupil.*" In this little book is one exercise, or more, adapted to every lesson in the Common School Speller. *All* the words of the Speller are not introduced into the sentences; but every word that is liable to be misspelled, or that needs to be explained, may be found there, defined, or correctly used, which is often the best kind of definition.

Every teacher has felt the need of some exercise for children, who are sitting idle, after having learned the next lesson they are to recite, or from indisposition to study. As the lessons of the Companion are all numbered, and of moderate length, the teacher can prevent the pupils from ever being able to say with truth, that they have nothing to do. He can even prevent the necessity of their interrupting him by asking what they shall do next, for he has only to say to them, "When you have no set lesson to occupy your mind, write the lessons of the Companion in their order, neatly and correctly, and place them where I can see them and correct them at my leisure." If the pupil cannot be trusted, he must be required to write a certain number of the lessons every day, or every week; and the teacher, by keeping a record of what he corrects, or by requiring the pupil to show up what he has written, may easily see that the required number has been written. Hereafter, under the head of *Neatness*, I shall give some directions in regard to the writing and preservation of such exercises; but now the object is to show the many advantages of these written exercises in orthography.

A few specimens of the lessons will enable me better to show their various uses.

LESSON LX.

CLASS 20. — *Words with* EA *like long* E.

Treecle is another name for molasses. Some careless *speekers* use the word learning for *teeching*. A *weazel* is a long-bodied animal, smaller than a cat. The *teazle* is a prickly plant, used to raise a nap on cloth. That *deeler* has a *meager* supply of goods. The *heeling* art has various theories. Be not *squeemish* or over-nice in small matters. Bissextile, or *leepyear*, is every fourth year. It was a *drearey* road for a *wearey* traveller. His old *beever* hat looked *greazy*. *Bohee* is usually called black tea. He was *impeeched*, or accused of treason. Do not *misleed* the simple.

LESSON XCIII.

CLASS 47, *continued, to show the irregularities of words formed from monosyllables ending in* LL.

She was handsome, and, what is better, good *allso*. *Allmost* every person has some redeeming quality. It is *alltogether* wrong to tease ill-tempered persons. He is *skillful*, and expeditious *withall*. The debt was paid by *installments*, or portions. The steeple above the *bellfry* was blown down. Those we love are *allways wellcome*. A *willfull* child must be subdued. He came not to destroy but to *fullfill* the law. The *fullfillment* of that prophecy is at hand. "My word shall *distill* like the dew," saith the Lord.

LESSON C.

CLASS 50. — *Words beginning with* WH, *which are too often pronounced badly, as if the* H *were silent.*

Wet the *wetstone* before you sharpen the knife. The *wig* party are not called so because they wear wigs. I wist not how to play the popular game of *wist*. *Wile* you live practice no dishonest wiles. He is not a *wit* the better for his wit. The sot *wines* when his wine is spent. Who can tell *wether* the weather will be fair? *Wither* must it be carried that it may not wither? *Wen* will the surgeons remove that wen? *Were* were they placed? *Witch* of the witches was called Hecate?

LESSON CCXCVI.

Class 86. — *Words misused, there being two or more words pronounced alike, but spelled differently.*

The *cession* of a court in England is called the ass'zes. It is impolite to make a noise with one's *chops* in eating. A *choir* of paper contains twenty-four sheets. There is no *choler* to his coat. We are bound to life by many *chords* or ties. A *sion* of one tree was engrafted on the stock of another. Citizens are sometimes familiarly called *sits*. When a witness is wanted, he is *sited*, or summoned to appear. Reading fine print always injures the *site*. Impressions of birds' *clause* have been found on rocks in Massachusetts.

LESSON CCCVIII.

Class 86, *continued.*

He was the last of the *profits*. *Quean* Elizabeth was a vain woman. John Adams died at *Quinsy*. A good horse will mind the *rain*. *Reign* is vapor condensed by cold. The Romans *raised* the walls of Jerusalem to the ground. No man could *raze* the dead unless God were with him. Some one *wraps* at the door. The jewel was *rapt* in cotton. The rising generation *reed* too much and think too little. "But little he 'll *wreck*," or care, "if they 'll let him sleep on." It is base to *reek* vengeance on a helpless foe.

It will be seen that the sentences are correctly written, so far as grammar, punctuation, capitals, &c., are concerned; but one word, to which the attention of the pupil is particularly called, is misspelled. He will know this word by its being printed in *Italic* type. The exercise, then, is, in fact, an introduction to composition, as well as to orthography, and I always found that such of my pupils as had written a course of these exercises, were acquainted with the mechanical part of composition, and rarely erred in those small matters of which even teachers are very neglectful.

But it has been objected to these lessons, that the spelling of words incorrectly may corrupt the eye of the child, which should never see any thing but what is as perfect as it can be made. I have known teachers to object to these lessons on this account, who had always been accustomed to the use of Murray's Exercises in false grammar, without perceiving any danger from the practice? There is no danger. The exercise is only a test of the accuracy of the eye, which sees the word correctly spelled a thousand times, and then sees it incorrectly spelled but once. The word, if ingeniously misspelled, may for a moment puzzle the learner, but then he settles the question on the spot, and writes the word correctly, to fix it in his mind's eye. What is more common than this mode of teaching? If I draw a circle to test the eye of my pupil, will he lose the correct idea of a circle because some portion of my curves are irregular? If I pronounce a word badly, or give a wrong inflection of the voice, to try the ear of my pupils, do I destroy the power of his ear correctly to distinguish sounds? I have even heard this misspelling of a word, once in a lifetime, complained of by teachers, who relished the letters of Jack Downing, and similar works, where false orthography runs through the whole volume, and who yet made no complaint of the pernicious influence of such examples.

I have said that no danger is to be apprehended from the misspelling of a word once in this manner, and I speak from experience. The lessons of the Companion, or similar ones, were used in my school for more than twenty years, and I hope the teachers whom I have had the happiness to meet at the several Institutes, will pardon me if I say that the want of such an exercise, in my opinion, was the chief reason of their appearing to such disadvantage. They lacked that critical discernment which my pupils acquired by writing these exercises themselves, and afterwards correcting the exercises of their fellows; an operation which I shall presently explain. But, one fact of every day occurrence settles this question, I think, beyond any doubt. Those who have any experience in printing, know that the most excellent spellers in the world are what are called proof readers, that is, persons whose business it is to read the first impressions from types, before the book is given to the public. I never knew an author, whether a teacher or not, who was not indebted to these men for many corrections that he had overlooked. If such almost perfect skill is acquired by the constant search for errors, it is clear that no harm can arise from a word's being misspelled once in the course of a whole book, in which, except in that one instance, it is always correctly spelled.

But, says the teacher, I have no time to correct such exercises. I pity the teacher who says this, and am half inclined to ask him, "If it will take longer to correct an exercise than to correct the pupil for the idleness or mischief that it might prevent?" But he *must* find time to correct a few for his own benefit; and, when he is quick at the work, and as sharp in detecting errors as a good teacher ought to be, he may easily procure assistance in the following way. After a few good scholars have written through the book, or even before they have completed the course, a new class may begin. Let these give their exercises to the teacher, who may pass them over to one of the few whom he can trust to correct them. When this one has done his best, let him pass them to a second, and he to a third, till the whole have inspected them, and exercised their skill in making corrections, and then, let them be returned to the writer. These inspectors, who are in fact "proof readers," will be benefited as much as the writer; especially if, occasionally, the teacher gives the exercises a final examination, to see how thorough his assistants have been in their inspection.

The best way to use the Companion is, to require every pupil to have the book and write the lessons in course; but, if the parents are too poor to get the book for their children, a case which, I am inclined to think, never exists in this happy country, or, if they think they are too poor, let the teacher get one book, and dictate a lesson from it, or write one on the black-board every day; or, let some monitor write it for him, and then let such of the pupils as please, copy and correct it. If the teacher cannot afford to buy one book for the benefit of his school, let him send to me, and I will give him one — and a word of advice into the bargain. I am sick of the constant complaint of teachers that they cannot persuade the parents or the committees to furnish the necessary books or apparatus for their schools; for, I believe that, if the teacher is active, and in earnest, the parents and committees will be so, and he may get almost every thing he asks for. Several young teachers have told me that they had changed their minds in this respect, for, as soon as they satisfied the committee of the utility of a globe, or an outline map, or a new book, a way was always opened to obtain it. Let my young friends try the experiment, and not complain until they are sure that the fault is not their own. Of old, parents, though evil, "knew how to give good gifts to their children," and parents, now-a-days, surely are not less liberal and indulgent.

As it regards oral spelling, I need not say much. My

method in the classes was to put out the word as it should be pronounced, and not, as is the custom of some, improperly pronounced, to indicate the letters that may not have their name sound in the word. The *whole class* pronounce after me, to make them attentive and to show that the word is understood. Then the first of the class spells the word, and if he spells correctly, well; but, if incorrectly, the next tries, and if he spells correctly, he goes above the other, who, instead of having a new word, is required to spell the word by which he lost his place. A new word is then given; the whole class pronounce it, and the third scholar spells it. If four, or five, or a dozen miss it, he who spells, goes up, and all who go down, separately spell the word they have missed. A new word is then given to the next that has not tried, and so on.

I know it will be objected to this method that it introduces rank or precedence, which many think worse than ignorance; but I never saw any evil arising from it, and its effect upon the attention and industry of the class is more than a balance for any imaginary evil that is said to proceed from it. This method enables the teacher to compel each child to take an equal share in the recitation; it enables complete class-lists of recitations to be kept; it saves the teacher the trouble, which is not trifling, of saying which shall answer; and it saves about one third of the time allotted to the lesson. The usual method of requiring him who misses a word to take a new one, always seemed to me unfair and unprofitable; — unfair, because it brings more new words to one pupil than to another, and this, too, when he is perhaps a little flurried by having missed; — unprofitable, because, until he who has missed a word spells it, you are not sure that he can spell it, and is benefited by having lost his place. My custom was to mark every word that was missed with a pencil, and then to put those words all out again at the end of the lesson, when I required them to be spelled simultaneously by the whole class.

Of this simultaneous spelling, or spelling in concert, I made great use. Before music was introduced into schools, this exercise and the saying of the multiplication table were my substitutes. To these I frequently resorted, if I wished to restore order or to cheer up the scholars. As words that had been missed were marked in my spelling book, I generally selected them, and, in the course of a term, many thousand important words would be spelled by way of amusement.

One custom was this. However the pupils were engaged, if I sounded my whistle, all business was instantly suspended, perfect silence reigned, and all looked to me, for no one else was ever allowed to whistle, the bell being the ordinary instrument for giving signals. I then put out a few words to be spelled by all, and the pitch of my voice always regulated theirs. In this way I would carry them, by degrees, from a low whisper to the loudest shout; then from one extreme to the other, omitting the intermediate sounds. Sometimes, in the midst of a word that they were spelling, I would sound the whistle; and as this meant that all should instantly stop, every one was careful to be attentive, lest he should spell a syllable alone after the rest had stopped. This may be called play but it was useful play, and when it was over, the children went on with their work more cheerfully and with renewed vigor.

I have often been asked whether I required my pupils, in spelling words, to pronounce the syllables separately. I never did, because it was of doubtful utility, and caused a great loss of time. I required a distinct pause after each syllable, but, as the syllables, if separate, would often be pronounced differently from what they would be in the word, I was satisfied with the correct pronunciation of the word, before and after spelling it. This was my custom before phonography had led to a more careful attention to the powers of letters; before any one dreamed of spelling by the power or sound, and not by the name of letters; and before any attempt was made to teach words before letters. If I taught spelling by the sound, as some now propose, I should certainly pronounce each syllable separately, but not, if the letters to be pronounced are called by their names.

Before leaving the subject of spelling, allow me to allude to one use that I made of the spelling book, which may be common to other teachers, but which has not fallen under my observation. When the words are arranged as in the Common School Speller, I know no better way to impress the rules and peculiarities of English pronunciation upon the learner's mind than to require him to read the lessons, that is, to pronounce every word of a lesson with care. Suppose, for instance, he had a fault of pronouncing words beginning with WH, as if there were no H, — a very common fault with us Yankees, — I should take him to the 50th class, which contains all the words beginning with WH, and I should make him pronounce them all in succession distinctly. If his fault was dropping the G at the end of words, I should turn to the 64th class, where, in giving directions for adding *ing* to verbs ending in E, some hundreds of examples are collected, the reading of which distinctly will perhaps entirely correct the fault. So with words ending in *ent* and *ence*, usually mispronounced *unt* and *unce;* the 52d class contains them all, and affords abundant materials for practice. I have already shown, under the head of Reading, that the Common School Speller contains the very tables that are necessary to enable the pupil to practise upon the fundamental sounds of the language.

One way of imparting interest to spelling lessons was common when I was young, but I do not hear much of it now. The boys of a class were accustomed to choose sides, and spell against each other. Those who object to giving precedence in classes will probably object to this kind of excitement also, but this would not deter me from occasionally resorting to it. I have seen such spelling matches produce some hard thoughts, but I do not believe this is a necessary consequence of the competition, for I never saw it among my own pupils in the course of twenty years. Before commencing, let certain rules be agreed upon. Mine were, as nearly as I can recollect, the following:

1. The lesson should be given before the sides were chosen.
2. The words should be spelled in some certain order, as, from beginning to end, from end to beginning, from right to left across the columns, or from left to right, so as to prevent any selection.
3. The word should be pronounced but once, unless the first speller requires it before he spells.
4. No speller should try twice.
5. If any speller prompts another, it must count one against his side.
6. If a pupil misspells, the pupil corresponding to him on the other side must try; if he spells correctly, it counts one for his side. If he spells incorrectly, the next on the other side tries, and if he gets right, he saves his side only, and neither party gains.

Matches of this sort are almost the only thing respecting my school days that I recollect with pleasure, and to the interest I took in them, probably, I owe the fact, that I was a good speller when I left school, although extremely ignorant of every thing but spelling.

At the end of every term, I was accustomed to review all

my classes in every branch, and to re-class the pupils. My method of reviewing in orthography was this. I selected about one hundred words from various parts of the spelling book, and without letting any pupil know the words I had selected, I required every child to spell every one of them, where the others could not hear her. As I could not hear them all myself, I employed, as assistants, the best of those who had spelled to me, and I never had any reason to suppose that they were not as faithful to their trust as I was to mine. The number that each missed was recorded, and the new classification was based upon this, and upon the class lists, in which the spelling of each scholar from day to day was recorded. In every other branch also, in reviewing the pupils, I always gave the same questions to every one, taking care, of course, that no one should hear another answer, nor know what the questions were before he was called on to answer.

The exercise of spelling, in some form or other, was never dropped in my school, even by the most advanced scholars. Every one was reviewed at the end of every term, and if there was any appearance of relapse, the pupil was obliged to spend more time than usual upon this exercise the ensuing quarter. Once, while I was reviewing my classes in this way, a young lady, aged sixteen or seventeen, who had received the highest honors of the public schools, and had so won the regard of her late teacher, that he was at great pains to recommend her to my particular attention, presented herself to be admitted as a pupil, for the purpose of *finishing her education*, as the common expression is. My children were taking a recess; and, being idle, I asked her if she would not like to amuse herself by spelling the sixty words that I had selected for the review of my scholars. She readily acquiesced, and missed thirty-two of the sixty. Lest she should feel mortified, I made light of it, and merely remarked that I supposed she had not practised much of late, and if she would like to revive her knowledge, I could let her teach a small class when she was not engaged in the higher studies which she wished to pursue. She made no objection, and went home, but, not coming again, I asked her cousin why she was absent, and was informed that she was not coming any more, for her mother did not wish her to go to a school where they did nothing but spell! My fidelity cost me a pupil, and I soon afterwards heard of her having entered another school, where, of course, she could "finish her education"——without learning how to spell.

ARITHMETIC.

Arithmetic is the all-absorbing study in the public schools of Massachusetts, and, probably, in those of every other state. As far as my observation goes, it occupies more of the time of our children than all other branches united. It is easy to see that the cause of this is the prevailing notion, that success in business depends upon skill in arithmetic. The thoroughness with which this branch is taught, is by no means commensurate with the importance unfortunately attached to it. Too much attention has evidently been paid to the higher parts of arithmetic, to the neglect of the very elements. One experiment that I made at every Teachers' Institute will show what I mean. So many of the teachers who led in the exercises of the Institutes, excelled in arithmetic and preferred to teach it, that I rarely touched upon it except to ascertain whether my fears were well founded, and in every instance they proved to be so.

One would think that nothing in the world could be easier than for a pupil to add up a single column of figures, and yet, in no instance have half the teachers of an Institute, on an average, been able to add correctly a column that amounted to over two hundred. Sometimes, not one fifth of them could do it, taking as much time as they pleased. They could extract a cube root, or perform a difficult problem in the rule of proportion, but they had never tried a long column of figures, and they were unable to master one. It rarely happened that those who added it correctly, did so with any thing like despatch. Ten or fifteen minutes was the time I usually allowed for the addition of such a column, but I usually added and proved it, that is, I began at the bottom and added it up, and then began at the top and added downward, in less than one minute. Many of these young teachers were better mathematicians than I, but I had attended more to the elements, and they more to the advanced rules. Of a thousand teachers, I found but one that brought up the sum correctly added before I had proved mine, and she did so but once. This first experiment led me to try further, and although a larger proportion performed correctly a common sum in addition, say, six columns of six figures each, and common sums in subtraction, multiplication and division, still, it was evident that they had not sufficiently practised these simple rules to do them with such despatch as I had been accustomed to see in my school, where, under monitors, the pupils had at least a hundred times the practice that children ever get under the master, in a school on the common plan.

I early saw that the use of books was unfavorable to despatch, and I made it a rule not to let a child cipher from a book, until she was very quick, and very accurate, in what are called the ground rules of arithmetic. My manner of teaching these rules may have had something peculiar in it, but it was rather the amount of practice than the method, which gave my pupils a degree of speed and accuracy that sometimes astonished strangers. I recollect that once an awkward teacher, from a neighboring state, visited my school, and as he had published an arithmetic and felt strong in this branch, he asked me to show him an exercise in it. I called out a class of about twenty, and gave them a sum in simple multiplication of which the multiplier was 8. They did the operation so quickly, that my visitor thought there was some trick in it, and he asked if I would allow him to set them a sum. He began to dictate, and to write his figures on the black-board, which was so turned that the pupils could not see it; but, his operations were so slow that the class grew impatient. He told them, at last, to multiply by 9, and, before he had multiplied the first two figures, some held out the sum to him and asked if it was right. "Stop a minute!" said he. As their numbers increased around him, "Stop a minute! stand away!" said he, knocking the misses with his elbows, "you put me out!" I beckoned to them to form a line, and wait patiently. When he had done, he examined their slates and pronounced them all wrong, and he was evidently pleased at this result. But, one of them instantly went to his sum on the black-board, and returned, saying that she believed the error was in his sum. He went over it again, and, after a long time, discovered that it was so. I asked him to try them again, but he declined, and most ungraciously added that "the girls bothered him." They would have done ten such sums to his one, and made their figures ten times as well as his were made. He was the author of an arithmetic, notwithstanding, and had taught for several years.

I do not consider that arithmetic is my *forte*, but the attention with which the few lessons I gave were received by my young friends at the Institutes, leads me to say a few words upon the elementary rules.

In adding a single column, say the following, which I place horizontally to save room, but the figures of which are to be added as if placed in one vertical column, I found that the pupils had various methods. Let the column be 8, 9, 6, 7, 9, 8, 8, 9, 6, 8, 9, 9, 8, 6, 7, 7, 9, 9, 8, 8, 7, 9, 8, 9, 7, 7, 8, 9, 8, 4, 9, 7.

Some cut the column into five or six parts, added the parts separately, and then added together their several sums. Some, as I dictated the figures, added each pair and set them down. Thus, when I said 8 and 9, they set down 17; 6 and 7=13, which they set down under 17, and so on. Others, as I dictated the figures, set all the 8's by themselves, all the 9's by themselves, and so with the other figures, and then said, 11 times 9 are 99; 10 times 8 are 80; 7 times 7 are 49; 3 times 6 are 18, and once 4 is 4. Then they had to add the several sums to find the total, 250. One marked the tens thus. He took the 8, and 2 from the 9, and made a dot; then he took the remaining 7 of the 9 with 3 from the 6, and made another dot; the remaining 3 and the next 7 making 10, he made a third dot. When he had finished, he counted his dots, and found 25 tens. Finally, another divided the column into tens, but made no dots. He said thus, dividing the figures as he went, 8 and 2 are 10, and 7 are 17, and 3 are 20, and 3 are 23, and 7 are 30, and so on.

When I told them that I had no such aids, they wondered; but the fact was, I had practised so much with my pupils that it was with addition as with the multiplication table; when asked how many are 6 times 7, I never calculate, for 42 is so connected with 6 times 7, that no calculation is necessary. So, when one figure follows another, I know what the amount must be, and make no calculation. I suggested, however, the following plan to the teachers, and, afterwards, their increased despatch showed that it was of some service to them. I placed ten or twelve 9's in a column, and said, "If I add ten to 9 what is the unit figure of the product?" 9 said they, of course. "Well, if 9 and 10 give 9, 9 and 9 will give one less than 9, viz., 8. So 9 and 8 will give two less than 9, viz., 7; and 9 and 7 will give three less than 9. viz., 6. As every one, therefore, knows what any number with 10 will make, let him drop 1 for 9, 2 for 8, 3 for 7, and he will readily find what he wants. Thus, in adding the column first given, say 8 and 10 would be 18, and, therefore, 8 and 9 will be one less, or 17+6 are 23+7 are 30+9 are 39+10 would be 49, 8 being 2 less, makes 47—two less than 7 will bring 5, and the next 8 added to 47 makes 55. The next 9 gives, not 65, but 64, and 6 are 70, and so on.

There is no trouble with figures under 7, nor, indeed, with 7 itself. To show how figures increase by the addition of 9, 8 or 7, they should be exercised on columns all nines, or all eights, or all sevens.

Of all the methods of *proving* a sum in addition, I have never found any equal to adding the figures in a direction contrary to that first used. If the pupil begins at the bottom, he should prove the sum by beginning at the top; for this entirely changes the combinations, and the child will not be so likely to run into the same error again, as he will if he goes twice in the same direction.

Another point in which children are generally deficient is numeration. I never set the sums for children, nor allowed them to copy from books, but always dictated the sum to be added, and required the children to write as I dictated, all together, if they used slates, and in turn if they stood before the black-board. I recollect once, that, after I had dictated a sum to the highest class in a school, and few or none had set it down correctly, the teacher, evidently distressed at their failure, said, "How could you mistake so, scholars, after I have shown you so many times! How often I have written such sums on the black-board, and told you how to read them!" I mildly whispered to him that the fault lay, I feared, in *his* having written the sums, instead of requiring the pupils to write them.

As soon as a child began to count, she began to write figures; just as she began to make letters, the moment she began to learn them. At the top of the black-board, I chalked, or painted, the figures 1, 2, 3, 4, 5, 6, 7, 8, 9, 0, as well as possible, and if the child was at a loss, she could look to the copy; if she made a bad figure, I rubbed it out, and pointed to the copy. It was no uncommon thing at the Institutes for me to be obliged to ask the young teachers what their figures were made for. If teachers do thus, what can be expected from their pupils?

The child begins to count his fingers, beans, marbles, or other objects, before he is required to write the figures, but as soon as he can write 1 and 2, he is required to add these together, and, if very small, he may mark against the figure as many units or ones as it represents, thus :

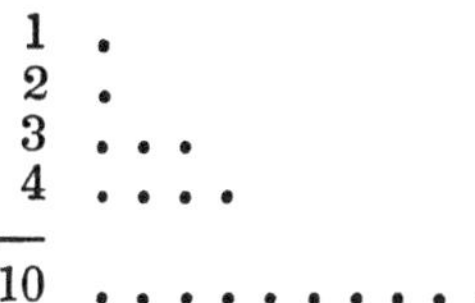

As soon as the column amounts to ten or over, let the teacher ask, how many tens and how many units are in the amount, and teach the pupil how to set the units under the column, and the tens on their left hand. He needs not to add tens until he has become expert in adding units ; but when it is necessary for him to learn numeration, let it be taught in this way. Write on the black-board as follows :

Millions.			Thousands.			Units.		
Hundreds of	Tens of	Units of	Hundreds of	Tens of	Units of	Hundreds of	Tens of	Units of
0	0	0,	0	0	0,	0	0	0,

Now give the child a single column that shall amount to more than ten. Let him set down the amount on the side of the slate. Suppose it to be 18, then ask. of what is 18 composed ? One ten and eight units. What is the one ten composed of ? Ten units. Then there are 8 units and 1 ten of units. See me write them under units of units, and tens of units. Give another column of figures, and do the same with the amount. Then, place so many sums under each other that they will amount to over a hundred. Suppose the sum to stand thus :

Millions.			Thousands.			Units.		
Hundreds of	Tens of	Units of	Hundreds of	Tens of	Units of	Hundreds of	Tens of	Units of
0	0	0,	0	0	0,	0	0	0
								3
								4
								5
								6
							1	8
							1	9
							2	7
							3	5
							4	6
						1	4	5

Ask the pupil now to add the column of units, and when she finds the amount, let her set it down in full on the side of her slate or black-board. Ask how many units and how many tens it contains, and let her set the units down, as she has been taught to do. Tell her she may put the tens under the other tens, or she may count them where they stand, and say, 3 tens and 4 tens, and 3 more tens, and 2 tens, and 1 ten, and 1 more ten, are 14 tens. Let her set down the 14 tens, as in the above sum, and then ask under what head does the 1 come. Perhaps she can tell how many 14 tens are, viz., 1 hundred and 4 tens.

Ask how many units or single ones make 10? How many tens make 100? In one hundred are how many tens? In fourteen how many units? What do the 1, 4, 5 stand for?

To impress this decimal increase upon the mind, then take a large square piece of paper and say, This paper we will call a hundred. How many tens are in it? Let us cut it into ten tens then. When it is so cut, take one of the pieces, and say this ten contains how many units? Well, let us cut it into ten units. The child will see the proportion between units, tens and hundreds, but he will see it more distinctly, if the teacher cuts up several hundreds in this way, and then lays them in piles to be added as if they were figures. Let us suppose such a sum to be composed thus:—

Hundreds.	Tens.	Units.	
●	●●●● ●●●●	•••• ••••	or 188
●●	●●● ●●	•••• •••	or 257
●●	●●●● ●●●	•••• ••••	or 278

Have a few spare tens and hundreds, and then ask the child to count the unit-pieces of paper. When he says 23, ask him how many tens are in 23? If he says 2 tens and 3 units, ask him to change some of his units with you for ten-pieces, and then ask him to lay the two ten-pieces on the other tens, leaving the three remaining units in a pile. Then let him count the ten-pieces, and when he says there are 22, ask him how many of them make a hundred-piece, and exchange hundred-pieces with him. Tell him to lay the two ten-pieces that remain, in the tens' place, and to lay the two hundred-pieces with the other hundreds. Then let him count the hundreds, and say how many there are. Ask him then to express the hundreds, tens and units, in figures, viz., 723.

Let him add several times in this way, and express the amount, or even write the whole sum in figures. When expert at this, give him the following:

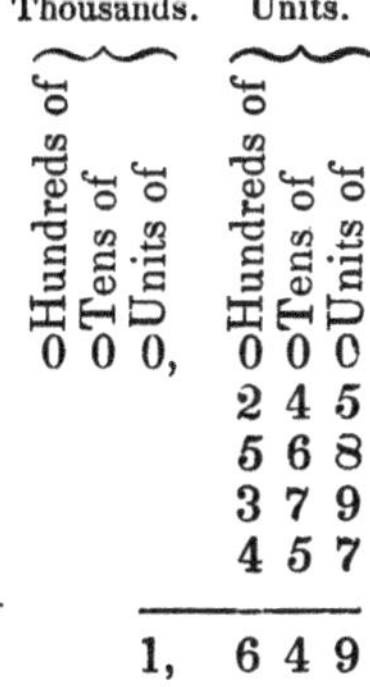

He can set down the units and the tens as before. When

he comes to the hundreds, tell him to set the 6 under the hundreds, and the ten of hundreds, making one thousand, must go into the next family, under units of thousands.

Then take a piece of paper ten times as big as a 100 piece, and call it a 1000 piece, that the child may see the tenfold increase of numbers towards the left.

By this time, he will understand the basis of numeration, and a more expeditious course may be tried as follows. Write the nine zeros, and place them in families as before,

Millions.	Thousands.	Units.
0 0 0,	0 0 0,	0 0 0

then ask how many figures must there be to reach to hundreds? How many to units of thousands? to units of millions? Write various sums under the zeros, and ask the children to read them. Introduce many zeros into the sums you write, and teach the pupil, that, if no other figure is to be placed under any zero, the place must never be left vacant, but filled with a zero. After the pupil reads easily any number you write, not exceeding millions, give him the chalk, and dictate, at first, as follows: Write three hundred and nine units! Write, in the line below, three hundred and nine thousands! Watch for the zeros to be put under the units, and then say, Write three hundred and nine millions! He will see that it is just as easy to write millions as units, if he recollects to place them aright.

If then you wish to dictate a number of sums to be afterwards added, write the nine zeros as before, and dictate the following sums, waiting, after you have named the millions till they are written down by the pupil, and then giving the thousands, and waiting till they are written, before you give the units.

000,000,000
306,460,099
87,087,807
960,096,906
9,009,090
90,600,006
756,000,010
7,007,007
70,070,070
700,700,700

8,808,080
67,068,000
964,064
7,907
89,000,089

When the pupil can write the above sums without mistake, the zeros may be removed from over the sum, and he may be exercised without them; but the teacher must be rigid in requiring the figures to be separated into families, and in requiring zeros to be inserted where no other figures come. If the pupil is told to write eight hundred and four thousand, and seventy-nine units, and writes them thus, 80479, the teacher must tell him to mark off his figures nto families, and ask him if 800 thousands are in the thousands' place. Or, he may ask how many figures does it take to make hundreds of thousands?

Many of the teachers whom I met at the Institutes, had evidently been accustomed to copy sums from books, and unaccustomed to write from dictation. The consequence was that they missed in addition, not because they did not add correctly, but because the sums that I dictated were incorrectly written down. All the subsequent rules must be made practical exercises in numeration, so that the place of every figure shall be as distinctly marked in the pupil's mind, as if it were written there.

When a large class are engaged in ciphering, and are allowed to bring up the answer as soon as it is found, there will be confusion unless something like the following rule is observed. Let me give the rule by showing how I managed in such cases.

Suppose the class contains fifty pupils. I dictate a sum for each to do on his slate. I always do it, and prove it, before any of the class bring it up; but, if the teacher cannot do this, the pupils must be required to form a line, those who do it first being nearest to the teacher. It is better that they should wait for him than for him to prepare the answer beforehand, for he needs the practice, and should compel himself to take it. As soon as he is sure that his sum is right, he must look at the first slate; if right number it 1, if wrong make a *w*, but say nothing. Then look at the rest, numbering those that are right in their order, and marking all that are wrong with *w*.

The teacher must also say how long he will wait for answers, and he must encourage those who do the sum wrong to try again. No one, after joining the line to show up, must make or alter a figure, and, if known to do so, he must go behind all that are in the line. This any honest pupil will do, if he detects an error while waiting for examination. When the whole fifty have shown their slates, or when the allotted time has expired, if 20 is the last number that has the correct answer, the teacher must tell all who did the sum incorrectly, that is, all who are not numbered, to call themselves 21. Let every scholar then write the number he has obtained on one corner of his slate, and keep it there.

Give a new sum, and mark the slates in the same manner, and let each pupil record the number he gets now, under the former number. When the lesson is over, let each pupil add up the numbers he has obtained, and let the teacher record the aggregate of each pupil on a list of names kept for the purpose. If he allows precedence to be taken in the class, the pupil whose aggregate is the least may stand first, and the rest according to their numbers. If the teacher needs to use his pupils as assistants, his class list of these exercises will show him the most capable.

To be more particular. Suppose the class consists of ten pupils, named A, B, C, D, E, F, G, H, I, J. The least aggregate of any one's numbers *must* be as many as the number of sums done, for he cannot be less than 1. Let the teacher then begin at the lowest number, say 8, if eight sums were done, and let him call every number, from 8 onward, till all are placed. Suppose the pupils have been numbered as follows:

	A.	B.	C.	D.	E.	F.	G.	H.	I.	J
1st trial	2.	4.	1.	7.	8.	5.	3.	10.	9.	6
2 "	1.	3.	4.	8.	5.	6.	2.	7.	10.	9
3 "	2.	3.	5.	6.	7.	4.	1.	9.	8.	10
4 "	2.	4.	1.	7.	5.	6.	3.	10.	9.	8
5 "	1.	2.	3.	8.	6.	5.	4.	7.	10.	9
6 "	1.	2.	4.	5.	9.	10.	3.	6.	7.	8
7 "	2.	1.	3.	4.	7.	10.	5.	8.	9.	6
8 "	1.	3.	2.	5.	8.	6.	4.	7.	10.	9
	12.	22.	23.	50.	55.	52.	25.	64.	72.	65

The Teachers' Class List then should be ruled as follows, and the record of the above lesson would stand as in the first column below.

A.	1	1	2	1	2	1	2	1	1	2	=	14	No.	1
B.	2	3	1	2	5	2	1	2	3	3	=	24		2
C.	3	4	3	3	4	3	3	4	4	1	=	32		3
D.	5	2	4	5	6	4	4	3	7	4	=	44		4
E.	7	7	6	6	5	8	6	7	6	5	=	63		6
F.	6	8	7	7	3	10	8	6	5	7	=	67		7
G.	4	5	5	4	1	9	5	5	2	6	=	46		5
H.	8	6	10	8	10	5	10	9	8	10	=	84		8
I.	10	9	9	9	9	6	7	10	9	8	=	86		9
J.	9	10	8	10	8	7	9	8	10	9	=	88		10

If the class have ten such trials in the course of the term, and the above columns represent the result of each trial, then the aggregate at the right hand shows the relative rank of the class at the end of the term. I kept such a class list in every branch that was taught in the school, and could at any moment tell the relative standing of every pupil, and select the best assistant in any branch where one was wanted.

When the children are ciphering on the black-board, there are various ways of keeping them at work. I will try to describe a few of them. Suppose the class to consist of six, and the exercise to be in addition. I first dictate one line of a sum to each pupil, as follows:

3,746,389,467
8,079,688,089
7,680,895,496
9,009,900,090
7,568,785,687
8,687,768,686

515
2 5 3

The pupils stand in a semicircle around the board, the

teacher or monitor standing on the left, the head of the class being always on the right.

FIRST METHOD.

Let the first child begin, and say aloud, "6 and 7 are 13." Let the next child say, "and 6 are 19;" the next, "and 9 are 28;" and the next, "and 7 are 35." The next sets down 5, and, if the children are very young, he sets a small 3 under the 5, as a guide to the next, who says, "3 tens carried to 8 tens make 11." Then the head begins again, and says, "11 and 8 are 19;" the next says, "and 9 are 28;" the next, "and [illegible] are 37;" the next, "and 8 are 45;" the next, "and 6 are 51[illegible] The next sets down 1 in the tens place, and puts a 5 un[illegible]r it. The next says, "5 hundreds carried to 6 hundreds make 11 hundreds;" the next says, "and 6 are 17;" and so on until the sum is finished.

As soon as possible, the habit of placing the number to be carried under the figure to be set down, must be dropped; for the children will be more attentive if they have no such aid.

If any one mistakes in the addition, let the next try, and go up, if precedence is allowed in the classes, but do not require the child who goes down to take a new number until his turn comes round again, for this will double his share of the work.

SECOND METHOD.

If precedence is not taken, let the teacher call on the pupils, not in course, to add, as in the former case, and ignorance of whose turn comes next will keep all attentive. This course gives the teacher much more trouble, however, and takes much more time.

THIRD METHOD.

Instead of saying 6 and 7 are 13, and 6 are 19, and 9 are 28, and 7 are 35, set down 5 and carry 3 — let the first child say, 13; the next, 19; the next, 28; the next, 35. Let the next set down 5, and the next, taking the next column, say 11; the next 19; the next 28; and so on to the end.

FOURTH METHOD.

Let the first pupil, or one designated by the teacher, add the whole first column silently, and, only telling the amount aloud, let him set down 5. Let another take the second column, and, declaring the amount aloud, let him set down 1. Let a third take the third column, and declare, and set down; and so on to the end.

FIFTH METHOD.

This method is called the silent method, and is useful when the teacher is engaged with a class, and wishes to keep the rest employed so as not to be interrupted by their noise.

The monitor stands with a sponge. The first pupil adds the first column silently, and sets down the result without saying a word. If correct, the monitor nods assent; if wrong, he rubs out the figure and says nothing. The next child then writes the amount as he made it; if right, it stands; if wrong, the monitor erases it. Not a word is spoken. If, when one has missed, the next is not ready to write, those below him who are ready, hold up the right hand, and the monitor points to the next highest to go to the board, and, if right, to go above both the one who missed, and the one, or more, that were not ready to correct him.

SIXTH METHOD.

This is the most animating, and resembles the fifth method, except that each pupil is furnished with a piece of chalk, and is at liberty to go and write down the amount of the column as fast as he can add it up. As this leads to great activity and a lively competition, the monitor or teacher must be very expert in the exercise, prompt in erasing errors, and careful to see fair play. If the pupils are seated in front of the board, no one should be allowed to write the amount of a column unless he goes from his seat to do it. Of course, after writing a figure, right or wrong, the pupil must take his seat before he tries again. If there are no seats for the pupils, so much the better. Let a semicircle be chalked in front of the board, and let the rule be that no one not toeing the circle, shall be allowed to write. Of course, every one that writes on the board goes to his place before he tries again.

If the teacher wishes to know how many columns are added by each scholar, he has only to lay a few counters under the board, and let each pupil who adds correctly, take one, and keep what he gets till the end of the lesson, when the number obtained by each may be recorded, and the rank of each assigned, if it be the custom of the school. Sometimes, when the scholars are very quick at figures, several will rush towards the board at a time, and the master or monitor being, of course, very active, the scene is very interesting, and faintly resembles the scenes in the Scotch schoolrooms, so graphically described by Mr. Mann and others.

In describing these methods, I have confined myself to addition, but the teacher will perceive that the other rules may be taught in the same manner, and it is unnecessary for me to give any examples. I do not know that these methods are peculiar to me. They are some of the many that I practised years ago, for I always endeavored to have a variety of methods, that the interest of the pupils might never flag. I even went so far as, once or twice a year, to alter the position of the seats, which were movable. My own desk, too, was wheeled by turns to every side of the schoolroom, and in this way all the interest excited by a new schoolroom was kept up in an old one. While thus shifting about, we once tried what is supposed to be a new plan, that of placing the teacher's desk behind the children, and after a fair experiment, I gave it up as having few benefits and many disadvantages.

In teaching Subtraction, I had very little, probably, that is not now common in the schools. The only method that I have not seen in any school is the following, which I learned from a German, twenty years ago. Suppose I am required to take the lower line of the following sum from the upper.

706,145,832
73,854,735

In teaching on the old plan I used to say, "Take 5 units from 2 units I can't. Borrow 1 ten from the 3 tens, and turn it into units, and add them to the 2 units, and say 5 units from the 12 units leave 7 units. Then, as I borrowed 1 ten and did not take it, the upper 3 is 1 more than it ought to be, and adding 1 to the 3 below and calling it 4, will be the same as if I changed the upper 3 into a 2 and let the lower 3 stand as it is. One I carry* then to the lower 3

*I use the term *carry*, but it is an incorrect term, because I really carry nothing from one figure to the next. When a column of units amounts to ten, I set down the units and really carry the tens to the column of tens; but, in subtraction, the operation is *giving* or *supposing*, rather than carrying. I have used the word *sum* also for operation, example, problem, &c., because the word is short and well understood, but its true meaning is *amount*.

makes 4 of it, and I say, Take 4 tens from 3 tens I can't. I borrow 1 hundred from the 8 hundreds, and, as 1 hundred is 10 tens, I add the 10 tens to the 3 tens, and say 4 tens from 13 tens leave 9 tens. Set 9 under the 3, and, as before, call the 7, 8, because when you borrowed 1 hundred from the 8 you did not take it away. It will be then 8 hundreds from 8 hundreds leave no hundreds; set down zero under the 7, and proceed to the thousands place," and so on.

If the teacher pleases, he can occasionally allow the pupil, when he borrows 1, to take it from the upper figure and change it. But this is often a more intricate operation than that I have described; for if the next upper place is occupied by a zero, nothing can be borrowed, and the next must be asked for a loan. Thus, in subtracting 1 unit from 1 thousand, the operation is as follows:—

```
1000
   1
────
```

Take 1 unit from no units, I cannot. Borrow 1 ten from no tens, I cannot. Borrow 1 unit from no hundreds, I cannot. Borrow 1 unit from 1 thousand units I can; and this brings us to the starting point again, so that, after borrowing like a loafer, I am no better off than when I began. Still it is well to borrow, and alter a few sums, to show what is meant by carrying.

```
3,461,034
  896,458
─────────
2,564,576
```

By the old method of carrying, the sum would stand as above; but, if, when I borrowed from the upper figures, I had taken what I borrowed, the upper line would stand thus after the operation.

```
2,350,924
  896,458
─────────
2,564,576
```

The upper line is so altered by this process that it cannot be recognized; and, as the figures now stand, the sum cannot be proved in the old way, by adding the smaller sum and the remainder together to equal the larger sum. It is often useful and necessary to preserve the figures of the larger sum, and it causes some trouble to restore them after the above transformation.

The German method to which I have alluded, does subtraction by addition.

```
3,461,034
  896,458
---------
```

In doing the above sum, I say to the first pupil, 8 and how many make 14? 6, he says, and sets 6 under the 8. As in addition, with which the child is acquainted, 1 must be carried for 14. Then say, 1 carried to 5 makes 6, and 6 and how many make 13? 7, says the child. Then set 7 under the 5, and carry 1 to the 4, saying, 1 and 4 are 5, and 5 and how many make 10? 5, says the child. Then set 5 under the 4, carry 1 to the 6, and so continue till the work is completed. As, at last, 1 will be carried to the vacant place of millions, the question will be, 1 and how many make 3? Set down the 2, and the sum is done.

My pupils have more readily fallen into this method than into the old one, and one method of applying it is very popular, especially in the silent exercise on the black-board. Suppose I am worth 375,484 dollars, and owe to several persons the following sums: 38,654 dollars; 87,263 dollars; 74,269 dollars; 69,745 dollars; and 80,676 dollars; required how much I shall have left after paying these debts.

```
 375,484  Minuend.
 -------
  38,654 ⎫
  87,268 ⎪
  74,269 ⎬ Subtrahend.
  69,745 ⎪
  80,676 ⎭
 -------
$24,872   Remainder.
```

I begin with the right hand column, and say, 6, 11, 20, 28, 32, and 2 make 34. I add as many tens as will make the top sum more than the amount of the column, and then what I must add to make the sums equal is what I must set under the column. Carry, as in addition, one for every ten. The first column amounting to 32, I borrow three tens and call the

4 over the column 34, and, of course, the column of 32 needs 2 to make it 34.

Then I carry 3, and say, 3, 10, 14, 20, 26, 31, and 7 are 38; set down 7, and carry 3; — and so on to the end.

The Germans, I am told, carry this method of Subtraction into Long Division also, and as it is a good exercise of the arithmetical memory, I will give a specimen.

```
7948 ) 54607.6845 ( 68,706
        ---------
        6919.6
        --------
          5612.8
          ---------
             492.45
             ------
              1557
```

I say 6 times 8 are 48, and 9 are 57. I set the 9 under the 7, and go on, remembering that I have 5 to carry. 6 times 4 are 24, and 5 to carry are 29, and 1 makes 30. Set down 1 and carry 3. 6 times 9 are 54, and 3 to carry are 57, and 9 are 66. Set down 9 and carry 6. 6 times 7 are 42, and 6 to carry are 48, and 6 are 54. Set down 6. 6919 is the remainder after the multiplication and subtraction. Then bring down the 6, and multiply by 8, &c. This method saves the making of 20 figures. The dots are used merely to show what figures are brought down.

It was the custom of my classes to do twenty or thirty sums in Subtraction in half an hour, and the difference between this amount of practice and that I obtained when at school, is somewhat remarkable. My teacher was so aged that, to my boyish mind, he divided the whole course of time with Methuselah. He wore a white wig, on the back of which the boys sometimes lodged chips and quill-tops. His vest was long, with pocket flaps that half covered his thighs. He wore breeches, white stockings, and shoes with large buckles. I never heard a word against his character, for he had none, and was so harmless that I can almost forgive the School Committee of Boston, who kept him in office a quarter of a century after he had become unable to do the duties of a master of this double-headed school of about 500 boys and girls. No boy had a printed Arithmetic, but, every other day, a sum or two was set in each manuscript, to be ciphered on the slate, shown up, and, if right, cop ed into the manuscript.

Two sums were all that were allowed in Subtraction, and this number was probably as many as the good man could set for each boy. This ciphering occupied two hours, or rather consumed two, and the other hour was employed in writing one page in a copy-book. Once, when I had done my two sums in Subtraction, and set them in my book, and been idle an hour, I ventured to go to the master's desk and ask him to be so good as to set me another sum. His amazement at my audacity was equal to that of the almshouse steward when the half-starved Oliver Twist "asked for more." He looked at me, twitched my manuscript towards him, and said, gutturally, "Eh! you gnarly wretch, you are never satisfied!" I had never made such a request before, nor did I ever make another afterwards. On the black-board, which was unknown in those days, a pupil may now get more practice in one hour than I got in one month.

In teaching Multiplication, I had no method that I have not seen in good schools of the present day. The Table was taught usually before the child began to cipher, for it was said and sung by the whole school for recreation, and the little children caught it from the older pupils before they were required to use it. If, however, a new scholar wished to learn it, she practised multiplying by 2 on the black-board till she knew the line; then she took 3 times until this was familiar. She was required too to rule 144 squares upon her slate, or on paper, and make Table after Table for herself without any guide or assistance.

It may be of use, however, for the child to know that he may begin to multiply on the left as well as on the right, and that Multiplication may be made Addition. Thus, if I wish to find 8 times 9678, I may do it in the old way from right to left:

```
  9678      or      9678
     8                 8
------              ----
77,424                64
                     560
                    4800
                   72000
                  ------
                  77,424
```

Or I may do it from left to right, thus:

```
  9,678
  8
 ------
 72,000
  4,800
    560
     64
 ------
 77,424
```

I say 8 times 9 thousand are 72 thousand, and I set down the whole amount. Then 8 times 6 hundred are 48 hundred, and set down the whole. 8 times 7 tens are 56 tens; and 8 times 8 units are 64 units. There is clearly a loss of time in this manner, but to a beginner it may communicate a clear idea of the contracted form in which the operation is usually performed.

Finally, the child may write the sum eight times, and add the sums together.

In Division the children must be required, at first certainly, if not always, to explain the common method by a process like the following:

```
6 ) 674,352        6 ) 674,352
    112,392            -------
    -------        600,000 | 100,000
                    70,000 |  10,000
                    14,000 |   2,000
                      2300 |     300
                       550 |      90
                        12 |       2
                           | -------
                             112,392
```

That is, instead of saying 6 is contained in 6 once, let the pupil say, 6 is contained in 6 hundred thousand 1 hundred thousand times. 6 is contained in 7 ten thousands 1 ten thousand times, and 1 ten thousand over. 1 ten thousand is 10 unit thousands, and 4 more unit thousands make 14 unit thousands, in which 6 is contained 2 thousand times, and 2 unit thousands over. 2 thousands are 20 hundreds, and 3 are 23 hundreds, in which 6 is contained 300 times and 5 hundreds over. 5 hundreds are 50 tens, and 5 are 55 tens, in which 6 is contained 9 tens of times and 1 ten over. 1 ten is ten units, and 2 units are 12 units, in which 6 is contained 2 units times.

I always found Long Division a more difficult operation to children than any other portion of the elementary rules, and some of my methods of explaining it may not be useless to young teachers, who should try to have more ways than one.

One way was to do Short Division long fashion, to show that there is no difference in the manner, but only in the difficulty of carrying the remainders in the mind. Thus the sum first explained:

6) 674,352
112,392

if done at length, and not in the mind, will appear thus

6) 674,352 (112,392	or thus:—	6) 674,352 (112,392
6		600,000
7		74,352
6		60,000
14		14,352
12		12,000
23		2,352
18		1,800
55		552
54		540
12		12
12		12

But the child soon learns how to multiply and subtract, and is only puzzled to know how many times the divisor *will go*, as the old term was, that is, how many times it is contained in the dividend, or a portion of the dividend. The rule for this is so simple that I should not waste a word on it, had I not discovered at the Institutes, that many young teachers have no rule but to try till the remainder comes less than the divisor. Let us take the following rule, viz.: "If the figures of the divisor amount to more than an equal number of figures in the dividend, one more figure of the dividend must be taken Then see how many times the first figure of the divisor is contained in the first two of the dividend, and this will generally give the right number of times for the whole sum, if the second figure of the divisor is less than 5. If it is more than 5, suppose the first figure of the divisor to be one more than it is, and then see how many times the supposed figure is contained in the first two of the dividend. Let us try this rule.

First with the 2d figure less than 5.

```
                        6294 ) 88469687 ( 14056
6 is in 8, once.               6294····
                               -----
                               25529
6 is in 25, 4 times.           25176
                               ------
6 is in 3 no times.              35368
6 is in 35, 5 times.             31470
                                 -----
                                  38987
6 is in 38, 6 times.              37764
                                  -----
                                   1223
```

Next with the 2d figure more than 5.

```
                        7846 ) 60298749 ( 7685
8 in 60, 7 times.              54922···
                               -----
                                53767
8 in 53, 6 times.               47076
                                -----
                                 66914
8 in 66, 8 times.                62768
                                 -----
                                  41469
8 in 41, 5 times.                 39230
                                  -----
                                   2239
```

This rule will not always succeed so invariably, but it will always come so near that the true number can be seen without further guessing.

The teacher, however, may always be *certain*, if, when he has any doubt of the rule, he multiplies the two first figures of the divisor to see whether what he has to carry will exceed the figures in the dividend. For example, take the following.

657489) 6473291476 (9

The second figure being neither more nor less than 5, it will not do to rely upon calling the first 7 or 6. 6 would be contained in 64, 10 times, and 7 would be contained 9 times. Is 9 right? Multiply the 6 and 5 of the divisor by 9, in the mind, and see if it exceeds the 647 of the dividend. 585 being less, the probability is that the whole 6 figures of the divisor will go into the first 7 figures of the dividend. Again, try the following:

89694) 8109687876 (

Call 8, 9, and will it be contained 9 times in 81? The answer is, certainly; because, if 9 is contained, any number less than 9, even $8\frac{9}{10}$, must be. But suppose the sum were

89694) 8,009,687,876 (8

will 9 be contained 9 times, or only 8 times, in the 80? Try the first two figures by 9. Nine times 89 are 801, which is more than the eight hundred of the dividend, and you may be sure 9 is too many, and 8 just enough.

A few dozen sums done by the class on a black-board, will make quite small pupils familiar with this rule, and will save them from a deal of trouble

The pupils must at first be taught what to call the figures of the quotient. For instance, when they find, as in the last example, that 89,694 is contained 8 times in 800968, the question must be settled whether the 8 in the quotient is 8 units, 8 tens, 8 hundreds, or what it is. The rule is easy; the 8 is whatever the last figure of that portion of the dividend used to produce it is. 800968 is used, and the first figure of the quotient is the same as the right hand 8, and this is tens of thousands. The pupil may then know that the quotient must contain five figures, or it cannot be right. I have sometimes required the pupil, in such cases, to set down zeros at the right hand of the first figure in the quotient, and rub them out and supply others as the sum proceeded. This will prevent his omitting to place zeros in the quotient when a figure has been brought down to the previous remainder, and the amount is not great enough to contain the divisor.

```
89694) 8,009,687,876 (8ØØ00
       717 552         93
       -------
        834167        89,300 times.
        807246
        -------
         269218
         269082
         -------
           13676
```

The only other point of arithmetic to which I shall call the attention of the young teacher, is a method of explaining what are called Compound Addition, Subtraction, Multiplication and Division. I once passed one of my classes, and found the monitor playing, as I supposed, instead of teaching her class in Compound Division. On inquiry, however, I found that she had been unable to make the class fully comprehend the operation, and she had adopted a plan not unlike that I have proposed for showing the increase of figures from right to left in decimal arithmetic.

She had taken large square pieces of paper which she called pounds. She had cut some of these into 20 pieces called shillings; some of the shillings into 12 parts called pence, and some of the pence into 4 parts called farthings. She had then chalked a sum on the black-board thus:—

	£.	s.	d.	q.
2)	3.	15.	6.	2
	1.	17.	8.	3

and she had placed 3 of the pieces representing pounds in one pile, 15 of the shilling pieces in another pile, 6 of the penny pieces in another, and 2 of the farthing pieces on the right of the other piles. Then she had begun to divide by 2, and had placed 1 pound piece under the 3. The pound piece that remained she cut up into 20 pieces, and added them to the 15. Then she placed 17 of the pieces under the shilling place. The odd shilling she cut into 12 penny pieces, which she added to the 5, making 17. Then she divided by 2, putting 8 pieces in the pence place. The odd penny she carried to farthings by cutting it up, and then dividing the 6 farthings by 2, she placed three farthing pieces in their proper order.

She then performed the same sum on the black-board, and compared the results. This was done by a monitor under fourteen years of age, who had never seen or heard of any such method of explanation; and it may well put to shame some teachers who have ventured to say that monitors cannot teach. I saw at once the simplicity of the illustration and immediately had suitable pieces of pasteboard prepared, not only to illustrate Compound Division, but Addition, Subtraction, Multiplication and Reduction ascending and descending, as the two operations are called. I had also a set of blocks to explain solid or cubic measure.

All such apparatus the teacher can get without expense, if he is as expert at whittling as a Yankee ought to be to uphold the national character.

MENTAL ARITHMETIC.

In Mental Arithmetic I did less at the Institutes than in written arithmetic, for the reason that other teachers preferred to devote themselves to arithmetic, and to me all branches were equally agreeable. It was my custom very early to introduce my pupils to this study, because it afforded relief to their minds, and, oftentimes, quiet and innocent amusement. It is hardly necessary for me to explain at large my course with beginners; for the Child's Arithmetic contains my plan, and has been recommended to teachers by Mr. Palmer in his Teacher's Manual, and by the authors of the School and Schoolmaster. The leading feature of the plan is the constant illustration of every elementary principle by the use of sensible objects. It contains full exercise for children from three to seven years of age, and, although primarily intended to be an introduction to Colburn's First Lessons, it is well fitted to precede any arithmetic that is fit to be used at the present day.

After the child is familiar with this little book, he will be prepared to relish those more advanced; and, in teaching these, the same system of illustration must be continued, whether the book provides for it or not. If the pupil has been properly taught the Child's Arithmetic, he will have a clear idea of the elements of calculation, will be accustomed to reason clearly, and to exercise his mind without distraction upon more difficult problems. By all means, oblige him to perform the calculations mentally, and without the aid of the book. It is not many years since a convention of teachers, in one of the counties of this state, were astonished at the unreasonableness of a gentleman, who required them to close their books, and to keep them closed, while he proposed a question for them to solve.

I shall not describe the various methods pursued by myself or others in teaching mental arithmetic, but shall content myself with giving an example or two as I have seen them performed by my friend William Clough, one of the most thorough teachers of this beautiful science that I have ever known, who lately taught one of our State Normal Schools, and is now Principal of an Academy at St. Charles, in the State of Missouri.

The peculiarity of his method of teaching is, that he requires the *reason* of every step to be more distinctly stated than usual, and he is careful to introduce many incidental questions that arise during the solution.

Suppose, then, the question to be the first in Colburn's First Lessons, p. 81, Letter B. "Four fifths of fifteen is six tenths of how many thirds of twenty-one?"

The pupil says, "Two and $\frac{6}{7}$ thirds of 21;" and then proves the answer as follows: "One fifth of 15 is 3;—four fifths of 15 are four times as much, and 4 times 3 are 12.—If 12 be six tenths of some number, one sixth of 12 must be one tenth of the same number, because one tenth of any number is one sixth of 6 tenths of that number. One sixth of 12 is 2, and 2 is the tenth of ten times 2, which is 20.—One third of 21 is 7, and 7 is contained in 20 two and six sevenths times. Therefore, 4 fifths of 15 is 6 tenths of two and six sevenths thirds of 21."

Among the incidental questions asked would, perhaps, be the following. "You say $\frac{1}{5}$ of 15 is 3,—how do you know this?" or, "Can you prove this?" The pupil says, "A fifth of 15 is fifteen times as much as a fifth of 1,—15 times one fifth of 1 is 15 fifths of 1;—5 fifths of 1 make 1; and if 5 fifths of 1 make 1, 15 fifths of 1 will make as many ones as 5 fifths of one are contained times in 15 fifths of 1—5 fifths of 1 are contained in 15 fifths of 1 three times; therefore, one fifth of 15 is 3."

Again, "You say 2 is the tenth of 10 times 2; how do you

know this?" The pupil replies, "2 is the same as one time 2, and one time 2 is the tenth of 10 times 2; therefore, 2 is the tenth of 10 times 2."

This is an abstract question, and I am not sure that it is the best I could have selected; I will endeavor, therefore, to give an example of what Colburn terms a concrete question. First Lessons, page 78, Question 19.

2. If 4 men can do a piece of work in 8 days, how many men would it take to do the same work in 4 days?

The pupil says, "8 men;—for if 4 men can do the work in 8 days, it will take 8 times as many men to do it in 1 day, because 1 day is an eighth of 8 days, and the less the number of days the more men it will require to do the work. One eighth of the number of days takes 8 times the number of men. 8 times 4 men are 32 men; therefore, if 4 men can do a piece of work in 8 days, it will take 32 men to do the same work in one day. If 1 day require 32 men to do the work, 4 days will require one fourth as many men to do the same work, because the more days there are, the fewer men will be required;—4 times the number of days will require one fourth the number of men;—one fourth of 32 men is 8 men:—therefore, if 4 men can do a piece of work in 8 days, it will take 8 men to do the work in 4 days."

3. Page 102, Question 39. "A man bought six sevenths of a cask of raisins for five dollars; what was the whole cask worth?"

The pupil says, "Five dollars and five sixths of a dollar." If the man bought six sevenths of a cask for 5 dollars, he bought one seventh of a cask of raisins for one sixth of five dollars, or for one sixth as much; because, one seventh of a cask is one sixth of six sevenths of the cask, and the less the quantity of raisins he bought, the less the money they cost; or, the less the number of sevenths of a cask he bought, the less the number of dollars they cost,—$\frac{1}{6}$ of the quantity of raisins, $\frac{1}{6}$ of the money they cost—$\frac{1}{6}$ of 5 dollars is $\frac{5}{6}$ of 1 dollar,—therefore, if a man bought $\frac{6}{7}$ of a cask of raisins for 5 dollars, he bought $\frac{1}{7}$ of the cask for $\frac{5}{6}$ of a dollar. If he bought $\frac{1}{7}$ of a cask for $\frac{5}{6}$ of a dollar, he bought $\frac{7}{7}$ of a whole cask for seven times as much, because the greater the quantity of raisins he bought, the more money they cost. 7 times 5 sixths of a dollar are 35 sixths of a dollar, which is equal to 5 dollars and $\frac{5}{6}$ of a dollar. Therefore, if a man bought $\frac{6}{7}$ of a cask of raisins for 5 dollars, the whole cask was worth 5 dollars and $\frac{5}{6}$ of a dollar.

The incidental questions might be, "How do you know that $\frac{1}{6}$ of 5 dollars is $\frac{5}{6}$ of 1 dollar? How do you know that 35 sixths of a dollar are equal to \$5 and $\frac{5}{6}$ of a dollar?"

4. Page 103, Question 46. "12 is $\frac{7}{5}$ of what number?" The pupil says, "$8\frac{4}{7}$. If 12 be $\frac{7}{5}$ of some number, $\frac{1}{7}$ of 12 must be $\frac{1}{5}$ of the number, because $\frac{1}{5}$ of any number is $\frac{1}{7}$ of $\frac{7}{5}$ of that number; $\frac{1}{7}$ of 12 is $\frac{12}{7}$ of 1—if $\frac{12}{7}$ of 1 be $\frac{1}{5}$ of some number, $\frac{5}{5}$, or the whole of that number, must be 5 times as much—5 times 12 sevenths are 60 sevenths, which is equal to $8\frac{4}{7}$—therefore, 12 is $\frac{7}{5}$ of $8\frac{4}{7}$." Several incidental or *review* questions would also be put.

5th. Page 105, Question 13. How many yards of cloth that is three quarters wide are equal to 7 yards of cloth that is five quarters wide?" The pupil says "$11\frac{2}{3}$ yards. If 5 quarters *width* require 7 yards in *length*, 1 quarter wide will require 5 times as many yards in length;—because 1 quarter wide is $\frac{1}{5}$ of 5 quarters wide, and the less the width the greater the length—$\frac{1}{5}$ of the width, 5 times the length—5 times 7 yards are 35 yards;—therefore, if 5 quarters wide require 7 yards in length, 1 quarter wide will require 35 yards in length; if 1 quarter wide require 35 yards in length, 3 quarters wide will require $\frac{1}{3}$ of that length, because the greater the width, the less the length,—3 times the width, $\frac{1}{3}$ the length;—$\frac{1}{3}$ of 35 yards is $11\frac{2}{3}$ yards;—therefore, $11\frac{2}{3}$ yards of cloth that is 3 quarters wide are equal to 7 yards that is 5 quarters wide."

This must suffice for arithmetic; and I shall say nothing of algebra, because I did not teach it at the Institutes, and, in my opinion, it ought never to be taught in the common schools. I shall never forget one occasion when some of Mr. Clough's pupils, who had never studied algebra, but who had been well instructed in Colburn's First Lessons, had a contest with some young teachers who had studied algebra, Tower's Intellectual Algebra furnishing the problems. The arithmeticians solved the questions by arithmetic in one fourth of the time required by the algebraists, and, except in quadratic equations, this disparity was kept up with ease. If it fell within the scope of this volume, I should more at large consider the popular error of introducing algebra into common schools of boys, and the all but folly of teaching it, in any school, to girls. I do not call in question the ability of the females to learn algebra, but the utility, and, of course, the policy, of teaching them what they will never use.

Let me add that if any young teacher wishes to see arithmetic, algebra, and mathematics taught as they should be taught, he cannot do better than to visit either of our normal schools; for, so different is the manner of teaching at these schools from the manner prevalent in the districts, that one who has often visited them can tell a normal pupil, by his management, about as readily as he can tell a veteran from a raw recruit.

Besides the usual method of proposing the question to the whole class, waiting a reasonable time, and then selecting some pupil to give the answer, and explain the process by which he arrived at it, I had another method, which, on some occasions, was very useful.

Every pupil was furnished with a slip of paper, about four inches by one. The question was given distinctly to the whole class; each scholar set the *answer* at the top of her slip of paper, and brought it, and laid it upon my book. If the answer was right, it was numbered from one onward; if wrong, I marked *w* against it, and she could try again, if there was time. To prevent confusion, only one showed her paper at a time, the rest forming a line, and giving up in turn. If any failed to get right, they were all numbered alike, the next after the last who gave the answer correctly. Nothing but the answer was allowed to be written on the paper.

At the end of the lesson, the pupil's name was written at the bottom of her answers, and the slip of paper furnished materials for the class record. In this way, every child had to do the work; and if any one who did not answer correctly requested an explanation, I designated some one who had obtained a number, to explain,—and sometimes several were called on, until some one made the process intelligible to the pupil who called for the explanation. This method I used much for practice, after a principle had been explained. Every pupil *stood* during the lesson; and as all were obliged to walk, the exercise afforded relief after confinement at any lesson that did not admit of such locomotion. If I do not forget it, I shall hereafter have more to say on the utility of standing and moving, as far as it can be done without confusion, during recitations.

WRITING.

When I first became a teacher, writing was an affair altogether different from what it is now. Metallic pens had not been introduced, and more than half the business of a writing-master was the making and mending of pens. After enduring this task one week, seeing that it made a slave of me, I called about twenty of the best pupils around me, furnished each with a knife, if he or she had none, and then made several pens before their eyes, explaining every part of the process. Then, each took a quill and cut just as fast as I did, waiting at every step to have the work inspected. When the pens were made, I tried each one, pointed out its defects to the whole class, and then showed them how to mend it. I then promised a reward to every pupil who made his own pens for a week; and that they might have practice, I told them I should never make another pen for any of them. I never had occasion to make one afterwards; but, from that time forward, I had pupils enough who could make as good pens as I could, and who made for the smaller children, and for their families at home.

Once, at least, in a term, I instituted a reward for the best pen. Let it not be supposed, however, that I selected one pen and gave a prize only to that; I could not be guilty of such injustice. My rule in this exercise, *and in all others*, was to reward *all* in proportion to their deserts. If there were ten bests, all fared alike, and the poorest, if at all deserving, had all that he deserved. If in any district school the goosequill is still used, I recommend to the teacher to try a similar course; and, if there is no other way to supply knives, let him buy two or three, and keep them to lend for this purpose, and for no other.

The course of teaching that I had adopted led me to see, at an early stage, that I must make every pupil learn to write, and that I could do this better, and in much less time, if I qualified myself to teach them. To compel myself to practise, I set all the copies for a long time, and never used what are called copperplate slips. When some of my pupils became good writers, I obliged them to set copies for the beginners, but, to the last, I always set all the copies for my best writers and assistants, and inspected all the copies set by the assistants. The only system of penmanship that I used was the very simple one to which I have alluded under the head of Spelling, and this I shall now attempt to explain somewhat more in detail.

Right against the wall, back of my desk, and in full view of the whole school, was a long black-board, about ten feet by eighteen inches, ruled like the specimen that follows:

The lines were cut into the board before it was painted, and, although the board was used constantly for seventeen years, the lines were sufficiently distinct to the last, and the board needed to be repainted only two or three times, and this work I did myself. I mention this fact, not to imply that my patrons were unwilling to pay for the painting, but because I put on a better coat than the painter would have done. I have often been told by young teachers that they should like black-boards, but the committee would not procure any. I have no respect for such teachers, for one who cannot get a wide board, and plane it, and paint it, has not ingenuity enough to be intrusted with a school. Besides, I do not believe there is a town in Massachusetts whose carpenters and painters are so mean that they will not aid the district teacher in getting up as many black-boards as he wants. While I was teaching at some of the Institutes, I showed the teachers how to paint diagrams on cloth, and when I found the village painter, and told him what I wanted, and *why* I wanted, brushes, pots and paints were placed at my disposal, and, in every case, compensation was refused. The charge that committees will not furnish black-boards cannot be well founded, except, perhaps, in cases where the committee have no confidence in the ability of the teacher to make any good use of them. But I maintain that the teacher, if he is fit to teach, is independent of the committee in regard to black-boards, and can make them himself without much trouble or expense.

Get a long black-board, then, and rule it as I have directed. The carpenters have a tool made on purpose to cut the lines into the board, but if such a tool cannot be obtained, the lines may be ruled with a chalk-line, and scratched in with a saw, or cut in with a penknife. They may be painted white on a black ground, but the writing never looks so well over white lines.

After the board is prepared, let every child have a slate, and let every slate be ruled exactly like the board. The teacher can do the ruling with a dull penknife or any sharp pointed iron. The marks, after a day or two's use, will not mar the writing, and, as only one side of the slate is ruled, work that does not require ruling may be done on the other. Three or four sets of lines can be marked on the slate, and the pattern just given is about the best in regard to size.

The distance between the lines 1 and 2 and 8 and 9 correspond, but the space between 2 and 3 is less than that between 7 and 8. 2 marks the height and 8 the depth to which letters not looped may go, and 1 and 9 mark the space in which the loop must be made. The five lines are for the body of the letters.

I cannot describe in ten pages what I could show on the black-board in ten minutes, but I must not entirely omit the directions for shaping and joining letters. Let the small letters be made first. Suppose a class of beginners to be before me, with their slates before them, and their pencils sharpened, and long, or else thrust into a tin handle or a goosequill, to make them so. Let the pencil be held properly at first, and much trouble will be saved in subsequent lessons. It is difficult to *describe* the proper manner of holding a pen, although it may be *shown* in a moment. The pen or pencil must never sink below the knuckle of the fore-finger into the hollow between that finger and the thumb; it had better not sink quite as far as the knuckle. It must pass under the end of the forefinger, and touch the side of the middle finger just below the nail. The most common fault of bad writers is turning the top or convex part of the pen towards the body, and the consequence is that the slit does not open, as it should, when the pen moves downward, but it does so when it makes the turn at the bottom of letters, where the most deli-cate line should be made. If the pen is held properly, the sides of the slit will open equally at the downward move-ment, and then, if the pen is not twisted, but carried round the turn and up, the slit is closed by the upward movement, and the finest hair line is produced.

In writing with a pencil, the upward lines can be made just as fine by lightening the pressure of the hand. If a pupil makes the upward lines as coarse as the downward, stop him at once, and give him a separate lesson in the art of bear-ing on.

To return to our lesson. Let me talk as if the class were before me, pencil in hand.

You see, children, I place my chalk on the second line and draw a straight, but leaning or inclined line, downward to the seventh. Now do the same on your slates. This mark is no letter, but it forms a part of several letters. Make these straight lines till you get the command of your fingers. Hold your hands so that you rest upon the little finger and the next to it, and only move the thumb, fore and middle fingers, in forming letters. Let me see how each makes a straight mark and holds his hand. Very well. Now, let the straight line only go down to the sixth line, and when you get there, light up your pencil, and begin to turn as you see me do, and when you have touched the seventh line, go up as lightly as possible to the fifth line. This forms the letter *l*.

If, now, instead of making another *l*, you place a dot where the top of *l* would be, then skip from 2 to 3, and finish the lower part of the *l* from 3 to 6, and curve it as before, you will make the letter *i*. I required you to make the dot first, because many persons are so careless as not to place the dot where the top of the letter would be if the *i* were an *l*. You see the dot must lean as the rest of the *i* does. If you begin half way between 2 and 3, and go down and turn as in *l* and *i*, and then, half way between the top of your letter and the third line, lay your pencil on the letter and draw a short line towards the right, you will have a *t*. Some care-less persons make a full cross at the top of *t*, but this is wrong.

To make *n*, you see I begin at the seventh line, and go up lightly to 4, then I curve, but do not bear on till I reach 3, when I bear on, and continue a steady pressure till I reach 7.

Then, touching the mark I have just made at 6, I go up lightly to 4, curve at 3, as before, and come down to 6, when I light up, curve at 7, and carry up a fine mark to 5. The fine mark is carried up, so that, if I wish to join on another letter the fine mark may be ready for it. An *m* is made like an *n*, the first part being repeated, beginning at 6. See now how I make it, and do the same on your slates. To make *h*, take the first mark that I taught you, from 2 to 7, then, touching it at 6, make the last part of an *n*. To make a *p*, begin half way between 2 and 3, draw a straight sloping line to 8, and then touching it at 6, make the latter part of an *n*. To make *u*, begin at 7, go up lightly to 4, then, beginning at 3, bear on, touch the fine mark you have just made a little below 4, go on to 6, curve as in *i*, and go up finely to 5. Then begin again at 3, bear on, touch the fine mark just below 4, and finish as if it were an *i*.

To make *v*, begin at 7, go up lightly, and turn as at the beginning of *n*. Go down to 6, bearing on, then curve, and go up lightly to 3, not flaring too much, then bear on, go down *by the side* of the fine mark, and not *on* it, as far as 5, then curve, and go up lightly to 4. To make *w*, you need only repeat the first part of *v*. To make *b*, the first part of a *v* should be lengthened by beginning at 2 instead of 3.

To make *j*, begin at 3, and bearing on, go down to 8, then curve, go up at 9, cross the thick mark you have just made half way from 8 to 7, and go up as fine as possible to 5. Dot the *j* as you would an *i* where the top of an *l* would come, on 2. *y* has the first part of *v* added to *j*, without its dot.

To make *o*, begin at 4, and go up lightly curving to 3, then begin to bear on harder and harder till 5, then light up, begin to curve at 6, turn at 7, and go up lightly to 4, joining as neatly as possible. Many begin to make an *o* at 3, but this is unsafe, for if it is badly joined it shows, and cannot be covered when *a*, *d*, *g* or *q* are made of the *o*. When *o* is well made, make *a* of it by placing the pencil on 3, and drawing it to 6, bearing on, and touching the *o*, but not cutting any of it off so as to spoil the oval, curve just below 5 and turn up finely as in *i*. To make *d*, make *o*, then begin at 2, bear on, touch the *o*, but cut none of it off, curve just below 5, and end as in *a*. To make *q*, make *o*, then begin at 3, go down, bearing on, to 8. To make *g*, make *o*, go down as in *q*, and curve, and go up as in *y*.

To make *c*, make a handsome dot on 4, touch the right side

of it, go up lightly as in *o*, curve as in *o*, except that, instead of joining where you began, you must let the fine mark incline to the right, and stop at 5. To make *e*, begin at 7, go up curving backward to 3, then finish as in *c*, taking care to cross the fine mark between 5 and 6.

To make *k*, begin at 2, and go down to 7 as in making *h*. Begin at 4, go finely to 3, curve and bear on between 3 and 4, but come down lightly to 5. Touch the fine mark just above 5, curve to 5, bear on from 5 to 6, and curve up as in *h*.

To make *r*, make the first part of *n*, go up from 6 as if going to finish *n*, but at 3 bear on, and go down beside the fine mark just below 5, and then curve up lightly to 4.

To make *s*, begin at 7, go up finely and without curving to 3, leave the fine line sharp at top, and touching it between 3 and 4, curve round, thickening most at 5, curving at 7, and ending in a neat dot on the fine line between 5 and 6.

To make *x*, begin at 7, go up curving, as if making an *o* backwards. Then make a *c*, taking care however not to bear on at any part of the *c*, and not to touch the *o* part above 4 or below 6.

To make *z*, begin at 7, go up lightly to 3, make a neat dot on 3, curve lightly and touch 3 again, then curve as you see me do, thickening most at 5 and reaching to 7, then leaving the angle sharp, curve on the 7th line, and go up with a fine line to 5.

To make *f*, begin at 7, and go up with a slight curve to 2, then curve to 1, begin to thicken in coming down at 2, and carry a steady pressure in a straight line to 8, then curve to the right, and go up without too wide a sweep to 5; touch the stem, but do not cross it, as is sometimes ungracefully done.

As the chief object of writing such large hand first is to give the child a free movement of the hand, which is more easily obtained with a pencil than with a pen, I have always required the curves at the top and bottom of letters to be narrower than is common in what is called old-fashioned round-hand. This will be seen in the specimen of letters on page 74, and the reason is, that nothing destroys the beauty of fine hand so much as too large a curve at the top or bottom; and if the child gets accustomed to a certain proportion in writing large hand he will preserve it, right or wrong, in small hand.

In writing large hand, no letter should be looped but *f*, *g*, long *s* and long *z* and *y*. In small hand, *b*, *h*, *k*, and *l*, are also looped. In large hand, the main stem of the *h* should be twice the height of the other part, but in small hand, it may be four times as high, including the loop. In large hand, *f*, *g*, and *y* go further below the body than the letter *f* goes above it.

Capitals extend from 7 to 1 upward. In old times, the G, J, and Y were carried from 1 to 9, but the fashion now is to set G, J, and Y upon the 7th line, and to carry Z down to the 9th. I think it is unsafe to make I for J, and the teacher should avoid this alteration, but G and Y, if well made, look better on the 7th, than on the 9th line.

Let not the teacher or parent expect any child to learn to write in a moment. It is not uncommon for professors of the art of writing to promise a good hand to the pupil in twelve lessons, whether he is apt to learn or not, and, I believe, whether he tries to learn or not. There is deception in this, not unlike that which is practised in teaching French, it being not unusual for professors to promise to teach a foreign language in twenty lessons to persons who have not, with every advantage of circumstances, been able to learn their own language in twenty years.

While I was a teacher, one of the most popular professors of writing visited Boston, and put up at one of the great hotels, the daughter of whose landlord was one of my pupils. She wrote a neat and very legible hand, but the professor, who wished to pay his board in the easiest manner, persuaded the landlord that his daughter wrote a very bad hand, and, in twelve lessons, he could make her write an elegant one. The father very politely asked my consent to the experiment, and I, of course, gave it, upon condition that she should not, in the mean time, write any at my school. The professor charged one dollar a lesson, and at the end of the course, as his bill for board was more than twelve dollars, he persuaded the landlord to give his daughter another course, which would *certainly* make her a quite accomplished writer. She took the second course, and one day afterwards she laid a specimen of her penmanship upon my desk, and said, in a somewhat triumphant way, "There, sir, what do you think of that?" "Is this the result of your twenty-four lessons?" said I. "Yes, sir," said she. "Here is what I wrote when I went to Mr. B., and here is what I wrote when I had completed the course." "Well," said I, "what does your father think of it?" "O, sir, he thinks I have made great improvement and don't you think so too?" "No," said I, "if I did not know the force of habit, I should say he had spoiled your handwriting; but, as you will soon forget all he has taught you, and go back to your former hand, the experiment will do you no harm." At my request, she gave me the two specimens of her work, and I laid them in my desk. "Now," said I, "Ann, tell me honestly under what circumstances you wrote the two specimens,—were they fairly written?" "Why, no, sir," said she, "I cannot say they were; for, when I first went to Mr. B., he told me to write that specimen without a copy, and although the pen was very bad, he would not mend it or get me a better one; but when I wrote the other specimen, after I had taken the two courses of lessons, he ruled my paper, and mended my pen fifty times." About three or four months afterwards, seeing the specimens in my desk, I called Miss Ann to me, and laying the *beautiful* specimen before her, I asked her to read it to me. It consisted of four or five lines only, but, after trying and guessing for some time, she confessed, what was quite apparent, that she could not read it. "Do you know what it is?" said I. "O, yes, sir," said she. "Now," said I, "see if you can read the other specimen." She read it with perfect ease, and confessed that, on the whole, it looked the best.

The fact was, the professor taught a style of writing which paid little regard to the peculiar form of each letter, and the letters looked as if they were all *m's* and *n's*. I have told this long story for two reasons. *First*, because I believe many a good teacher has been injured by comparisons made by injudicious parents and committees, between what such professors *promise*, and what regular teachers, under many disadvantages, *perform*. If the professor is really a good penman, and does nothing but teach his art, and if the pupil attends to the lessons, as persons usually do under such circumstances, punctually, carefully, and with a deep feeling of what is expected of them, and of the extraordinary expense incurred, much improvement may be made. But this will all be lost, unless the pupil frequently, and for a long time, practises upon the lessons received; and, as not one in a hundred does this, almost every pupil of twelve-lesson-professors relapses into the handwriting to which he was accustomed before he was *reformed*. My second reason is, that the story teaches the importance of two rules, which teachers should always insist upon, first, that the writing shall be legible, and then that, if possible, it shall be elegant.

I would gladly give directions for the formation of the capital letters, and also some rules in regard to printing, but my book threatens to be too voluminous, and I must desist, or omit entirely other matters of at least equal importance. Let children, then, begin to write early. Let them write large hand before small. Let them write on the slate freely before they write on paper. When they write on paper, let them use a lead-pencil before a pen. Let them write much freely and almost carelessly, to acquire a free movement of the hand, but let the teacher require every regular copy, and every exercise in orthography, grammar, &c., to be as well written as if it were a set exercise in writing. If the teacher is a good penman, he can carry this instruction into every exercise of the school; but, if he is not a penman, he cannot teach penmanship, any better than a clown can teach manners.

DRAWING.

I KNOW not how I can better explain my notions on this subject, than by giving the preface of a little volume that I have published on the subject, entitled:

THE EYE AND HAND;

Being a Series of Practical Lessons in Drawing, for the Training of those Important Organs: Adapted to the Use of Common Schools.

PREFACE.

Experience has fully demonstrated that Drawing may be introduced into Infant and Primary Schools with great benefit to the children, and with beneficial effect upon the discipline of the schools. Every child, however young, should have a slate, and it will require no great skill on the part of the teacher to chalk some familiar object on the black-board, and request those children not otherwise engaged, to copy it. The evil of our primary schools, and the greatest evil, because productive of most other evils, is, want of employment; and yet how easily a teacher could keep a hundred children constantly and pleasantly engaged, if he knew how to draw.

The apparatus of primary school-rooms does not admit of any great variety of lessons; for, often, the little pupil has no desk, and, of course, no opportunity to use rules, pens, and paper. No matter,—much may be done without any apparatus but the slate and pencil; much that will be an excellent introduction to the drawing of maps, and to the study of Arithmetic and Geometry. Besides the drawing of common objects, which exercise the taste, a regular course of drawing may be given, which will train the eye and the hand, and be to drawing what the four fundamental rules are to Arithmetic, the basis of all the more advanced movements.

When Napoleon was emperor of France, he established a national system of education, and one of the earliest studies was Drawing; not fancy drawing, which is hardly subject to any fixed rules, but that portion of the art which *is* subject to them, and for which directions may be given as certain as any rule of mathematics,—on which, in fact, drawing as a science depends. The emperor ordered the Bureau of Instruction to prepare a drawing book of this sort for the national schools, and the book so prepared by M. Francœur, was eminently successful.

The following book is a free translation of the French Manual, and as far as my practice and my judgment are to be depended on, the effect of the course of instruction here proposed is to produce wonderful freedom and accuracy in the use of the eye and hand. Those who have seen the elegant writing, printing, and map-drawing, performed by my pupils, should be informed that those exercises were done by children who had also been trained to draw according to the system here proposed and explained, a system more simple, more practicable in our common schools, and more economical, than any other that I have seen.

The first lessons are *Lines*, horizontal, vertical, oblique, of various prescribed lengths, which the pupils are gradually taught, without the use of any rule or dividers, to draw perfectly straight, and to cut into halves, thirds, quarters, inches, tenths, &c., thus illustrating the earliest exercises in fractions. Then *Angles* are introduced and gradually explained, and, by practice, the child is soon enabled to draw an angle of any prescribed number of degrees. Next follow *Triangles*, *Squares*, *Pentagons* of all sorts, parts of which are prescribed, and the rest required to correspond. *Pyramids*, *Prisms*, &c., come next. Then *Circles*, *Ellipses*, *Ovals*, are introduced, with *Cones*, *Cylinders*, &c. &c. Next, these exact rules are applied to the drawing of *Urns*, *Vases*, the *Orders of Architecture*, &c. &c., and finally, the elements of drawing in *Perspective* are given. All these lessons are expected to be performed without the use of instruments, but, directions for making the same figures with instruments are given in an appendix, and simple problems, in the simplest rules of arithmetic, are given, to enable the pupil to calculate the contents of a square, a polygon, a prism, cone or cylinder,—an exercise of the utmost importance to the mechanic, who wishes to draft his own plans, calculate contracts, and be independent of others.

The exercises are confined to lines, and do not attempt to teach shading. Directions are given at every step, so that a teacher who knows nothing of drawing, may, by following the rules, learn the art while teaching it to his pupils, and the correction of their work will soon give him an exactness and facility of eye and hand, that will surprise him. Such was the effect of my practice in this way, that, to this day, I rarely use any rule or dividers for drawing lines, or describing circles.

In teaching drawing to the young, I would not exclude fancy drawing, because this cultivates the taste as well as the eye and the hand; but there is no such system in it nor can any be introduced. I should, therefore, introduce fancy figures occasionally, as I would introduce spelling from reading lessons, to vary the exercise and give life to it. The main reliance, however, must be upon that part of drawing which is subject to rules, which does not depend upon arbitrary taste, and which may be conducted systematically to any extent of skill and accuracy. If the teacher requires aid in the delineation of common objects, he may find elementary drawing books in great abundance, or he may place real objects before the pupils; and, if they practise the lessons of this book first, they will afterwards apply their knowledge and skill to the delineation of natural objects without the awkwardness and fear that usually mark the efforts of beginners.

I am satisfied that drawing and writing are nearly allied, and may be introduced into primary schools much more early than is generally supposed; and, as there can be no doubt of the utility of these branches, and as they serve admirably to fill up the otherwise idle hours of school time, it is to be hoped that, if teachers do not voluntarily introduce them, the Committees will require them to be introduced, not to push aside other studies, but to banish indolence and all its evil consequences from our schools.

I believe that drawing may be taught to children as soon, or even sooner, than they can be taught to write. In preparing a book to train the eye and hand of pupils, I was aware of the fact that most teachers of drawing are entirely unacquainted with any rules of the art, except those which relate to the manner of holding and using the pencil, that is, in making marks and shading figures. Of course, the children will get instruction in this part of drawing more easily than in that which is less common. A course of lessons, therefore, that had a bearing upon the scientific part of the art, was a desirable thing, and such I endeavored to furnish to the young teacher. The book is accompanied with such complete directions, that I need not repeat them, but shall content myself with giving a few plain directions to aid teachers in drawing objects of taste, which may not be embraced by the rules of the book, but which, as I have said in the preface, should be interspersed among the more severe exercises of the book, as a reward or relaxation.

By all means let the pupils draw *outlines* first. If they have any choice of pencils, let them use a soft one in preference to a hard one, and make the line as lightly as possible, that it may be easily erased if not well made. Whatever the picture to be drawn, let the *whole* outline be drawn first. Then examine it carefully, and fix the outline by a plainer mark with a harder pencil. If the object to be shaded be an animal,—a horse, for instance,—begin at the head and shade downwards. If a landscape, begin at the top, which is generally the more remote part of the picture, and then there will be less danger of erasing the work by rubbing your hand over it. Indeed, the neat workman will always keep a piece of paper between his hand and his work, to prevent any erasure, and any soiling of the paper. For a general rule, the deepest shades belong to the remotest objects. If you draw a circle and wish to shade it so that it shall resemble a ball, the darkest shade must be at the circumference, and the centre of what was the circle will be the lightest, and will represent that part of the ball nearest to you.

These hints will enable the teacher, not only to keep his pupils employed, but to make diagrams and other illustrations of his lessons. He may even go further, and by the same rules paint illustrations on cotton cloth with great ease. At one of the Institutes I gave the teachers a lesson in the art of painting on cotton; and then, to ascertain whether I had been understood, I called on such as thought they could not paint a copy of what I had painted, to hold up a hand. Several hands, of course, were raised; and, to their surprise, I picked out the most faint-hearted of them, and requested her to come forward and draw and paint an object similar to that I had painted on the cloth. She said "She could not do it to save her life." To please me, however, she made an attempt to draw and shade the figure, which was the large bone of the arm, and she did it well, and with great ease and dispatch.

All that is necessary is to take a piece of cotton cloth, and tack it as tight as possible upon a board, (I used a common folding-board.) Then, with a crayon or lead pencil, draw an outline of the object to be painted. The paint to be used is common black paint, such as is used to paint common wood-work. It is made by mixing lampblack and linseed or painter's oil. A little spirit of turpentine may be added, if you wish it to dry speedily. Do not make the paint too thin. My rule is to mix it on a pane of glass, and of such consistency that it will just not run off. A common stiff hair-pencil will do to paint over the outline, but a stiffer brush, made of bristles, and no larger than a common hair-pencil, is preferable, because it overcomes more readily the fuzz which is found on the surface of most cotton cloth. For the same reason, in printing letters on this cloth, I generally use a stick made of a piece of shingle a tenth of an inch wide, and about as thick as the shingle is, in the middle. With the flat side I mark the thick part, and with the edge the thin part of the letters.

After the outline is painted with the small brush, the best way to shade the figure is the following. Take an old paint-brush that has been worn down until the bristles come to an edge like a wedge, which wedge must not exceed an inch in length. Place the edge lengthwise on the outline, bear on, and, as you draw the brush forward, light up the hand. Of course, the darkest shade will then be at the outline, and the lightest near the centre towards which the brush is drawn. If there is no wish to give the figure a rounded appearance, rub the brush on a piece of cloth or board till it makes a mark of the desired shade, and then rub the brush over the figure. Diagrams painted in this way will last very long, and, if soiled, may be washed and look all the better for it. A little practice will enable the teacher to overcome any obstacle that will arise, and in this way, he may ornament his school-room, and prepare illustrations which will be as much more intelligible than mere words, as one example of painting would be more effectual than this imperfect description of the process.

GEOGRAPHY

A Lecture on "The Best Method of Teaching Geography," delivered before the American Institute of Instruction, at Hartford, Conn., August, 1845; by WILLIAM B. FOWLE. *Re-published from the fifteenth volume of the Institute Lectures.*

IN rising to address you at this time, I feel the embarrassment which always attends any attempt to address a mixed audience upon the details of instruction in any branch of science; for, if the subject is only treated in general terms, there are always some to accuse it of having no practical bearing; and, if it is treated in detail, a larger number, perhaps, will find it dull and uninteresting. I would gladly have avoided the task altogether, but your committee were so polite as to invite me to lecture, because I had some score years of experience as a teacher of the branch which they proposed for my subject, and I had done so little for the Institute, that I did not feel at liberty to decline, however serious were my misgivings as to the result.

The subject proposed by your committee was, "The Best Method of Teaching Geography," by which they probably meant *my* method, taking it for granted that no honest teacher will for a moment use any method but that which he considers the best. But a serious difficulty met me at the outset; for, what did the committee understand by the term Geography? I knew that this term, etymologically considered, meant a description of the earth in all its appearances, permanent and changeable; but the committee must have used the word in a more restricted sense, and how was I to get at it? I applied first to that leviathan of lexicographers, Dr. Johnson, and he said "Geography is *the* knowledge of the earth." *The*, we are told by an admired grammarian, is the *definite* article, although, as in this case, all that is *in*definite in the definition seems to proceed from the use of *the*. But, allowing that the Doctor meant, "Knowledge of the earth," the question naturally arose, *What* knowledge of it? Its origin? its structure? its superficial features? its artificial divisions? its changes? or, what part of the various knowledge that has been collected from age to age? To ascertain the kind or degree of this knowledge, I thought the definition of particular departments of it would aid me, and turning to the word Geology, I found that to mean, "The Doctrine of the Earth." I then, of course, turned to the word *doctrine*, and found that to mean, "The principles or positions of any sect or master." Not perceiving that I had made any approximation to the desired point, but more than ever convinced of the absurdity of requiring children to study lessons from the Dictionary, I turned to the word Topography, and found this to be, "A description of particular places," by which, I suppose, the Doctor meant, "A particular description of places;" for, if a description of particular places is topography, then a description of *all* places is not topography.

I resorted, then, to the definitions given by our best geographers, but, instead of repeating these, which, by the way, are often greatly at variance with the contents of their textbooks; I prefer to give a paragraph from the Library of Useful Knowledge, which not only describes what I consider to be the great mistake of all geographical textbooks, but which proposes nearly the plan that I have pursued from the beginning, and which I shall endeavor to recommend in this lecture. "Universal Geography," says the author, whoever he may be, "is the science that conveys to us a knowledge of the earth, both as a distinct and independent body in the universe, and as connected with a system of heavenly bodies. The figure, structure and dimensions of the earth; the properties and mutual relations of its parts; the features of its surface; its productions and inhabitants, and the laws which govern or partially affect it as a heavenly body, are all included in the comprehensive term of Universal Geography. This definition," he goes on to say, "or rather, this description of the objects of geography, serves as the basis of M. Malte Brun's elaborate work, but it manifestly embraces a great variety of subjects commonly called, and treated under distinct heads of, natural philosophy. To avoid, therefore, the confusion of ideas to which the extensiveness of this definition may give rise, it will be convenient to reduce its terms within the limits usually assigned to geography. And we are the rather induced to do this, because *the interests of science have been promoted, in no slight degree, by a judicious and well defined arrange ment of its parts, which at once excludes a great number of fanciful resemblances, and, like a division of labor in mechanical employments, renders every branch more easy to be acquired, and more likely to be extended and improved.*" "In its proper and more confined sense," he concludes, "geography comprises a knowledge of the figure and dimensions of the earth, and the situation of places upon it; of the natural and political features and divisions of its surface; *and of its various productions and inhabitants.*" This latter definition, with the exception of the last clause, may be assumed by the lecturer, but "the description of the various productions of the earth" approaches so nearly to Botany and Geology, and "the description of its inhabitants" approaches so nearly to Natural and, perhaps, Civil History, that they had better be referred to the books devoted to those important but distinct sciences.

If we examine the books that are most used in the schools of the United States for teaching geography, we soon come tc the conclusion, that, if all they contain is geography, then this is the most comprehensive name ever given to a science, and we shall be led, perhaps, to suspect that Dr. Johnson was fully aware of what he said, when he defined geography to be "THE knowledge of the earth," *par excellence.* I know not that I shall do injustice to many of these textbooks, if I say that every thing is found in them but what ought to be there; for, really, when the proper materials *are* there, they are so buried under other matters, that they are with difficulty found. In most of them, besides topography, and a smattering of geology and astronomy, we find history, botany, zoölogy, meteorology, and all the other *ologies* appertaining to natural history, with theology, chronology, genealogy, manners and customs, the statistics of war, education, sectarianism, internal improvement, law, physic, agriculture, commerce, manufactures, philanthropy, and most other human concerns. Now, all these subjects are very important, and every well educated person should know more, much more of them, than is contained in these geographical textbooks; but it is questionable whether an adult mind would be much improved by reading or learning by rote such knowledge, however important, given as it is, without system, without due proportion, without judgment. But, if such desultory remarks are of doubtful utility to adults, what must they be to children, who generally come to the study of geography long before they have studied any of the subjects just enumerated? It was the custom, when the spelling-book was almost the only secular book used in our schools, tc crowd a smattering of almost every thing else into it, and I have one that contains, besides its vocabulary of words, the elements of reading, grammar, arithmetic, geography, astronomy, rhetoric, theology, penmanship, and a variety of other matters, more necessary then, when the Bible and spelling book were the school-boy's library, than such a medley is in our geographies now, when every division of human science has an appropriate textbook, in which it is systematically treated. The good sense of the community has long ago banished such extraneous subjects from the spelling book, but will it sift the geographies also? Many of those subjects are as much related to spelling as the others are to geography; for, spelling, unless accompanied with writing, reading and grammar, is but half taught, and this fact the people are beginning to perceive.

What I have called the extraneous matter of geographical textbooks often constitutes about three quarters of them, and, no doubt, it is introduced to fix the geographical facts in the memory by association or some other sympathetic influence. But, if this is a sufficient excuse for introducing such fragments of various knowledge, how important is it that the most striking and apposite illustrations should be selected. Yet, I find no such judgment exercised; so that the *aid* afforded by the associated knowledge only increases the burden. For instance, one popular author, who relies much upon the aid of pictures, when treating of the geography of America, gives us a view of Columbus leaving Palos, in Spain; but how will this help the child to remember the shape, features, natural or artificial divisions of America? It introduces an historical fact, and may recall *Spain* to mind, though the site of Palos, the subject of the picture, is no where described. In his larger geography, the same author gives a picture emblematical of the United States, viz.: an Indian astride a flying eagle. Then we have a picture of the Resignation of General Washington, but, as we are not told where it took place, it is not evident what *geographical* fact it is to impress upon the memory. This incongruity is not confined to him, however, for another amiable and excellent author, whose book is a mass of facts, that render it, in my opinion, unfit to be used by children, while they show his unusually extensive acquaintance with the earth and all that appertains to it, gives a Roman Catholic procession in Guatimala; some peasants dancing in France: and many similar pictures, not peculiar to the country where they are given, and not likely to operate as aids to the recollection of any geographical fact any where. But this will suffice, and I need not produce examples from inferior authors. I am not unacquainted with the power of association in assisting the memory, but I have been accustomed to associate unknown things with those that are familiar, and I cannot be deceived into the belief, that, where there are no common points of resemblance, any thing is gained to the memory by having two facts to remember instead of one.

So with the description of places, customs, &c. &c., which are to be committed to memory; they are rarely connected with the thing to be remembered with them. For a general rule, those who have studied the textbooks in common use, are ignorant of the location of places and the physical features of the earth, exactly in proportion to the quantity of words they may have committed to memory. My heart has sunk within me when I have examined children, whose memories had been thus taxed at the expense of health, and of years of precious time far worse than wasted. Who does not know how eager such children are to recite as soon as they have committed a lesson to memory? One would think the recitation was to fix it forever in the mind, whereas it is really only a device to let it escape and make room for its successor; it being a law with these unsubstantial things, as with solid bodies, that no two can occupy the same place at the same time.

While I was at school, geography was first introduced as a regular exercise, and, on the whole, the method of instruction was more rational than that which has since prevailed, although its result was very similar. The chief book used was an abridgement of Dr. Morse's Universal Geography, but it was *read* only, and not committed to memory. It was never explained to the pupils, and being quite unintelligible, was, of course, very uninteresting. The only portion that was tolerable, was a description of the animals of this country; and this was to the desert a sort of oasis, which we visited, in the course of our reading, only about once a year. The book contained one or two maps, but we were never required to examine them, and, in most cases, they were soon torn out, and thrown away as the most useless things in the world. To beguile the tedious hours of idleness, which then, as now, constituted the larger part of school time, such of us as retained the maps were accustomed to play "hunt for places" on them. This was a standing game for years, and to this I am indebted for all the knowledge of geography that I brought away from school, although, whenever I was detected in this forbidden exercise, I was severely punished. I do not recollect any more of that book than I should if I had committed it all to memory, but I recollect how I hated Dr. Morse for making it. Another book, used at the same time, was Bingham's Astronomical and Geographical Catechism, a small book which I committed to memory in a few months, and recited regularly eight or ten times a year, without understanding a word of it, for it was never explained to me. In connection with oral teaching, I prefer books that ask questions, and require the pupil to search the atlas for an answer, without furnishing one ready to his hand, or a key to one in the shape of the first letter. But the little Catechism gave an answer to every question, and a departure from the very words of the book, although the idea was retained, was deemed an error, as well as the height of presumption. There was no association in my mind between any description in these two books and any spot on the maps, but many of those descriptions were indelibly associated with certain black-and-blue spots elsewhere.

I have remarked that the extraneous matter of our geographical textbooks is of but little value when learned; let me enlarge a little upon this idea. Who does not know that when a new edition of a geography, a *revised* edition, I mean, is printed, the old edition is no longer fit for use? Why is this? The author of the larger geography used, until lately, in the Boston schools, tells us, in the preface of one of his editions, that it was first published in 1819, and, after two editions, was stereotyped, or placed beyond alteration. Soon, he adds, it was necessary to re-write it entirely, and then, after two more editions, it was stereotyped, or fixed again. Unfortunately the world would not stay fixed to accommodate the types, and, in a subsequent page, we are told that the book "may be expected to remain as it is, until a considerable change shall become desirable," that is, until an unusually large portion of it becomes incorrect! The author of a later and more popular geography, but by no means a better one, informs us in his preface, that "The introduction of a great variety of books into schools in the same department of knowledge, by rendering the information uncertain, the expense greater, and the progress less rapid, is an evil of which many have complained." But how is this evil to be remedied? How is the *greater expense* of using *various* books, that may correct each other, instead of "rendering the information uncertain," to be remedied? Let us see. "To obviate this," continues the preface, "the author has resolved to give his work a periodical revision, which will be repeated and continued regularly once in five years thereafter;" which seems to mean that, instead of buying several books of different authors, the pupils will only have to purchase several editions of the same book. But the expense is of no importance compared with the fact, that, after a child has studied a book five years, the new edition will show him that, if what he has learned is retained, it is incorrect, and, of course, useless to him.

Now, whence arises this absurd, nay, cruel necessity for change? Not because the world has changed; it is essentially the same it was when Noah went forth from the ark four thousand years ago;—not even, because the divisions made by man have essentially changed, for, every where, except perhaps in our own country, these divisions are what they were one generation at least ago. Is it not evident that the new book must be made to rectify matters that should never have found a place in the old one? What is the object of teaching geography in our schools? Is it not the same as that of teaching arithmetic, reading, spelling, and the other common branches—to give the child something that will be of service to him when he becomes a man? And is there not enough that is permanent on the earth, to occupy the few months, or even years, that are devoted to the study of geography? Have the oceans ceased to heave since the Almighty gathered them to their place? Have the countless rivers ceased to run since they were poured out from the hollow of the Almighty hand? The everlasting hills, have they moved again since they fled from the wrath of Him who uplifted them? No, no, no, nor will they, till the dooming angel shall plant his right foot upon the flood, and his left foot upon the earth, and swear by Him that liveth forever and ever, that time shall be no longer.

But let it not be supposed that I would reject all such aids as would interest the child in the permanent, and, as I think, proper subjects of geographical instruction. The competent teacher may often suggest some circumstance to engage the pupil, and give him an interest in the thing to be remembered If you wished to express the fact that there is such a country as Italy, and its peculiar form, upon the mind of a child, you might tell him about Rome as it was and as it is; when its material wall included but one hill, and was so low that it was overleaped in derision, or when its spiritual wall inclosed all Christendom, and aspired to include heaven; when it subdued the world by knowledge, or enslaved it by ignorance; when the dark oracles of the Sibyl, or the bright oracles of God, were shut up from the people; you might tell the child all this, but what would he know of the *geography* of Italy? Not one tenth as much as he would if you showed him the map, called his attention to its boot-like form, and required him to draw a dozen or more outlines of it. The textbook used in the Boston schools was as copious as any, and the instruction conformable to it, probably, as thorough; and yet, in the remarkable Report of the Examining Committee of those schools in 1845, we are told, "That each scholar (of five hundred selected from the first division of the highest class of each school) was required to sketch on paper an outline of Italy, and many attempted it, but, of the whole number, only *seventeen* made a drawing, which could have been recognized as a representation of Italy, by one who did not know what the scholar was trying to do."

Again, if you wished to impress the geographical outline of the Spanish Peninsula upon the pupil's mind, would you tell him of Ferdinand and Isabella; of the repulse of the Saracen invaders, and the invasion of Mexico; of the enfranchisement of Spain and the establishment of the Inquisition; of the slaughter of infidel Moors, and the more modern butchery of Christian hosts? You might do all this without giving the pupil any idea of the *geography* of Spain. But, if you should show the pupil a Spanish dollar, and call his attention to the Shield, whose form is exactly that of the Peninsula; to the Castle and the Lion, Castile and Leon, whose union freed Spain from the Saracens; to the two pillars, emblems of the Pillars of Hercules, Gibraltar and Ceuta; to the motto that entwines them, "*Ne plus ultra*," "there is nothing beyond," and then explain to him this limit of ancient geography, which Spain herself was the first to pass, my word for it, you would not only give him some definite ideas of the geography of Spain, but you would give an interest, that never existed before, to Spanish dollars.

By such means, the well-furnished teacher may enliven the details of study; but I have always found that, where the book is what it ought to be, and the black-board and pencil are constantly used, there is but little need of other excitement, and the name of a country becomes associated with every geographical peculiarity of it. I will not go into all the details of the method by which I contrived to impress all the important features of the globe upon the minds of my pupils, for this would be uninteresting, perhaps, even to teachers, and he who wishes to read them may find them in the books which my peculiar method of teaching compelled me to publish. I shall, therefore, only say briefly, that, when called on to teach a child geography, my custom is, first to show the child a map or plan of his own town; then to point out its connection with other towns; how these towns form counties, and how the counties form the state. Then I should take the map of the United States, and point out Massachusetts and the neighboring states, showing how they combine to form the Union. Next, I should take the map of North America, and pointing out the United States and its territory, I should constantly keep the eye of the pupil upon the decreasing size of Massachusetts. I speak of *maps*, because these are in every school, but the globe is far better, whenever it can be obtained. Then on the globe, or a map of the world, I show the connection between North and South America, the wide space of water between the continents, the New World on one side, and the Old World on the other. I show him the whole globe, how we live on it, and how it turns round; then I recall his attention to his native state, and when he has a distinct idea of its place on the globe, I return to his own town, or to his own state, if I have no suitable map of the town to enable me to make that the point from which our future lessons are to proceed. I then require the pupil to draw as good an outline of his town, county or state, whichsoever I must begin with, on the slate, black-board or paper, or on all of them. When he can do this decently, I let him fit the contiguous states upon it. If his book has little or nothing in it relating to his own state, he may draw the outline of every state in the Union, separately, several times, without entering into minute details; but if he has a map of his own state, and his book can serve him as a guide, let him draw a map of good size, and mark first the mountains on it, and be told that these are the most important feature in a country, and generally indicate the high lands from which the rivers rise. Then let him mark the rivers, and be sure to make him understand that they run from the highlands to the sea, *downhill* always. Then proceed to the other geographical divisions of land and water, dotting the important towns, and talking about the face of the country, as if it were outstretched before you.

If something like this familiar survey had been attempted in the schools to which I just now referred, do you think that, when their five hundred elect scholars were asked, "Do the waters of Lake Erie run into Lake Ontario or those of Ontario into Erie?" only two hundred and eighty-seven could have answered correctly, and "if we take into consideration," as the committee say in their report, "what is unquestionably true, that many of those who did not know, answered by guess, and they were just as likely to guess right as wrong," would it have been a fact, as the committee assert it was, that "much the largest portion of our best scholars could not tell which way the waters run, in spite of all the fame of Niagara?" Surely not; and, after this exposure, whatever textbook may be used in those schools, you may depend upon it that the pupils will never row their teachers up these Falls again.*

Before leaving the native state of the pupil, be sure that a general idea of all its important points is obtained, so that the child can readily tell its parts, as you draw them on the board, or point them out on the outline map. Then let him take a neighboring state, and do the same by that, and so extend his knowledge to the rest, gradually travelling over the world, learning no descriptions by rote, but visiting every place often, and impressing *things*, not words, upon the mind. If the teacher, while pointing at the map, can enliven the lesson by a pleasant anecdote, description, or picture, so much the better, and any teacher may do this, if he faithfully prepares himself for the lesson; but woe unto the story if it needs to be formally committed to memory!

The first time I go over the world with a pupil, I do not hurry, and I am not too particular. The next time I require more. At first, the states and countries of the world are

* A subsequent report of the committee declares that great improvement has been made in these schools since this lecture was delivered, and the liberal appropriation for globes and outline maps, and the increased activity of the teachers, show that, ere long, Boston will be herself again.

drawn separately, and of a small size ; next, the smaller states are grouped, and so, at each course over the world, the space included in the maps is extended. I required no maps to be drawn for exhibition, but, once a year, I selected a fair specimen of the work of each pupil, and bound the whole neatly, as a sort of landmark from which to measure the progress of the pupils. The volumes that I have thus preserved are among the most valuable memorials of my pupils and of my labors.

After a basis is thus laid, the children are ready to enjoy history, voyages and travels, and all books that describe the countries with whose geography they are acquainted. It was always my custom to select a good newspaper, and read it, or suitable parts of it, to my more advanced classes. If the name of a place was mentioned, we determined its direction and distance from home ; and if the name was new to the class, they noted it upon paper, and at the next lesson were expected to tell all they had gathered relating to it. To meet such exigencies the school was always furnished with the best Atlases and Gazetteers ;* but these often failed us, for the newspapers are always in advance of books, and we were often obliged to go into the world, and get instruction from men who know more of the actual world than they do of books. All arrivals and departures of vessels, most advertisements, and, indeed, almost every part of the paper, besides imparting the knowledge of what was actually going on in the world, made the pupil acquainted with its geography, and afforded me countless opportunities of imparting that useful and practical knowledge which the child will never pick out of his textbooks, and the want of which makes our mere book-learned pupils as unfit for business, as if what is learned at school is only to be used at school, having nothing to do with the outward world.

In this way, I would teach geography to young children and to all beginners ; but, if they are required to learn history also, they should connect it with geography. My plan was always to read the history to the class, requiring them to look at the maps. Each pupil also drew an outline map on paper,

* Perhaps no more useful assistant has been afforded to teachers than the UNIVERSAL PRONOUNCING GAZETTEER lately prepared by THOMAS BALDWIN, of Philadelphia, assisted by many distinguished scholars, foreign as well as native. This is one of the *Books of Reference* that should be in every School Library, and should be placed there by School Committees.

and, as fast as places or other objects, such as r vers, mountains, &c., were named, they were marked on the map, and, if there was room, the event and its date were recorded by their side. Maps were prepared, adapted to the different epochs in the history of a country; especially if such divisions of the country as were not natural and permanent were seriously altered. In the history of England, for instance, the first map represented England as it was when first invaded by the Romans. The second represented it as it was when the Romans left it. The next, divided under the Saxon Heptarchy; the next, after its reünion under Alfred; then in the reign of Elizabeth, and then in our own times. Sometimes, in teaching ancient history, we hung a large outline map before the class, and marking the place of each event with both the ancient and modern name, and inserting no name unknown to history, we formed a sort of historico-geographical map, which the pupils all copied for private use. I need not go further into these details; the plan, probably, is not so novel now as it was twenty years ago, when I adopted it, and I have said as much as the intelligent and industrious teacher needs, and far more than the indifferent one will use.

If it be asked, as it reasonably may, why not begin at once with history, and let geography come in by the by? I answer, because history is not geography, and no history will touch upon a hundredth part of what relates to the geography of a country. Books of voyages and travels are better than history in this respect, but, as I have already hinted, a good newspaper is better than all of them. But there is another serious objection to this indirect mode of teaching geography and it is, that the time usually spent in school forbids this course of instruction. If the meagre compends of history used in our schools be adopted as a guide, the child will know as little of geography as of history; and if the larger histories are employed, a general acquaintance with geography would require nearly the whole threescore and ten years allotted to mortals, and not merely the few years of a school life. No, — geography is as much a science as geometry, and it can be picked up by reading history no better than geometry can be picked up by reading works on astronomy The elements must first be systematically learned, and then the cognate sciences may, and should, aid and illustrate each other.

In teaching geography to the young, a question of some

importance is, *how*, or rather, *where*, shall we begin? The prevalent opinion among the best teachers is, that we should begin at *home*. Some go so far as to say, we should begin at the school-room, fix the points of the compass, teach the direction of the roads, the boundaries of the district, the contiguous districts, the boundaries of the town, the situation of every pond, stream, hill, and other important object in it, and then proceed to the next town. This, on the whole, is the true plan, and the natural one; but you may have perceived that, in describing my course, I first gave a general idea of the world, that the child might know what and where home was, and this course had been forced upon me by the attempt to teach entirely on the *home* plan. When I marked the cardinal points on the floor of my school-room, the little geographers would ask, "What does north mean, sir? Why is north always there? Do we live on the top or bottom of the world, sir?" &c. &c., questions that may very easily be answered in one lesson, which I have always found the pleasantest lesson the child ever learns. With the exception of this one lesson then, I would begin as near home as my means of illustration would admit. But, alas, how defective are these means! Suppose that, in obedience to the directions in a geography published in this very city,* the teacher should begin at the school-room. He will naturally look into the book for information as to the vicinity, but so far from finding any at the beginning of the book, he finds not one word about Connecticut until he reaches the one hundred and ninety-fourth page, and of three hundred and fifty-two pages, but *one* is devoted to Connecticut, and nearly half of this is a picture of Yale College. Another popular geography, containing three hundred and twelve pages, and published also in Hartford, gives your state but *one page and a half*. A third geography, published in New York, and much used, gives Connecticut *three* of its two hundred and eighty-eight pages, including, however, a view of Hartford, and what would be a view of Yale College, if the trees did not conceal all the buildings. The geography perhaps the most extensively used in this country, and published in Philadelphia, out of three hundred and thirty-six pages, allows Connecticut about *two*, including a picture of a school-house, and a wagon of emigrants going west; but whether the wagon points out the

*The Lecture was delivered at Hartford, Conn.

object of the school, or whether both these objects are peculiar to this state, we are not informed. Finally, the geography until lately used in the schools of Boston, and, I think, published in that city, contains three hundred and thirty pages, and spares *one* to Connecticut, but then, it is a *whole* page, without the drawback of a picture. The number of pages devoted to Massachusetts in each of these books, is hardly greater than is given to Connecticut, and yet our children learn nothing of our state, but the few pages I have named, and can you wonder that they know as little of Massachusetts or Connecticut as they do of Tartary or Ethiopia? I hope these details will be excused on account of the important bearing they have upon our schools. Few of our children ever go beyond the limits of our state, and no geographical knowledge can be so important to them as the knowledge of that state with which they are so intimately connected; and yet, for half a century, we have been contented to let them study every thing but this, apparently supposing that a competent knowledge of their own state is born with them, and, being an instinct, needs no cultivation.

Some most important apparatus has been provided of late for the instruction of the young in the elements of geography; I refer to black-boards and outline maps. These seem to be all the teacher would require, if he were what he ought to be; but as he is what he is, some textbook must guide him, or he and his scholars will all be lost, if they wander a furlong from home. Black-boards may be made a substitute for outline maps, but they serve better as helpers, and it is far better to use both, and always to have a globe at hand to correct the wrong impressions which children are so apt to receive from maps, however drawn. If not familiar with the globe, they will be constantly inclined to think the surface of the earth flat as a map. Being accustomed to hold the northern part of their maps elevated, they will naturally connect the idea of up with north, and of down with south, and, perhaps, to this we may attribute, in a great measure, the mistake in regard to the course of Niagara river, to which I have before alluded, for its course is almost directly north. The presence of the globe is also necesssary to prevent the mischief that arises from using maps drawn, as they must be, on various scales. The map of the world must correct this error, if no globe is at hand; but the map of the world is on a plane, and needs a globe to correct itself. Sometimes, to correct erroneous notions, I have hung

maps upside down before the class. The outline map is a safe assistant, in so far as it presents only such points of geography as are always true and unchangeable, and is not apt to be crowded with the less important matters which obscure other maps. The practical teacher may accustom the child to look upon it as upon the earth's surface; he may point out the general features of the country, the elevations and depressions, and their connection with the source and course of rivers; and a few lessons of this sort, that require no book, would save the poor children, and the poor rivers also, a deal of *up-hill* labor.

The textbooks would be a less important concern, if the teachers were all they ought to be; but we have reason to believe that the character of our teachers has of late been greatly improved, though not, perhaps, in proportion to the additional duties imposed upon them. Before they could become expert in teaching those elementary branches which satisfied our fathers, new branches have been introduced, until we seem to be in danger of having a surplus of colleges, without any good schools. It would, in my opinion, be wiser far to teach a little, well, and to have the instruction such only as will be available in the world. Small as the amount of learning is, that our children acquire at school, a large portion of it is as unfit for use as if it were never intended to be used. Grammar is any thing but learning the correct use of language; geography is pantology, as I have shown; the too early introduction of algebra has made almost a negative quantity of common practical arithmetic; those who have mastered book-keeping, seem to understand only the *waste;* proficients in astronomy cannot tell the Little Dog from the Great Bear; profound botanists descant on the structure and repeat the hard names of exotics, without knowing the name, or the class, or the virtues of the plants on which they daily tread; and thousands, who are reported to have mastered a foreign language, cannot pronounce a word of it correctly. This ought not to be so. Progress is desirable, but not at such an expense. Let me, however, return to my subject. Geography is a science that may, in a great measure, be exhibited to the senses, and it is the duty of the teacher to call in their aid in every possible manner. If the countries cannot be brought under the eye of the pupil, the best maps of them must be; and when, in this way, a clear idea is communicated to the mind, there is no need of committing words to memory.

And, in attempting such illustrations, let not the young teacher be discouraged at the idea that he may not execute a map as readily, or as well as a veteran teacher might do it. Whether he knows *how* to go to work or not, let him rely or the perfecting power of practice. Be not afraid, therefore to attempt whatever others have done, and let no fear of failure or love of ease induce you to shrink from any real improvement. Above all, do not impose upon your pupils any system of instruction which mocks them with a show of learning, while, by leaving no useful and permanent impressions on the mind, it really inflicts upon the innocent a punishment not unlike that of the guilty Danaïdes, who were condemned to be perpetually filling with water a vessel whose bottom was full of holes.

As my general ideas on the subject of geography are contained in the preceding lecture, I shall endeavor now to give such a particular account of my manner of teaching, as will enable the teacher to carry out those ideas which have not been sufficiently explained.

I lay it down as an axiom, that geography, adapted to common schools, must be limited almost entirely to *topography*, and such views of the surface of the earth as do not properly belong to any other science. When narrowed down to this, it may be understood by children, for it may be made an exercise of the senses. When I commenced teaching, the geographical textbooks were not essentially different from what they are now. Then, as now, they contained much irrelevant matter, which was either neglected by the learner, or, if learned, was not only forgotten, but seemed to prevent all attention to such parts of geography as were really intelligible to children, and worthy of being remembered.

While instructing at the Teachers' Institutes, I have had a good opportunity to verify all my fears upon the inutility of teaching geography by means of the common class books. It is but fair to conclude that the thousand teachers whom I have met, had been as carefully instructed in geography as any pupils that have ever issued from our common schools and academies. They had all learned books by heart, and had taught their pupils to do the same. Of the descriptive part of geography they remembered very little, and so far from being able to sketch a picture of any country from memory, on the black-board or on paper, the majority of them did not venture to draw a map from a copy placed before them, and many had never attempted to do this. When called on to name islands, or rivers, or even towns, — to *name* them, not to describe their situation or other peculiarities, — their list was soon exhausted; and they were always astonished at the fact which this experiment revealed, for the first time evidently, to themselves. I hope they will excuse me for alluding to what some may think it my duty to conceal; but the great reform to which I am assured that my few imperfect lessons has led, satisfies me that they themselves would now use this argument, the strongest that can be produced, of the insufficiency of our popular textbooks, and of the prevalent method of teaching geography; for, surely, if the best pupils of our schools become teachers, and, after teaching, are still deficient in a tolerable knowledge of the easiest part of the science, topography, time has been wasted, money has been wasted, health has been squandered; all, pupils, teachers, parents, have been deceived, and a thorough reform is needed, is demanded.

I do not speak at hazard on this subject; I saw the futility of this whole system of instruction, the first year of my teaching, and from that time to this, I have avoided it, with how much reason, my pupils, and the young teachers with whom I have so lately compared systems, must determine. I do not fall below any one in my estimate of the importance of studying the history, climate, products, natural history, geology and other peculiarities of each portion of the earth; I only differ from others in regard to the time when these may best be connected with topography, and to the manner of that connection. But I have touched upon this in my lecture, and must now proceed to my lesson.

Let me suppose, then, that a class of small children stand before me, ready to receive their first lesson in geography. I should proceed with them somewhat in this manner.

My little friends, do you know what is meant by the earth? — Dirt, says one. — What we live on, says another.

Can you see the whole of the earth we live on? — No; I guess we can't.

Why not? — It is so big, says one. — It is so long, says another.

No; these are not the reasons. When you approach a town what do you see first? — The houses, says one. — The highest trees, says another. — The steeples, says a third

Why do you see the highest things first? When asking this question, stand a short thing and a long thing beside each other on a level form or table, and ask again, Why should I not see the bottom as well as the top of these things?

Let the pupils guess as long as they please, and then chalk part of a circle on the black-board, if you have not a large globe, and drawing something for a man on the topmost part of the curve. (I always drew what are called "dot and line men" for such purposes.) Draw another line from his head, so that it shall touch a remote part of the curve and glance off in a straight line, then make a steeple or tree whose top shall rise above the line, thus:

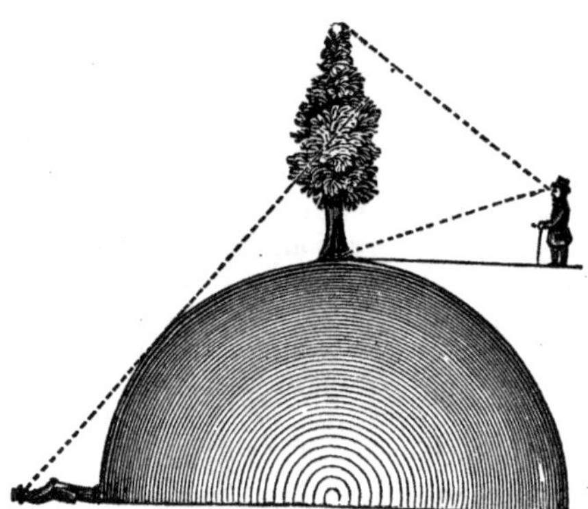

Then ask, Can any one tell now, why one little man sees the top of the tree before he sees its trunk, and why the other man sees the whole tree?

There 's a *swell* between them, says one, at last.

Well, wherever you stand on the earth, it is just so, and this swell, among other things, has led men to think that the earth must be round, like an orange or an apple.

This earth is not only round, but it keeps turning round all the time. Here run a long pencil or a wooden skewer, through an apple or a round potato,* and say, The earth turns just so, and always in the same direction.

* I mention this rude apparatus because it is common for district teachers to complain of the want of globes and other expensive apparatus. when good

Does it turn on a stick, sir? — No, it turns on nothing. God made it, and turned it, and his power keeps it turning just as certainly as if it turned on an axletree.

Now, stick a pin into the apple, and say, there, Mary or John, suppose that pin to be you, and the pin's head to be your head. There you stand! Well, the earth turns entirely round in a day and night, or, what is the same thing, in twenty-four hours. How many hours will it take it to turn half way round? — Twelve hours, says some one. — Well, let us turn it half round, and put another pin at the top, right opposite the other.

But, says John, looking big with his discovery, if we turned round so, we should fall off, should n't we, Mary? — I think we should, says Mary, unless we are fastened on somehow or other.

No, the earth draws you to itself, and keeps you on in spite of yourselves. — How can it draw without arms? says one. — Why don't we see it draw? says another.

Did you ever see a loadstone or a magnet? children. — No, sir, or Yes, sir. — Well, here is a small one. Do you see it draw this needle? — Yes, say they all. — Where are its arms? Can it draw without arms? — Yes, it does; I see it draw. — No, you do not see it draw, you only see the needle move towards it.

Well, says one, we don't move towards the earth; we are touching it. — Jump up, John, as high as you can, and don't come down again. — I can't stay up, says John; I must come down. — Yes, if you get away from the earth, you are drawn right back towards it. The earth is like a great magnet, and draws you as this little magnet draws the needle.

Here is a stick of sealing-wax. If I rub it a moment on my woollen coat, and place it near little pieces of paper or quill-feathers, it will draw them in the same manner.

The largest things are drawn the hardest. When I lift you, John, I only pull you away from the earth, which is trying to hold you down. I am larger than you, and the same strength that would lift you would not raise me, for the earth draws me much harder than it does you. The resistance that you meet with when you try to lift any thing is

substitutes, that cost nothing, are scattered on every side of them. For a general rule, the best apparatus for schools is that which costs the least.

called its weight, but there would be no weight, if the earth did not pull as it does.

But this has not much to do with geography, my young friends. I only showed you this apple, and turned it to show you that some parts of the apple turn faster than other parts.

How can that be, sir, if all turn round in the same time? says Mary.

See for yourselves. John, stick a pin into the apple as far from the two ends of the stick as you can. Very well. Now, stick one as near one end of the stick as you can. Very well, again. Now, stick one half way between the other two. Very well. Now see me turn the apple, and tell me which goes the furthest in once turning round.

This one in the middle, says John, goes the furthest, and that hardly goes at all — it only turns round the end of the stick. — Well, if one goes so much further than the other in the same time, which must move the fastest?

I did n't think of that before, said John. — Well, then, the parts that go the least distance, and turn the slowest, must be the very spots where the ends of the stick are, must they not?

Yes; unless the earth waggles sometimes, says Mary.

But it never waggles, as you call it; it always turns just so, as exactly as this apple must turn on this stick, and all I have been saying to you was intended to teach you this; for the earth has two spots that almost stand still while all the rest turns, and these two spots are always in the same part of the earth, and men call them the *poles*, because the earth turns on them as exactly as if they were the ends of a pole. One is called the North pole, and the opposite spot the south pole. Anything that points towards that pole, points north, and the north, of course, is always one way. On some steeples, you see N.-S. and E. W. under the vane, and this means that, when the vane points to N., it points north, and when it points in the opposite direction, it points to the other still spot, which we call south. When you face the north spot, or pole, the right hand points to no such still spot, but we say it points east, and the left hand points west.

Now let the teacher instantly mark on the floor, or on the ceiling of the school-room, which is the preferable place, these four chief points; and, if he wishes further to please the class, let him ask each child in which direction his home lies; in which the sun rises or sets; in which direction the church is, or any hill, or other visible object well known to the child.

Now take a globe,—any one will do,—and show the child the State, or the spot on which he lives. Make him see how small it is compared with the whole earth, or globe, or world.*

Let him tell which pole is nearest to his home. Then, while you turn an apple on the stick, let him chalk or scratch a line round it, just as far from one pole as from the other. Let the *pupil* do this, for it will delight him, and he will never forget the name of that circle, nor why it is drawn there, and called the Equator, or equaller. The teacher should always let the pupils take part in the illustration, if they can.

Then you may ask him in which half he lives, the northern or the southern? Which way from his home the equator lies? &c. &c.

If you please, you may let him mark a parallel to the equator that shall pass through his home, and a meridian that shall do the same.† But, the object of this first lesson should be to teach the child what is meant by *north*, and what relation *home* bears to the whole globe.

When this is done, you may proceed at once to teach, from home, all that is important in the town, in the neighboring towns, in the county, in the state, in the United States, in North America, in the Western continent, in the wide world.

But, previously to doing this to any extent, it is desirable to teach what is meant by a map; what the divisions of land and water mean; and how they are represented on the globe, and on maps.

Take the Atlas, and lay open the map of the Eastern and Western hemispheres. Then take the apple, and cutting it from pole to pole, open it as if there were a hinge on the side nearest to you, and lay it down on the two hemispheres. If the atlas contains a map of the northern and southern hemi-

* *Earth* having reference to the substance, *globe* to the form, and *world* [whirled] to the motion.

† An interesting and expeditious method of drawing circles, parallels, meridians, &c., without instruments, is described in the introductions to my Elementary Geography and Common School Geography, and with, as well as without, instruments in my "*Eye and Hand.*"

spheres, cut another apple at the equator, and open that, and laying it down, show how the poles come in the centre, and why the circumference is the equator.

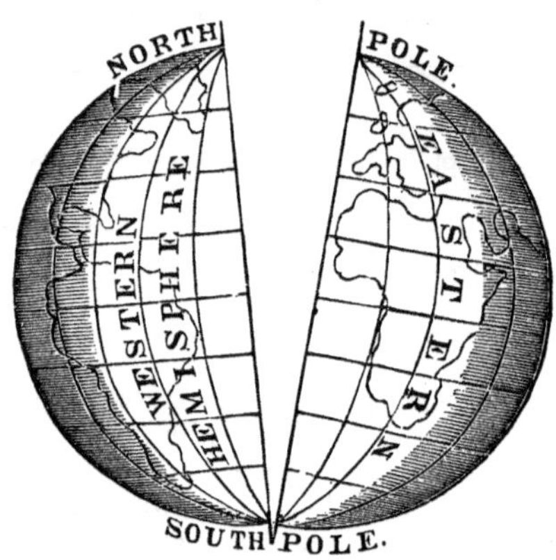

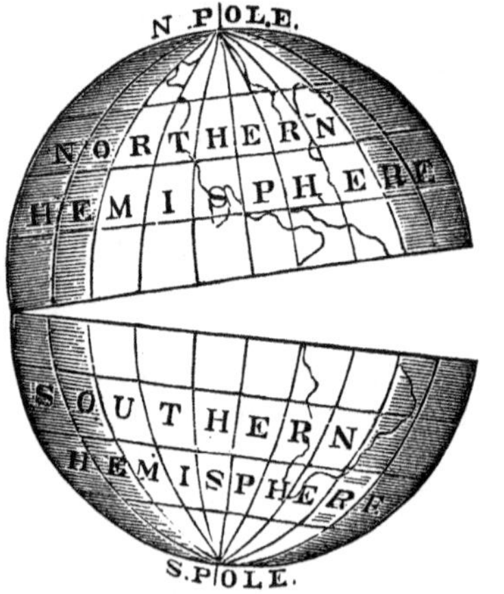

To show the divisions of land and water, take the globe, if you have one, and, if not, a map of the hemispheres. Show how land is marked, and how water. Place your pen on various spots, and ask, "Is this land, or water?" When this is understood, proceed to minor divisions.

Point out the oceans and the continents,—all the oceans and all the continents. Show, by comparing the map and the apple, how the oceans are divided. Show what an island is, and let each child, in turn, point to one, as long as any new ones can be found. Show what a peninsula is, and let them point out peninsulas as long as they find any. Then take lakes or seas, explain each, and let the children show them as long as they can. Be sure to take one division at a time, for in this way you are to teach what the divisions are. After the child knows them, you may review him by pointing to them promiscuously, and asking to what division they belong, whether islands, lakes, or what?

I believe my Geography was the first, in this country at least, that taught the geography of every country, by any system that classed the divisions of land and water, and it is still the most thorough in regard to this sort of classification.

Until lately, the Massachusetts child had no means of learning the geography of his town, county and state; and, strange as it may seem, it is true at this moment, as it has always been, that no geography, except mine, furnishes means of learning even an outline of the geography of Massachusetts. Two or three pages have been all that could be spared to this important state, and these are all that our children have been taught. The consequence is, that they often know less of the geography of their own state, than of China or Ethiopia, and some teachers, that I have met, could not mention a dozen towns of Massachusetts, and tell in what county they were situated.

My Elementary Geography for Massachusetts children, after giving a due proportion of general geography, devotes one half of the book to Massachusetts. There is a map of every county, and every town in each county is distinctly marked on the county map, and described in the book.

Furthermore, I have prepared a large outline map, much larger than that published by the Legislature, on which every town is marked and bounded, with its prominent hills, ponds, streams, villages, &c. &c. This is intended to be suspended before the class, when they are reviewing the lessons learned on small maps in the book, which correspond to this large one. The teacher, too, with a fescue, will frequently travel over the large map with his class, and make them as familiar with every county, town, river, railroad, &c., as they are with the road to church.

I know not how I can further illustrate my method more effectually than by giving a brief analysis of my Common School Geography.

At first, such a general idea of the world, as has just been given, is attempted. Then a few questions, to be answered by an examination of the map of the world, are given, but so given, that the child, by searching the maps, can find out the answers, without a key, and without troubling the teacher. For instance, instead of asking the child where the Atlantic Ocean is, the question is, "What large body of water separates America from Europe and Africa?" He knows water from land, and he has been taught by previous questions where the five grand divisions of land are situated. Every question throughout the book is based upon knowledge previously attained, but a test of the accuracy and thoroughness of the child's knowledge of one lesson is applied in the next that follows; for, after the child has, by searching, found out the answer to the question above mentioned, he is met with the question reversed, thus, "Where is the Atlantic Ocean?" Every question in the book has its reversed question of this sort, and the object is, not only to enable the child to learn the lesson by his own exertions, but to prevent a defect not unlike that which is often seen in arithmetic, when children can tell how many 7 times 9 are, but cannot tell how many are 9 times 7.

After a very general idea of the world, as a whole, is thus given, the map of Massachusetts is taken, and questions relating to that are asked in the same manner, and afterwards they are put in another form, as before described. The Geography contains a small outline of Massachusetts, in which the counties only are represented. While learning the relative position of the counties, the child, however young, is required to copy the map on the slate or black-board repeatedly. I have met with many teachers who pretended that they could not do this, but I never met with a child who studied geography and refused to draw such a map as I have mentioned. Children love to draw, and although at first, their work is very imperfect, the idea or picture in the mind is more correct than that on the slate, and practice will soon render the latter very exact, and the former almost indelible.

Since the first Teachers' Institutes were held, the number

of teachers who require their pupils to draw maps has very greatly increased. Many, however, still shrink from it, because they are unused to the exercise, but this obstacle will soon be removed by the practice they will acquire in examining the work of their pupils. Many who can draw cannot print; but how soon they will learn the form of letters when they once attempt to make them! The method of teaching the alphabet that I have proposed, will, if pursued, remove all objection on this score.

But maps drawn on the slate, and on the black-board, are soon erased, and are rarely drawn with so much care and accuracy as those done on paper. Let the children, therefore, immediately begin to draw on paper also. In this exercise no instruments should be used but the eye, the fingers and the pencil or pen. It is more important to train the eye and the hand than to have a perfect drawing; and no one who has not seen the effect of practice would believe me were I to relate some instances that I have witnessed, in very young pupils, of almost perfect accuracy attained without the aid of any instrument, even a common rule or dividers.

The immense advantage of such a trained eye and hand to man or woman must be seen without an argument; and yet, although by early training it may be acquired by almost every one, how few have even a tolerable degree of skill or accuracy in this exercise. At the risk of making my book too large, I have already given some instruction in this matter of drawing, and, therefore, I shall only say here, that, if the drawing of maps were not the most effectual method of fixing the topography of countries in the memory, its value as an exercise of the eye and hand should make it an indispensable exercise in every school.

But what sort of maps shall be drawn by beginners? Small ones, by all means. The rule should be to draw the map that relates to the lesson in preference to any other, and to put upon it only such rivers, towns and other divisions of land and water as are mentioned in the lesson. A specimen of this course is given in my geographies, by which any teacher can be guided, whether his pupils use the book or not.

It will save the teacher much trouble if, at the outset, he writes on a sheet of paper, the order in which maps shall be drawn, and puts it up in some place easily accessible to the pupils. They will not then be troubling him with the question, "What map shall I draw next, sir?" In my Geography, the map of the United States furnishes twenty pages of lessons, and while the class is learning these, separate maps of every state should be drawn on the slate, and on the black-board, and finally, for preservation, on paper. The children will learn the lessons the first time sooner than they will draw all the maps, but they will do better to go over the questions again than to proceed to another map.

Let all the maps be drawn on paper of uniform size say an eighth of a sheet of letter paper; this the teacher must require, and he must require every piece to be neatly torn or cut, and this the child can easily be taught to do. Let him fold the paper once, then scrape the edge to be torn with his thumb or finger nail, and then carefully tear it, or cut it with a dull knife. Let him then fold, and scratch, and tear again, till the paper is of the right size. This uniformity of size and neatness of edge may seem to be a small matter, but I can assure the teacher that, if he does not *always*, IN ALL THINGS, attend to such matters, his pupils will always be deficient in neatness and order. After my pupils had drawn their maps in this way, and shown them to me, they were required to fold them up uniformly, as a merchant folds his letters and bills, maps in one file, orthographical exercises in another, and so with other branches, and each exercise was required to be labelled so that its contents might be known without taking it from the bundle. I verily believe that, by this course, I did more to induce a habit of order and neatness, than I could have done by all the lectures that I could have preached, if I had done nothing but preach, for the whole term of a school life. The neatness with which some of my pupils filed and labelled their exercises would have done credit to one of our Pearl street accountants.

This care of exercises had another good effect. No loose papers were seen strowed over the desks of the pupils; the books were not thrown into the desks any how, but every thing in the desk was arranged in order, and I made it a point to examine every desk often, to commend the neat, and to warn or instruct the careless. I may say more on this subject when I come to the subject of neatness, but I must now return to the description of the manner of drawing maps on paper, with ink.

There is an order to be observed in the drawing of a map, and the pupil must be taught first to draw the outline with a lead pencil; next, he must ink it neatly with a pen. Then, if ever, he must color it. Next, let him draw the rivers and mountains. Then let him make the little o that marks the situation of towns, and then let him print, not write, the names, so that they will bear upon the o, and not be so far from it as to appear to belong to something else.

In coloring maps, only three or four good colors are needed. India ink, Prussian blue, lake, gamboge and green verditer, are enough; and as no child would use a large cake in a long term, and small cakes are generally of poor quality, the teacher should purchase some large cakes, and cut them up, so that a piece of each of the five colors named will only cost about as much as one whole cake of either. The best way to use these paints is to rub off a little of each color upon a saucer or other piece of crockery ware. One hair pencil will do, if well washed before the color is changed; but, as hair pencils can be bought for about a cent apiece, the neat pupil will try to have a hair pencil for every color. A little mug of water will be found useful, if it be only to prevent the dirty practice of wetting the brush with the mouth,—a practice not uncommon in schools where painting is taught, and not always free from danger, some paints, especially the greens, containing poisonous ingredients.

In shading the shores of a country or of a lake, India ink should be used, and to do the work perfectly, the pupil should have two brushes. With one he must draw a small portion of the coast neatly, and, while it is wet he must take the other brush, which is clean, but wet, and spread the India ink from the shore outward. Do but a little of the shore at a time, for, if the ink dries before it is spread with the wet brush, it can never be well spread afterwards.

Let us now return to the description of my Geography. At the first lessons, specimens of map-drawing are given, that the pupil may see what is expected of him. The lessons proceed from his own state to the United States, North America, South America, Europe, Asia, Africa, Australia, and Polynesia. Every country is treated systematically; that is, each division of land and water is by itself. Nothing is to be committed to memory, the practice of examining and drawing maps most effectually communicating and fixing the ideas.

After every map has been gone over in this way, there is a series of lessons in what are called Voyages and Travels

Questions are asked which oblige the child to travel over every map, and describe the countries, rivers, seas, &c., that he passes over. Among other lessons, an account of the voyages of Columbus, Cook, La Peyrouse, Vancouver, and Kruzenstern is given, and this sort of exercise may be continued to any extent by the teacher.

But the child thus far has only studied the countries separately, and a General Review is now provided for, in which all the countries, towns, rivers, islands, and other divisions of the whole world are introduced, not with a table of statistics to burden the memory of the child, but in such order as to show the relative size of each, and enable the child to compare known countries and objects with the remote and unknown.

An appendix follows, in which some of the maps, especially that of Massachusetts, is more particularly described than at the beginning of the book. Next come practical exercises on the latitude and longitude of places; the difference of time produced by a difference of longitude, and of climate by a difference of latitude; to all which is added a list of names used in the book, in whose pronunciation there is any difficulty.

In the Geography thus briefly described, there are three peculiarities not to be found, I think, in any other.

1. It contains little or no matter that may be considered changeable. In most cases, a revised edition of a geography differs so much from former editions, that the new books will not class with the old, and the teacher must be troubled with different books in the same class; or must form two classes; or must throw away the old books as worthless. The permanent materials of the Common School Geography will prevent any evils of this sort.

2. The second peculiarity is the order and distinct classification which pervade the whole book. There is no jumbling of all the sciences together. Pure geography only is taught, and this is taught in order. Instead of introducing history, philosophy, and a variety of other matters to impress the topography of a country on the memory, the child is taught to travel over the territory, and draw its outlines, until a never-fading picture is delineated in the mind.

3. The book, though not a large one, is sufficient for any district school, and contains within itself the materials for never-ending progress, if the directions in the book are fol-

lowed by the teacher. The first time the child goes through the book, he is required to give one particular only. When asked where is Boston, for instance, he will say it is the capital of Massachusetts. Next time he may be required to tell its situation at the east of the state. Next time he goes through, he may say it is mostly situated on a peninsula, at the head of Boston Bay, which is an arm of Massachusetts Bay. Next, he may give all that has before been given, and add its latitude and longitude ; — or, a class may be required to name some town, or island, or river, in turn, as long as any mentioned in the books have not been named. Confine this operation to one country until all the names of every division of land and water are familiar ; then include the whole continent ; then the whole world. After they can readily name all the towns, or all the islands, &c., in the book, let them be allowed to take their maps, and go as much further as they please. The mere *naming* of the place or thing, however, must not suffice, but some particular relating to it should be described, so that there can be no question that the child knows where it is situated. I generally required my class to stand during this exercise, so that they could have no access to books or maps. Then they answered in turn, trying but once, and sitting if they could recollect no new name, or named what had previously been named by another.

As far as my knowledge extends, this was the first book that recommended the reading of newspapers to the upper classes in geography. Every teacher knows that, much of the geography taught in our schools is not such as is of every day use in society and common life ; and perhaps nothing so completely shows what should be taught for geography as these very newspapers. All that is doing in the world is there recorded long before it gets into books. The mere record of arrivals and clearances is an excellent lesson. The reading of the news shows in what the books are deficient, and if, while the teacher is reading, the children, atlas in hand, find the places mentioned, or, slate in hand, record them, to be found against the next lesson, a fund of geographical knowledge will be acquired, that may be sought for in vain among the pages of the textbooks.

Every child that studies geography should be taught to draw maps. Next to the orthographical exercises and the correction of false grammar, in which I had hundreds of manuscript exercises, which I intend, one of these days, to publish in the form of a third part to my Common School Grammar; next, I say, to these, for its effect on the industry, and, of course, on the discipline of the school, is the drawing of maps. How infinitely superior to the common practice of sitting idle, or even of committing lessons to memory, would be the directing of children to draw maps on a black-board, or on a piece of paper. *Never let a child have it in his power to say, "I have nothing to do."* I believe that, for more than twenty years, no pupil of mine could ever say this with truth.

Once a year, it was my custom to let every pupil draw a map to be bound in a volume, and kept as a record of the ability of each, and as a landmark of the progress of the school, as a whole, in this branch of manual skill. I furnished to every pupil a piece of paper of uniform size, and left it to her to draw what map she pleased, and to ornament it as her taste might dictate. I have preserved many such volumes, and they are to me precious memorials of pupils who are now mothers or teachers, or inhabitants of that better country not mentioned in our geographies. It is not unusual for parents to bring their children to see what "mother did when she was of their age;" and it often happens that the first and last map the pupil ever drew, is preserved in these volumes. In one of them are eight maps, drawn by children, five or six years of age, who were not studying geography, but who, seeing what the others were doing, requested permission to draw a map for the book. The outline, printed names, and coloring, are entirely their own, and their names and ages, well written by themselves, are at the bottom of their maps. What would not many men and women give for such a specimen of the work of their earliest days! Every district school should have such a book annually bound like the School Register, and sacredly kept as the property of the town.

A LECTURE

On the "Uses and Abuses of Memory in Education;" delivered at Rochester, N. Y., before the Convention of County Superintendents of Common Schools, and first published at their request, by WILLIAM B. FOWLE.

GENTLEMEN, — The subject on which I propose to offer a few plain remarks for your consideration, is Memory — Memory, that wonderful faculty of the mind which alone perpetuates the product of all the others; which resuscitates the past, and enables us to lay up for future use the knowledge we may acquire by study or experience.

What, then, is Memory? The aged will perhaps tell us that it is a gloomy treasure house of regrets; the young, that it has no existence; the fortunate, that it is a paradise to which his constantly receding footsteps would fain return, but from which he is constantly driven by the flaming sword of his onward destiny, — while, to the disappointed, memory is a barren waste, without one verdant spot; a cheerless desert, where the monuments that rise over buried hopes, never cease to cast their deep shadows upon the present scene. In this sense, memory is very much what our propensities and habits, our virtues and vices, may make it; but the memory with which teachers have to do is less poetical, — a more matter of fact affair, and as such only would it become me now to speak of it.

As all discipline of the mind depends upon a proper education of this wonderful faculty, it is important, surely, that we should endeavor to ascertain what it is, and we naturally go to the metaphysicians and put the question to them; but the definitions of these philosophers are as various as they are unsatisfactory. Whilst all acknowledge that memory is a faculty of the mind, all have been puzzled to tell how it is connected with the mind, and how it operates.

One maintains that it is only a continued but weakened perception, (that is, a feeling not repeated, but forever felt.)

Another says it is only what remains after a sensation, (like the vibration of a string that is never to be struck again.)

A *third* declares it to be a sensation, or an idea renewed (but he could not tell us what renews it.)

A *fourth* tells us that it is a sort of sensibility so delicate that it can be affected by a past sensation, (as a place once struck is susceptible to a slighter blow afterwards; but we are not told how, or by what the repeated blow is given.)

A *fifth* has called memory that faculty which experiences anew what has been already perceived, with the consciousness that it has been previously perceived; (but this is a statement of facts, and no explanation of them.)

A *sixth* describes memory to be a power of the mind to revive or recall former impressions.

A *seventh* insists that memory is not itself a faculty, but an attribute of every other faculty, and this, it appears to me, is the only theory that a teacher can tolerate for a moment.

But, although the descriptions of this mysterious faculty have been so various, not so have been the systems of instruction based upon them, for these have been very uniform, and, I fear, uniformly erroneous. All the theories of memory, but the last I mentioned, agree that it is a single power of the entire mind, and that it only requires an act of the will for the mind to perform one act of memory as well as another. In other words, the common notion seems to be, that every mental storehouse is fitted up for the same kind of goods, and it is the duty of the teacher to fill all alike; and this attempt at filling is often carried on until school days are over, when the mind, no longer controlled, for the first time discovers its own fitness and capacity, and begins to accumulate treasures entirely different, perhaps, from those which had been forced down, notwithstanding the disgust and nausea that always accompanied the operation.

We do not know what the mind is, and we can hardly expect to understand all its faculties. But, as in the case of electricity and the subtler fluids, if we cannot ascertain the *nature* of memory, we may ascertain some of its laws; and by this method we may approach nearer and nearer to that seat of the mind, which is surrounded with clouds almost as impenetrable as those tremendous shades which involve the eternal throne; and though mortals may not hope to be admitted to the secret place where light actually dwelleth, we may, we must ascertain something more of its nature and of its laws, or the very *light* that is in us will continue to be darkness.

I have said, that various as are the theories of memory, the use that is made of it in education is altogether too uniform. So prevalent is the error on this subject, that when men speak of memory, it rarely happens that any other operation of the mind is meant than that which we exercise in common with parrots, I mean *the recollection of words.* You, who are teachers, know, that when parents bring their little unfledged angels to you, and wish to make you sensible of their prodigious talents, the burden of praise almost uniformly is, that they can commit ever so many pages at a lesson. Commit! — yes, and commit suicide at the same time. It is this notion, this mistaking of the mere memory of words for the *whole* of memory, that I consider the unpardonable sin of teachers and bookmakers at the present day. I hope my remarks will not be considered as those of one, who, having laid aside the harness, has no better use for his leisure than to make observations upon those whom he has left in the traces; but rather as the remarks of one, who, for twenty years at least, has practised what he now preaches, and who has reason to believe that thousands of his late fellow-laborers would be glad to adopt the system he recommends, if those who superintend their schools would second their endeavors, and supply the means of communicating *ideas* instead of *words.*

Let us consider for a moment the position I have assumed, that the memory of words is generally considered the whole of memory. What is the first employment of the mind in the nursery? Learning to say things by heart; that is, to say them heartlessly. When I was at a dame's school, I learned the Assembly's Catechism, — the compend of it that was then printed in the N. E. Primer, — so thoroughly, that I could repeat it backwards as well as forwards, and understood it one way just as well as the other. When the dame had visitors, I was often brought forward to perform this feat, crab-fashion, to the great amazement of the visitors, the glorification of the venerable dame, and to my own great edification in Christian knowledge and humility! God forgive her, if she erred in teaching me the first step in that narrow way, whose gate she opened with love if not with judgment!

Then the child reads books without having them explained, and generally without any examination by the teacher, — for who, until perhaps very lately, ever heard of examining a child in his reading lesson, except perhaps to correct the pronunciation of a word, or to settle the power of a dash or comma, — although the reading lesson may be the best medium for conveying useful knowledge to the mind, the best opportunity for teaching the definition of words, the precious occasion for inculcating a healthful taste for substantial food!

Then, at an early age, English grammar must be studied, *committed*, I mean, for the words are by no means synonymous. The words of some manual must be said or sung for a given number of years, until the child arrives at that *ne plus ultra* of philology, "a substantive or noun is the name of any thing that exists or of which we have any notion, as *man-virtue-London;*" and then, if the child is at a loss to know exactly what sort of notion "*man-virtue-London*" is, he will not fail to learn what it is "to be, to do and *to suffer*."

Geography, of course, cannot long stay uncommitted. A book is placed in the child's hands, containing on an average, about 350 pages. The committing of this to memory is generally the work of years, and, by the time the task is done, the world has so changed, that more than half the book contains is incorrect, and the only consolation the poor victim has is the consideration that, if what has been learned is not true, it will do no harm, for it has been forgotten as fast as it was learned.

Next, the child must study history—*study* history! That is, he must commit page after page to memory, or, at least, such paragraphs as have been adjudged a sufficient answer to a stereotyped question. The meaning of the language is not elicited by any impertinent inquiries; the geography of the country at different epochs is not allowed to interrupt the thread of the narrative, and the practical and moral conclusions are left, as the gramarians say, *understood.*

I could add to this summary, astronomy, botany, the various branches of natural history and natural philosophy, the modern and ancient languages, and all the branches usually tormented in our higher schools; but I have said enough to illustrate my remark, that common school education is generally conducted as if there were no memory but that of words, and as if this were all that is essential to the proper development of ideas, and the full exercise of every intellectual faculty.

Leaving the school for a moment, let us look abroad into the world, and see how facts corroborate this opinion. If you select half a dozen persons of good intelligence, it is probable that the memory of each will be different from the others. You will, perhaps, hear the *first* deploring his wretched memory, which cannot recollect his children's names, and, in the next breath, he will hum a tune that he has heard but once, perhaps, half a century before *Another* says he cannot remember the name of a person, but if he has seen a man once, he never forgets him, and yet he complains of a treacherous memory! A *third* had no memory at school, and could never learn his lessons; but he can never forget the brutality of the master, who regularly flogged him for not doing what he would gladly have done if he could. He "never can forget," and yet he has no memory. A *fourth*, perhaps, has travelled much, and can describe most particularly every route or every object he has seen, but as he sometimes forgets an appointment or a message, he laments that he has no memory. A *fifth* can never quote a line of poetry, and concludes she has no memory, although the chronicles of scandal are engraved on her memory of adamant, and she is not unlike one of our western mounds, the capacious receptacle of worthy characters that have been slain, and from which the curious may at any time extract the sad memorials of human frailty. A *sixth*, in fine, who cannot recollect the text at church, or a single sentiment of the discourse, will tell you how long her poorer neighbor has worn the same bonnet, and how every person in church was dressed; or, perhaps, she recollects every christening for more than half a century, to the great annoyance of advanced spinsters and old bachelors, who would prefer to have this matter confined to the family Bible.

If this be a true picture of life, it follows that every person has a memory for something, and *that* something is usually what occupies the strongest faculty of the mind, and, of course, affords the greatest pleasure. A musician will be more likely to remember tunes than sermons; a mechanic will remember the form and operation of machines, better than any written description of them. The painter will recollect the color of a dress, and the dress-maker the fashion or cut of it. An angry person will remember an affront, and a benevolent person will never forget a kindness. Shall a man who remembers words most easily, say to any of these, you have no memory? or shall he take airs because he can remember *words*, when they are so fortunate that they can remember only *things?*

One thing is certain, the memory of words is no criterion of intellectual power. Some of the greatest talkers have been the shallowest logicians, and some of the greatest linguists have been the greatest simpletons. In fact, the memory of one class of facts is no pledge for the memory of any other. and few persons have ever been distinguished in every department of memory. But we are told that this committing to memory strengthens the mind and leads to a habit of application. So it does. It does strengthen this particular faculty, it does lead to a habit of application, but only to words, considered *as* words, and not as embodying ideas. Let me not be misunderstood. I am not contending that a great verbal memory, and great general scholarship, great practical knowledge, are incompatible, but only that one branch of memory, like the high priest's rod, has swallowed up other branches as large as itself, and is likely to die of repletion.

Remarkable verbal memories are almost the only ones that have been recorded, and yet every one can recollect remarkable memories of other faculties. I spent much time with Zerah Colburn before he went to Europe. He was then about five years old, and could neither read nor write. His manners were so rude that he knew not the use of a knife and fork, and when placed at table, he stabbed a large sausage, and holding it impaled on his fork, he placed both elbows on the table, and nibbled alternately at the ends until the sausage disappeared. And yet this untutored child performed calculations which involved so many figures, that I could not have repeated them from memory after a week's application, but he made the calculation, and gave the answer in a few seconds. When he was exhibited in London, he was allowed to overwork this faculty, and it was destroyed, as the *verbal* memory usually is, by the excessive exercise of it.

How common it is to hear a teacher complain that his pupil will not attend, has not the faculty of attention. But children are never destitute of attention. The reason they do not attend to the lesson in hand is, that they are attending to something else. Attention, like memory, is an attribute of every faculty, and it is only where there is no desire that there is no attention. A stupid boy may forget his lesson, but he will not forget his dinner, and the same operation that puts one man into an ecstasy, puts his neighbor to sleep. Children, at school, usually prefer one study to another; what they like they attend to, and what they do not like — and this is what they have the least capacity for — they disregard. Now, I conceive the greatest, the highest effort of teaching to consist in so clothing useful subjects with interest, that those who may not love them are still induced to attend to them. This exercises the weaker faculties, and increases their ability. As the hand or foot acquires strength and skill by judicious exercise, so does every faculty of the mind; and as the muscles lose their power and skill by inaction, so does every organ of the brain. If a child is malicious and quarrelsome, vindictive and passionate, you have only to give him cause and opportunity for the display of his malevolence, to increase its power. But place this child where his passions will not be excited, treat him with unvaried kindness, cultivate his reason and his moral sentiments, encourage him to acts of benevolence, and set him an example, and in time his lower propensities will become less active and less powerful, if not entirely subdued. I do not pretend that all evil dispositions can be made good ones, nor that all memories can be made equal, for I know that there are original and irreconcilable differences; but I also know that the worst disposition and the weakest memory may be greatly improved.

After the view which I have taken of memory, it may reasonably be expected that I should endeavor to show how education should be conducted if the view be correct, and it be important to improve the *whole* mind, and not merely a portion of it. May I be excused, then, if in doing this I speak in the *first* person, for it is in this person that I have taught for twenty years,—and ought I not to add, that when I declare what *may* be done, I only describe what has actually been done?

As it is certain, then, that the intellect of a child under five or six years of age is immature, I should pay less attention to that than to the senses, on whose power and correct perceptions so much of the future intellectual progress depends. Most children are very observant of the ten thousand objects of nature and art that surround them, but they are generally left " to find out by their learning," that is, to find out without instruction, the qualities and peculiarities of what they see. The senses are allowed to take care of themselves, as if they could not go wrong, could not acquire bad habits, and must come out right at last. It would lead me too far if I should follow out this idea, but I have alluded to it that your own minds may do so. This early cultivation of the senses is a delightful exercise to children; and clothing, as it does, all he objects around them with interest, instead of promoting sensuality, the surest basis is laid for intellectual and moral progress. Conversation, then, with children, about common things, their form, size, color, number, order, feel, smell, taste, sound, &c., next after the fear of God, is the true beginning of wisdom.

I should allow the little ones as much liberty as is consistent with tolerable order. I should give them little or nothing to commit to memory, and make their exercises light, and vary them often. I should not be distressed if they did not know their letters in six months or six years, for they can be taught ten thousand things more important; kindness, obedience, reverence, truth and justice, will do them far more good than the alphabet. If I see any evil propensity displaying itself, if I cannot demonstrate the impropriety of it, I shall not punish until I have exhausted every means of preventing its indulgence. Prevention is the great principle; for to my mind nothing is more unwise and unjust than the laws which regulate even the best Christian communities. We allow the young to run unmolested until they break the law, and then we punish them. If a boy discovers ever so vicious a propensity, and we are sure that crime must be the consequence, we cannot touch him until it is too late; we cannot restrain him; *it is against the law to save him.*

If the little child shows an uncommon aptness for one thing more than another, I never allow the predominant faculty to be overworked, but I turn my chief attention to the weaker faculties that need encouragement. What is generally called genius and talent is only the predominance of one faculty over the rest. This must be carefully educated, but the others must be well attended to, also, or we shall see another example of genius without a well-balanced mind; wonderful talent without common sense; genius that can create other worlds at pleasure, without being able to get a decent living in this. The merry little being learns to talk, to sing, to think — little thoughts, of course — to draw, to count, — anything but her money — to play, dance, and be happy, and to make others so.

But it will not be long before the child will *desire* to read; and, perhaps, of late, no question has exercised the minds of teachers so much as how the first lessons in reading shall be given. With the old plan of teaching the names of the letters first, and then their various powers, you are acquainted; the new method, which has found friends in the highest rank of teachers, proposes the teaching of whole words first, without regard to the elements of which the words are composed.

Of course, the learning of one word is no help to the pronunciation of a new word; at least, I have never seen words placed in any book on this plan, so that the first words learned are a key or help to those which follow.

I do not deny that a child may learn to read a few words in this way sooner than he will if he waits to become acquainted with the letters, but I have always found that pupils who are allowed to skip the elements of any art or science, and revel in its pleasant things, are never willing afterwards to go back to those elements, which, though omitted at first, must be learned some time or other. Now, as no one pretends that the names of the letters and their powers need never be learned; but, on the contrary, as they all recommend this, at a later stage of the business, the question seems to be whether, in the end, the new method does not cause a loss of time and an increase of labor.

But we are told the new plan is more pleasant to the child; he prefers words with meaning, to letters and syllables without. I think, however, that this objection to the old plan relies for its force entirely upon the defective manner in which the alphabet has usually been taught. If it be important to connect ideas with letters, I would engage to connect as many with a letter as with any word. It would be difficult to illustrate this position better than by reading a short extract from a work called "The Youth of Shakspeare," which, in the quaint style of that day, "runneth of this wise."

"Mother," said young Shakspeare, "I pray you tell me something of the fairies of whom nurse Cicely discourseth to me so oft. How may little children be possessed of such goodness as may make them be well regarded of these same fairies, mother?" "They must be sure to learn their *letters* betimes," replied she, "that they may be able to know the proper knowledge writ in books, which, if they know not when they grow up, neither fairy nor any other shall esteem them to be of any goodness whatsoever." "I warrant you I will learn my letters as speedily as I can," replied the boy, eagerly. "Nay, I beseech you, mother, teach them to me now, for I am exceeding desirous of being thought of some goodness. But what good *are* these same letters of, mother?" inquired he, as he took his hornbook from the shelf. "This much," replied Dame Shakspeare; "by knowing of them thoroughly, one by one, you shall soon come to be able to put them together for the forming of words; and when you are sufficiently apt at that, you shall thereby come to be learned enough to read all such words as are in any sentence, which you shall find to be only made up of such; and when the reading of such sentences shall be familiar to you, doubt not your ability to master whatsoever proper book falleth into your hand, for all books are composed only of letters, as I shall teach thee straightway." The lesson had not proceeded far, when the draper's wife came in. "And what hast got here, prithee, that thou art so earnest about?" asked Mrs. Dowlass. "A hornbook, as I live! And dost really know thy letters at so early an age?" "Nay, I doubt I can tell you them *all*," replied Master William, ingenuously, "but, methinks, I know a good many of them." Then pointing at the several characters, as he named them, he continued: "First, here is A, that ever standeth astraddle. Next him is B, who is all head and body and no legs. Then cometh C, who bulgeth out behind like a very hunchback. After him cometh D, who doeth the clean contrary, for his bigness is all before. Next;"—here he hesitated for some few seconds, the others present regarding him with exceeding attentiveness and pleasure—"next, here is—alack, dear mother, do tell me that fellow's name again, will you, an' it will go hard with him if he escape me."

Think you that a child taught the alphabet in this or any similar way, would ever be tired of his lesson?

But let us suppose the child has passed the threshold, *what shall he read?* Not, surely, such books as are levelled down to his intellect, for these will keep the intellect down. It is better to give him books that he can understand when explained, and this explanation it is the duty of the teacher to give. I would have the child understand just enough to enable him to take an interest in the book, but I would have it always beyond his easy grasp. Bring the book down to the child's capacity, so that he can understand every word, and every idea of it, and he will never wish to read it a second time, and will make no progress in ideas or in reading, if he is compelled to read it. If I may compare great things with small, I will say that the Creator does not teach us to read in the book of nature in any such way. We are interested in every page that he has spread before us, but we understand very little of it. On the second perusal, we learn something more; and the more times we read, the better we understand, though we are sure we shall never master the great volume. There is a just medium in this matter, and he who consults the nature of children will observe it. Children, if I know them, prefer to read such books as require not only a constant stretch of the understanding, but even of the imagination; and such are the best for them, if they are to be read more than once.

But some utilitarians would have all reading books for schools filled with lessons in useful knowledge, and, of course, would exclude the greater part of our best poetry and works of imagination.

It is true that much useful matter may be introduced into school books, and, other things being equal, instructive lessons should be preferred; but the great object for which reading is taught in schools must not be lost sight of in the attempt to introduce a little of all sorts of knowledge, which will never make children good philosophers, and which will assuredly prevent them from becoming good and impressive readers. Show me a teacher who prefers to use books on this mistaken plan, and I will show you one who knows nothing of reading as an art.

In teaching English grammar, I would require little or nothing to be learned by rote. If there is any real difference between the parts of speech, the child should be obliged to think it out, instead of seeking the information in a dictionary. Moreover, in teaching English grammar, I would be sure it *was* English. Our language is more simple in its structure than any other, and I would teach it in all its simplicity, whatever might be the fashion. Not one child in a thousand studies any other language than his own, and yet every child is obliged to learn grammars that were constructed on foreign models. Because Greek had one article, two adjectives were set apart from the rest and called articles, that English grammar might not appear to lack this part of speech. As Latin nouns had six cases distinctly marked by a different termination, so English nouns must have cases, although they undergo no change, or only one in the singular, which renders the word no longer the name of a thing, — of course, no longer a noun. Because the Greek and Latin, and some modern languages, in their various modes of speaking, vary the termination of the verb, we also must contrive to have five modes, not because *we* have any change of termination, but because we ought to have! Because the Greeks and Latins, by the addition or change of terminations, counted forty or fifty methods of expressing tense or time, we, who have but one such change of termination, like the simple jackdaw, are strutting about with our borrowed feathers, and pretending to be classical peacocks.

In teaching geography, I should require no lessons to be committed to memory.

The author of the larger geography used in the Boston schools, has told us that it was first published in 1819, and, after two editions, was stereotyped, or permanently fixed. Soon, he adds, it was necessary to re-write it entirely; and then, after two editions, it was stereotyped or fixed again; and he says it may be expected to remain as it is, till a *considerable* change shall become desirable,—that is, till an unusually large proportion of it is false. In the mean time, it must be borne in mind, thousands and tens of thousands of children are learning such geographies, with the certainty that what they learn, if remembered, will soon be of no value. The world will not stay fixed, as the unlucky book does, and when there is so much certain and permanent knowledge to be learned, is it not cruel to trifle with the young mind thus? It is bad enough to have to commit to memory what is true, but it seems unpardonable to oblige a child to "commit" what is already false, or avowedly soon to become so. Let it not be supposed, however, that the geography alluded to is singular in this respect—I believe it is like all others that are popular; and a late most popular author solemnly promises in his preface not to change his book oftener than once in five years, right or wrong. It is said of one of the worthy governors of New Amsterdam, that because the wind had a troublesome trick of changing, he was accustomed early in the morning to fix the city weathercock for the day; and in what does his conduct differ from that of the author last mentioned?

Again, it is generally conceded that the true way to learn geography is to begin *at home*, and travel no faster than we get acquainted; but, as geographies are made to be *universally* used, this beginning at home is impracticable. A geography adapted to any particular home, would not be likely to have an extensive sale. The utmost we may ask then is, that they shall give a particular account of our own state. Well, how far have they done this? Mitchell, out of 336 pages, allows the empire state but 4, and these include 3 pictures that were not executed by Raphael or Benjamin West. Olney's geography allows your great state

4 pages out of 288, and these 4 include 3 engravings, not by the same great masters. Smith allows you 4 pages out of 312, and he can only afford 1 engraving. Woodbridge, in his new edition, thinks that 2 pages out of 352, with 1 picture, are enough for New York; and the other authors are no more liberal. Poor Massachusetts is allowed room in proportion to her size; and yet these books furnish all the knowledge that our children are required to learn of their respective states.

If you wished to learn the geography of a *town* instead of a world, how would you proceed? Would you go to one farmer and ascertain whether he raised wheat or oats? to another to know how many men he employed? how many pigs he raised, or how his potatoes yielded? Would you visit the schools to see how many children attended? how many pupils there were of each sex, and how many teachers? what school books were used and what abused? and *whether they were purchased because they were cheap, or because they were good?* Would you visit the several clergymen and ascertain how many sects there were, and how many of each sect? which expended the most money, and which had the most virtue to show for it? No, indeed; you would know that these things have nothing to do with geography. You would walk round the boundaries of the town, and see how other towns bordered upon it. You would travel every road and learn where it led to; you would visit every pond and every hill, and sail down every stream; you would learn the locality of every church, of every school-house, and every other public building; you would learn the limits of every school district; the remarkable caves or rocks; the quarries, and every thing that could be considered *permanent;* you would draw a plan of the town, till you were familiar with every part of it.

Then, if you wished to learn the history of the town, you would have some lines to go by, some points to measure from. You could lay out the farms of the first settlers, and cut them up as their descendants did; you could plan new roads and future improvements, and your accurate knowledge of the unchangeable features of the town would never cease to be of service. Statistical tables are valuable to the political economist, to the historian and antiquarian, and such may prepare and preserve them for reference; but what would they think if asked to learn such tables by heart? We cannot travel over the world as we may over a town, but we may travel over maps till the face of the globe is familiar, the great natural features, those characters which the Creator has engraved on the everlasting rocks, and not what transient man has scratched upon the shifting sand.

The celebrated Rousseau ridicules the custom of teaching history to children, and he relates an amusing anecdote, which shows that history was taught in his day very much as it has been since. He was spending a few days in the country, and a fond mother invited him to be present at a lesson in ancient history about to be given to her son. The lesson related to that event of Alexander's life, when, being dangerously sick, he received a letter informing him that his physician intended to poison him, under pretence of giving him medicine. Alexander handed the letter to the physician, and while he was reading it, drank off the medicine at one draught. At dinner, the conversation turned upon the lesson, and the young historian expressed so much admiration at the courage of Alexander, that Rousseau took him aside and asked him in what the wonderful courage consisted. Why, said he, in swallowing such a nasty dose of physic at one draught. His kind mother had dosed him almost to death, and he hated all medicine like poison. Still, the history was not lost upon the child, though it was misunderstood, for he determined that the next medicine he had to take, he would imitate Alexander. "If it be asked," adds Rousseau, "what I see to admire in that act of Alexander, I answer, that I see in it the proof that the hero believed in the existence of human virtue, and that he was willing to stake his life upon his belief. The swallowing of the medicine was a profession of his faith, and no mortal ever made one more sublime."

History, as taught in schools, should be a practical application of geography. My method of teaching it, was to read the history to the class, explaining every word, and illustrating every sentiment, as far as possible, by maps, books, engravings, medals, relics, and conversation. Then I required the pupils to read the lesson for themselves, and be prepared to answer such questions as I might propose. I never taught ancient geography except in connection with history, and never without a constant comparison of ancient geography with modern. In this way there is hardly any branch of human knowledge that was not brought to the aid of history, and in return illustrated by it. But, set a child to learning the compend by heart, or only so much as will serve for an answer to certain set questions, printed and adapted to the very words of the answer, and what does the child acquire but a distaste for what is only a dead letter, and a love for tales and romances, and that trashy reading which is too well understood, and whose spirit, as well as letter, killeth too often both body and soul?

But, it may be asked, would you not cultivate the memory of words at all. I answer that the ordinary intercourse of society will do much towards educating this memory, but there is one school exercise, which, when not perverted, is peculiarly fitted for this purpose; I mean *spelling*, although spelling, if properly taught, is not merely the learning of words, but the expression of sounds, and the acquisition of a correct pronunciation, which is rarely acquired in any other way. Perhaps no one branch taught in our common schools has been so badly taught as this, and in no department is there such a general complaint of deficiency, and such a loud cry for reform. Whence is this? Certainly not because correct spelling is not universally considered indispensable to a good education, certainly not because there is any dearth of spelling books. Will you bear with me a few minutes longer, while I endeavor to explain the cause of the deficiency which is so notorious?

First, then, spelling has been treated as an inferior branch, in which to exercise a pupil was to degrade him. Hence the higher classes have generally been excused from spelling, or have only spelled occasionally, without having regular and set lessons. Now, spelling must be taught at school, or the chance is a thousand to one that the adult will never make up for the neglect. The reason of this is, not so much the incapability of adults to learn, as their unwillingness to come down to the only effectual way of learning, that is, *by lessons from the spelling book*. It must be this, for adults read the words constantly, write them frequently, and understand and use them better than children do; and yet they seldom correct words that they have been accustomed to misspell. The reason uniformly given by adults, who continue to spell ill, is, they were not properly drilled when young.

The *second* reason why spelling has retrograded in our schools, has been the pretended improvement of spelling books. Thirty or forty years ago, little or no regard was paid to pronunciation; and any person who *chewed* his words was laughed at as a flat, or sneered at as a pedant. About that time Walker's Dictionary was reprinted in this country, and spelling books began to be made on his plan. The test of gentility, thenceforth, was pronunciation, and not orthography. Figures and other marks were introduced into spelling books, and relying upon these, the classification of words began to be neglected, until it was almost disregarded, and the difficulty of learning to spell was increased just in proportion to this neglect. Who needs an argument to show that a proper classification facilitates the learning of every art and science, and that on the association thus produced, the memory in a great degree depends for its power? The great desideratum of a spelling book is that it shall be choice, but sufficiently comprehensive in its vocabulary, simple, but exact and thorough in its classification; and that it shall teach the true pronunciation without appearing to do so, and *without drawing off the pupil's attention from the naked word.*

The *third* reason for the decline of spelling was the introduction of definition spelling books, and the custom of giving spelling lessons from dictionaries. If attention to the marks and figures that indicated the pronunciation, took off the scholar's attention from the orthography, much more so did the affixing of a definition. The definition became every thing, and the orthography only a secondary object. The vocabulary of a definition spelling book was so curtailed from necessity, that it was altogether insufficient for the purpose of teaching orthography, and the words of a dictionary are so numerous that it is the labor of a life, a *school* life, to spell it through once. You see the consequence; in the definition spelling books, many common and useful words were omitted, and the attention was distracted between those that were left and their definitions; while the length of time required to go through a dictionary, rendered a familiar acquaintance with the definition or the orthography absolutely impossible. And had the definition been retained, what would it have been worth? Common words are generally mystified by a definition, and seldom explained. The other day, in preparing a new work to oblige children to *write* the words of their spelling books, I wanted a simple definition of a *flounce* and of a *periwig*, both common things, and well understood. I turned to the most popular, and really the best school dictionary, and found the definition as follows:

Periwig. Adscititious hair.

Flounce. A loose, full trimming, sewed to a woman's garment so as to swell and shake.

I then asked an intelligent child what sort of hair he thought "adscititious hair" was.—"I don't know," said he. "Is it hair that is all in a snarl?"—I then asked an intelligent girl what she should call "a loose, full trimming sewed to a woman's garment so as to swell and shake," and she said at once, "an April fool."

So much for the definition of *easy* words. I then had occasion to look out the word *Imbricated*, and found that it meant "Indented with concavities." I asked a miss who was reading, the meaning of the word *anodyne*, and she looked in the dictionary, and mistaking the *a* which denoted that the word was an adjective, for a part of the definition, she said *anodyne* meant, "a mitigating pain."

If the memory is treacherous, the definition will soon escape, almost as soon as it is learned, or it may be applied to the wrong word. When a class of young misses was once reading to me, the word *wedlock* occurred, and, as usual, I asked the meaning of it. "I know," said a lively little girl, who had "studied dictionary," as she called it, at another school; "it is something they fasten barn-doors with."*

I believe this is a fair specimen of the aid that children get from definitions obtained in dictionaries; for, as I have said, if the words are common, no definition is needed, and a large proportion are of this description; and if the words are not common, the definition will not be understood, or will be immediately forgotten.

The *fourth* cause of the decline of spelling, is the attempt to teach spelling from reading lessons. I have already hinted that the true place to teach a child the *meaning* of a word is not in the dictionary, where it may have a dozen meanings apparently contradictory or perfectly unintelligible, but in the reading lesson, where the word is used, and where its very use often defines it. The faithful teacher will never miss this opportunity to explain words, not only because the interest and the intelligent reading of the particular lesson depend upon it, but because he will never, in any other department of instruction, have so good a chance to teach the correct meaning and use of words. But this is a very

* As I have seen this anecdote elsewhere, and may be suspected of appropriating what is not my own, it may be proper for me to say that it was first published in one of my Reports, many years ago.

different exercise from spelling; and just so far as it is excellent for teaching the meaning and use of words, it is unfitted to teach spelling; for, if it be true that the affixing of a definition diverts the attention from the orthography, it is evident that the sentiment, and the interest of the narrative, will do so in a greater degree. Every scholar knows the extreme difficulty of printing correctly; but this does not arise from the ignorance of the author or the printer, but from the constant tendency of the sentiment or thought to divert the attention of the proof-reader, whether author or printer, from the structure of the words themselves; and hence their custom of spelling the words instead of pronouncing them, or the reading of sentences backwards, to destroy the sense and fix the attention upon the naked words.

But spelling from reading books is attended with another serious disadvantage. The number of words spelled will not be extensive, and many words in common use will, perhaps, never occur at all. Besides, those that do occur, occur in utter confusion; and, for this reason, neither teacher nor pupil can ever know how many words he has learned, nor of how many he is ignorant. The presumption is, that the words of a spelling book include all that will occur in useful, but not strictly scientific books, and in profitable conversation; and these will be spelled and written over and over, until they become familiar; and when teachers will go back to this old plan of using the spelling book, and not till then, will they be able, in my opinion, to remedy the defect which all acknowledge to exist. It will not do to say that spelling is not worth the trouble of acquisition, for I think no one will deny that spelling is like charity in one remarkable respect; for a man may understand all mysteries and all knowledge, and yet, without correct spelling, — be nothing.

If I did not believe that the prevalent mode of committing books to memory was *cruel* as well as incorrect, I should not be so anxious for the reform. The custom has been, and now is, for the teacher to set a lesson to be learned at home, and it not unfrequently happens that the parents have the hardest part of the work to do, for they have to direct the child, to encourage him in the disagreeable task, and then nurse him in the sickness that follows constant study when he should be taking exercise. I wonder that parents have not come to the conclusion that they may as well *set* the lesson as *teach* it, and so have the credit of it. Who does not know that nineteen-twentieths at least of every lesson committed to memory, are immediately forgotten? I should as soon think of employing a child to bring me water in a basket, as to learn lessons by rote. What would you think of a farmer, who, instead of taking his boy into the field, should send him to a school, where he would be required to commit an agricultural catechism to memory?

It would not require much shrewdness in the farmer to guess what would be the result of this sort of education. He would instantly reject it, and the next morning, perhaps, send his child to school to be taught geography, or natural philosophy, in the same irrational manner!

Some years ago, I wrote a dialogue* for the amusement of my pupils, and as it not only exhibits the folly now under consideration, but also the kindred folly of crowding a little of every thing into the young mind, with your permission, I will read a page of it.

A mother in search of a school for her child, accosted a young teacher as follows:

Mother. Are you the mistress of this school, miss?

Teacher. I am, madam.

M. Your school has been highly recommended to me, and I have concluded to place my only daughter under your care, if we can agree upon the subject of her studies. Pray what do you teach?

T. What is usually taught in preparatory schools, madam. How old is your little girl?

M. She is only five, but then she is a child of remar-kable capacity.

T. I should not think she studied many branches at present, madam, whatever she may do hereafter.

M. Indeed, she is not so backward as you imagine. She has studied astronomy, botany and geometry, and her teacher was preparing to put her into Latin, when ill health obliged her to relinquish her school.

T. Have you ever examined her in these sciences, madam?

M. O yes, indeed. Fraxinella, my dear, tell the lady something of geometry and astronomy. What is astronomy, my dear? Ask her a question, miss, any question you please.

T. What planet do we inhabit, my dear?

* Since published in the "Familiar Dialogues" of the author.

C. Hey?

T. What do you live on, my dear?

C. On meat, ma'am; I did not know what you meant before.

M. No, my dear, the lady wishes to know what you stand on now; on what do you stand?

C. On my feet, mother; did she think I stood on my head?

M. Fraxinella! dear, you have forgotten your astronomy the three days you have staid at home. But do now say a line or two of your last lesson to the lady; now do, dear, that's a darling.

C. The equinoctial line is the plane of the equator extended in a straight line until it surrounds the calyx or flower-cup, for the two sides of an *isuckle* triangle are always equal to the *hippopotamus.*

M. There, miss; I told you she had it in her, only it requires a peculiar tact to draw it out. I knew she would astonish you.

T. She does, indeed, madam. You speak of the *plane* of the equator, my dear; will you be good enough to tell me the meaning of the word *plane?*

C. *Ugly*, ma'am; I thought every body knew that.

T. How many are three times three, my dear?

C. Three times three?

T. Yes, how many are they?

C. I don't know. Mrs. Flare never told me that; she said every body knows how to count!

T. She taught you to read and spell, I suppose.

M. No, I positively forbade that. I wished to have her mind properly developed, without having her intellect frittered away upon the elements. But I see your school will not do for my daughter. I was *afraid* you only taught the lower branches. Come, Fraxy, dear, let us call on Miss Flourish; perhaps she is competent to estimate your acquirements, and finish your education.

I have thus, in a very familiar way, endeavored to expose the too prevalent error of attempting to cram all sorts of knowledge into the mind through the single avenue of the verbal memory, to the neglect of all other kinds of memory, of the external senses, and of the reasoning powers. The first great principle which should guide us in the education of children is, *to teach only what is necessary and proper, and what the child is competent to understand*, and the next is, *to illustrate, explain, and demonstrate it, as far as possible, to the understanding and the senses.*

I have given you the result of twenty years' observation and experience; and whether I am in error, or whether the common theory of memory and the common system of instruction are in fault, you, gentlemen, must judge.

ENGLISH GRAMMAR.

If any one branch taught in our common schools is very badly taught, that branch is English grammar. Whatever may be the textbook used, the object undoubtedly ought to be, to teach the child to speak and write correctly and with ease; and, if the teacher is competent, this object may be attained with any of the popular textbooks, or even without any of them.

Unfortunately, however, the number of district school teachers who are skilful in the use of language is very small, although many are acquainted with the technics of grammar, and can analyze sentences made by others with tolerable facility. To such, and to all teachers, let me say, that their time will be better spent if they begin earlier to teach the *use* of language, leaving the grammar to come in, as it originally came, after the language has been formed.

To enable the teacher to do this, he must begin early with the child, and make every exercise bear upon this. In my remarks on reading and orthography, I have shown how a beginning may be made, and I shall endeavor not to repeat what I have said.

I should begin to teach English grammar, then, when I begin to teach the English language; that is, when I begin to teach reading, spelling and talking. The mischief has been, that children have been allowed to read without intelligence, to spell without any application of the words, and to talk without care, although they talk before they read, or spell, or write; and being allowed to talk badly, the chief object of teaching technical grammar afterwards is, to undo what has been previously done, but what should have been avoided. If parents only felt the importance of speaking correctly, and even elegantly, in the presence of their children; if they paid a hundredth part as much attention to language as they do to dress and external appearance, we should hear little of grammar, except as it affords directions for foreigners who wish to learn our idioms, and have not time to do so by practice in writing and speaking it.

Unfortunately, not one child in a hundred is so situated that he is not exposed to evil influences in this respect; and the time is far distant, I fear, when, in the family and in society, the use of language will be so free from error that the young will insensibly learn to speak correctly, and be so familiar with good usage that they will not need to resort to grammars to know in what it consists. Several years ago, a young Frenchman, who had been educated in Paris at great expense, undertook to teach French in Boston. He was an excellent scholar, and yet one day he pointed to a countryman of his who passed us in the street, and remarked, "That man is an upholsterer, and has taken no pains to perfect his pronunciation, but I would give all I am worth to be able to pronounce French as correctly as he does." "How did he arrive at such perfection?" said I. "He was born at Tours," said he, "where French is more correctly spoken than in any other part of France, and he speaks well from habit. I shall never equal him." The teacher cannot, perhaps, counteract entirely the evil influences of home, and of intercourse with the illiterate and unrefined, but he may do much by the force of his own example, and by untiring vigilance in regard to the faults of his pupils.

Before children are readers or writers, they are often great talkers; but how rarely do we hear of a teacher's engaging in conversation with such pupils, or indeed with his most advanced pupils; and yet, what exercise could be more proper or more useful than for the teacher to call his little class around him, and converse freely and affectionately with them upon the thousand subjects that interest their opening minds? Besides the exercise in grammar which such a conversation would afford, how completely might the teacher win the affections of the children, and lay the basis of mild and yet effective discipline; and how easily could he impress upon the yet unsullied heart the great principles of conscience, morality and religion. Were I again to undertake to teach, this exercise would be one of the first that I should introduce into every class; but, when I was a teacher, I was blind as my fellows in this respect, except that I was accustomed to converse with my oldest pupils on the subject of their next composition.

It is to be regretted that so few teachers are fitted to converse with their pupils in this manner, but this should not prevent them from making the attempt; and I err greatly in my judgment, if they do not soon find that in this exercise, as in philosophy, action and reaction will be, at the least, equal.

If he cannot trust himself without a text, let him take some common thing,—a piece of money, for instance,—and ask the little ones its uses, and such other particulars as will lead them to tell what they know on the subject. He may even appoint the subject of conversation the day beforehand, and let them think upon it before they come to the class. I know that many teachers will say they have no time for such an exercise, and I suppose they have not; but I think every one can make time for it, by thus employing some of the minutes that are worse than wasted in teaching useless things, or in teaching even useful things in a useless manner.

I have already shown how early the child may be taught to write, and how usefully he may be employed in writing little sentences from his books, from dictation, or from copies set on the ruled black-board. Every sentence that the child writes in this way is a lesson in grammar, and in the use of language, which is, or ought to be, the only object in learning the grammar of one's own language.

When I was at school, composition was not taught, and, although I received the Franklin medal for English grammar especially, I am not aware that I ever wrote a word of composition until I left school, and I am sure that I never wrote one as a school exercise. I entered what is now called the Eliot school, in Boston, at the early age of six years, easily passing for a child of seven, because as large as my brother, who was eight. We read one verse, and spelled one or two words, every day. My class consisted of twelve forms or long benches, each holding six or eight boys. Each form, on successive days, said grammar, as it was called, and my turn came only once a fortnight, unless I got above others in spelling, which elevation, of course, brought the grammar lesson somewhat earlier than if I had remained stationary. Six lines of the grammar were the least quantity that was taken for a lesson, but we might say more if we pleased, and he who said most went to the head of the form. Such was the horror in which this exercise was held, that boys, whose turn it would be to say grammar the next day, would miss words in spelling, so as to drop into a lower form, and put off the evil day. Others, who had an opportunity to rise into the doomed form, intentionally spelled the words wrong, and staid down.

The recitation was generally made to some boy of the highest class, and it was never accompanied with any explanation. When a boy had said every word of the grammar book through three times, he was promoted to the first class, which alone was allowed to make that wonderful application of grammar which is technically called parsing. The textbook I first learned was the *Young Ladies' Accidence*, by Caleb Bingham, with whom, after he became a bookseller, I had the pleasure of serving my apprenticeship, and whose partner I had the honor to be until his death. If this were the proper place, it would give me great delight to sketch the character of this excellent man, who was the earliest reformer of education in Boston, and perhaps in these United States. No reading books were so popular as his American Preceptor and Columbian Orator. No spelling book was more used than his Child's Companion in our primary schools, which, at that time, were private or select schools for children under seven, and kept by females; and his little grammar, called "The Young Ladies' Accidence," because, when he made and named it, the author was teacher of a select school for girls, was the first grammatical textbook used in the public schools of Boston. I must be contented, however, with barely saying that Caleb Bingham was a good scholar; a very successful and much beloved teacher; a gentleman in the best sense of the word; an humble, devout, consistent, and charitable Christian,—one of those whose purity of heart enables them, even here on earth, to see God.

Before I had learned the Young Ladies' Accidence once through, it was superseded by a little abridgment of Murray's Grammar by "A Teacher of Youth;" and this I recited twice by rote,—a few lines at a lesson, before I was initiated into the mysteries of parsing. How far this change of books went towards finishing my English education may be inferred from the fact, that, when, at the age of thirteen, I went to the public Latin school, and the teacher, by way of examination, asked me what was the perfect participle of the verb *love*, I could not answer him. It is not to be wondered at, therefore, that I hated grammar, had no faith in the utility of teaching it as it was then taught, and determined to reform the method, if I ever had a good opportunity.

But the teacher must use some textbook, and the question

is, how shall he use it? To answer this question fully, it would be necessary to give particular directions for the use of every one of the hundred or more textbooks that have been prepared to explain, or modify, or simplify, the system proposed nearly half a century ago by Lindley Murray. I can not be expected to do this, and must be contented with one general remark, viz., Whatever be the textbook, as soon as a principle is stated, do not advance one step further until it is understood, and applied to actual practice. How this may be done, I have attempted to show in my Common School Grammar, to which I must refer the young teacher, since to explain any textbook would be to write a grammar as large as that to which I refer.

But the most popular grammars used in the United States abound in difficulties, and, by perplexing the teachers and disgusting the pupils, they fail to aid either in the great work of using their mother tongue with facility and effect. Something is fundamentally wrong. All teachers and all pupils feel this, and yet no reform that has been proposed reaches the difficulty, or, in any considerable degree, obviates it. Will the reader bear with me while, at some length, I point out what I consider to be the evil, and endeavor to propose an adequate remedy for it.

The first school that I undertook to teach was to be conducted on the monitorial plan, and the monitors, as usual, formed the highest class, and were under my special instruction. The first time that I endeavored to give them a lesson in English grammar, I found that they all applied to the dictionary to ascertain to what part of speech a word belonged. As the same word, in different circumstances, might belong to different classes of words, and the pupils seemed never to have exercised their ingenuity in attempting to class words by the use that was made of them in the sentence, I directed all dictionaries to be banished, and the definitions of the various parts of speech to be thoroughly learned before the next lesson. When the time arrived, I selected a sentence from the reading book, and I shall never forget it. It was, "David smote Goliah." "Well," said I to the first pupil, "what part of speech is David?" "A noun, sir." "What is a noun?" "A substantive or noun is the name of any thing that exists, or of which we have any notion." "Is David, in this sentence the name of any thing that exists?" "No, sir; David died long ago." "Is it the name of any thing of which you have any notion?" "Yes, sir; I have some notion of him as a very small man, and a king." As the object was only to ascertain the part of speech, I asked the next pupil what part of speech *smote* was. "A preposition, sir." "A preposition!" said I, with astonishment, "pray what is a preposition?" "Prepositions serve to connect words with one another and to show the relation between them." "Very well," said I, with all the importance of a teacher who felt it his duty to expose the ignorance of his pupil, "what words does *smote* connect?" "David and Goliah, sir, for there is nothing else to connect them." "Yes," said I, somewhat flurried, "but what relation does it show between them?" "Not a very friendly one, I should think, sir," said the pupil. I was struck with the truth of the answers, and had the honesty to say, "You are right, miss, or the definition in your book is wrong."

This incident shook my faith in the perfection of Murray's Grammar; and the long course of study which followed, resulted in the settled conviction that *Murray's* Grammar is far from being synonymous with *English* grammar, and that any time spent in teaching it is worse than thrown away. This may seem a bold assertion, when it is recollected that, perhaps, hundreds of persons have published grammars founded upon Murray's, and the schools of our country, from one end to the other, for nearly half a century, have known no other, and half the teachers, and nearly all the parents, seem to have adopted the notion, that to throw aside this very popular grammar would be to throw aside the English language itself.

Twenty-five years ago, when I first struck for reform, the charge of wishing to corrupt, or, at least, to alter the language, was urged against me with no little violence, although I never proposed any such alteration, and was mainly anxious to preserve the "well of English undefiled." I have had the pleasure of seeing several of the improvements I then recommended very generally adopted, but much rubbish yet remains to be removed; and as, in teaching this branch, I differ from my brother teachers still more in regard to the matter to be taught than in regard to the manner of teaching it, I will venture to give the reasons for my conduct somewhat at length.

The human mind being essentially the same in every man, it would be strange, if, in some important respects, there was not a degree of similarity in the languages which their common wants have created. All languages, for instance, would be likely to have words that were the names of objects that could be the subject of sense or of thought. They would have words also to distinguish several individuals of the same name from each other, and they would have another class of words to express the actions that any object may perform. Beauzée* expresses the same idea when he says, "Reason produces every where the same results; it establishes every where the same sorts of words to represent, under similar circumstances, the same kind of ideas; it subjects words to the same kinds of service, and it fixes the relations between them as the ideas are related of which they are the signs." A grammar whose object is merely to show in what respects all languages agree, is called a general grammar; but languages do not agree in every respect, and a general grammar would never enable us to learn those peculiarities which are confined to a single language. How shall we learn them, then? Is it not by studying such grammars as set forth these peculiarities in the clearest light, unmixed with the peculiarities of any other language? Now, if it can be shown that the grammars in common use, called English grammars, do not exhibit the peculiarities of our language, but, on the contrary, so mix up its peculiarities with those of other languages that no distinct idea of English grammar is contained in them, ought we not instantly to discard them all, and to endeavor to find some one that shall be fitted to do the work that they can never accomplish?

To understand this remark, let me give an example, taken from the Latin language. We there find that the verb, or word that expresses action, changes its termination more than a hundred times, and, without the addition of any other word, changes its meaning as many times. Thus, —

Amo	means	I love.
Amabam	"	I was loving.
Amavi	"	I have loved.
Amaveram	"	I had loved.
Amabo	"	I shall or will love.
Amavero	"	I shall or will have loved.

Amem	"	I may or can love.
Amarem	"	I might, could, would, or should love.

* *Beauzée*, author of "Grammaire Générale, ou Exposition Raisonnée des Éléments nécessaires du Langage," etc.

Amaverim	means	I may have loved.
Amavissem	"	I might, could, would, or should have loved.
Ama	"	Love thou.
Amare	"	To love.
Amavisse	"	To have loved.
Amor	"	I am loved.
Amabar	"	I was loved.
Amabor	"	I shall be loved.
Amer	"	I may or can be loved.
Amarer	"	I might, could, would, or should be loved.
Amator	"	Be thou loved.
Amari	"	To be loved.

Here are twenty forms of a Latin verb, each having a different termination, and each a difference of meaning, as I have shown by the English translation that I have placed opposite to them. Now these changes of termination are called *tenses* in Latin grammars, and, with one or two exceptions, each of these has five other variations to express the other persons in the two numbers. Thus,

Amo, I love; *Amas*, thou lovest; *Amat*, he loves;
Amamus, we love; *Amatis*, ye love; *Amant*, they love.

The Latin verbs, therefore, have really more than a hundred such changes of termination.

Now, how is it in our language? How many terminations have we; or, if these changes of termination are called *tenses*, how many *tenses* have we? Let us see. We have —

Love, lovest, loveth, loves.

Loved, lovedst.

Six in all! and, surely, there must be an amazing difference between the *particular* grammar of the Latin language and that of English, and this point of difference, of course, it would seem to be the duty of the makers of English grammar-books distinctly to set forth. They have done no such thing; but, on the contrary, they have said that we have as many tenses as the Latins have; and English children, who could learn our six terminations, which make but two tenses, in five minutes, are compelled often to waste years in learning the translations of the hundred Latin tenses, although not one in a thousand will ever see the Latin words.

This multiplicity of terminations has been called an advantage, and is said to add richness to the Latin tongue; but it seems to me, that, if it is an advantage to have an alphabet of a few letters, by the transposition of which we can express all, and more than all that can be expressed by the countless hieroglyphics which the alphabet superseded, the English language has an advantage over the Latin in being able with six words to express all that can be expressed by their hundred, and this without any loss of strength, or any fear of mistake.

This will suffice for an example, and the question naturally arises, "How came English grammar to be so strangely perverted?" Fortunately, this question can be satisfactorily answered. But, if it be asked why disturb the course of instruction by introducing a new system into the schools? I answer that this question should have been put to Lindley Murray when he proposed his grammar; for the grammars before his day hardly departed at all from the true idiom and structure of our language. The teacher who has not access to any good library, and who takes,—as, I trust, every Massachusetts teacher, who deserves the name, does,—the *Common School Journal*, will find in the third volume a brief analysis of some of the early grammars of our language, an analysis which was made, I believe, by a gentleman, who, if I can judge from his initials, W. H. W., saw in those grammars what the true principles of English grammar were, and seems to have approved them, and, nevertheless, went away and constructed a grammar of his own, which, if possible, departs further than Murray's does from the simplicity of truth, and does not appear to be in the least improved by the critic's researches. The analysis, however, as far as it goes, is fairly made, and the following is the result.

Lilly's Grammar. This was a Latin grammar, though, in a second part, it touched upon English; "but," says W. H. W., "both parts are devoted to the grammar of the Latin tongue." The fact is, nobody studied English grammar when this was published, in 1513.

Ben Jonson's Grammar, 1640. W. H. W. says of this grammar The author attempted to force the English language to the Latin idiom." This grammar was written in English.

Dr. Wallis, 1653. "This learned man endeavored," says W. H. W., "to free the language from the trammels imposed on it by other writers, *but he sometimes fell into the opposite extreme.*" Dr. W. classed adjectives, pronouns, possessive cases and participles, with mere adjectives, and allowed no moods, and only two tenses, to verbs. As his grammar was in fact the basis of my Common School Grammar, I shall say more of it than the critic did, and shall hereafter endeavor to show that Dr. Wallis fell into no extreme, as the critic erroneously supposes.

John Brightland, 1710. The critic says, "*He thoroughly, investigated every department of the subject, and his work presents a striking contrast with many of our modern hasty and superficial productions.*" He makes but four parts of speech, —nouns, adjectives, verbs and particles. Pronouns he calls nouns; the article and the possessive case he calls adjectives. He has no moods, and only two tenses. Participles he calls adjectives. The auxiliaries he calls principal verbs, and the verbs after them infinitives with *to* understood, as did Wallis and Ben Jonson. Under the name of particles he includes adverbs, prepositions, conjunctions and interjections.*

Gough, James and John, 1750. The critic says, "This is a production of little merit;" but he gives no particulars in regard to the parts of speech.

James Harris, 1751. The Hermes of Harris is a *general* grammar, and should not have been mentioned by the critic among English grammars.

A. Fisher, 1753. Four parts of speech, the same as Brightland's. He has no moods, and but three tenses. He allows but two cases, having no objective.

The British Grammar, 1762. This anonymous grammar has eight parts of speech, and calls the article and adjective subdivisions of the noun. It has but two cases, four moods and five tenses. It allows no potential mood, and no second future tense, but, in other respects, is like Murray's Grammar, of which it was probably the basis.

It is not known who was the author of this grammar, but he is entitled to the infamy of having led the way to a fatal

* These were the conclusions of a man who, it seems, had "thoroughly investigated every department of the subject of grammar!"

relapse into the wretched system, from which Wallis had so patriotically redeemed our language.

Dr. Priestley, 1762. This very learned author had no moods, and but two tenses. "He also asserts," says the critic, "that we have no more business with a future tense than we have with the whole system of Latin moods and tenses."

Dr. Lowth, 1763. Dr. Webster says that Wallis and Lowth are the two ablest writers on English grammar. Dr. L. allows but two cases; has four moods, omitting the potential of Murray; and three tenses, adding the future to the present and past of his predecessors.

Dr. Johnson, about 1763. This grammar was prefixed to the great dictionary. The critic says it cannot be regarded as a complete system of English grammar. It contains one bright remark, however, which the critic seems to cite with disapprobation. Dr. J. says, "Our language has so little inflection or variety of terminations that its construction neither requires nor admits many rules." He also objects to the use of new terms or names in grammar.

Dr. Ash, about 1763. This grammar is mentioned, but nothing is said by the critic to enable the reader to form an idea of its plan, except that the author called it an Introduction to Lowth's Grammar. Dr. Ash rejected the passive voice, and called participles adjectives.

William Ward, 1765. Of Ward the critic says, "He was strongly inclined to the old system of instruction, and used his influence to revive many useless terms, which had been rejected by Wallis and Lowth." Has not the critic done the same thing in his own grammar, published in 1846?

John Burn, 1766. The critic gives no idea of his system, and might as well not have named him.

James Buchanan, 1767. "Stolen chiefly from the British Grammar," says the critic.

The ill health of W. H. W. prevented him from continuing the list any further, but he brought it far enough to show that, originally, English grammar was made entirely subservient to the Latin; then, some noble minds, led on by Dr. Wallis, broke the shackles, and made a proper English grammar; and, finally, men of less genius and learning began the retrogression, which ended in the production of Murray's Grammar, *et id genus omne*.

I promised to say something more of Dr. Wallis's Grammar, but let me first say a word or two of the man.

Dr. John Wallis was a distinguished professor of geometry in Oxford University, one of the founders of the Royal Society, and one of the secretaries of the famous Westminster Assembly of Divines in 1644. Before he was honored with the professorship, he was a clergyman, and, probably, a teacher, for he taught several deaf mutes to speak, and wrote a valuable treatise on the best method of instructing them. It is to be regretted that no one seems to have thought of simplifying the labor of teaching these unfortunates by adopting the English Grammar of this true philosopher, who to this, no doubt, owed much of his success in teaching them to articulate words. Dr. Wallis made some valuable discoveries in natural philosophy, and his mathematical works led to many important improvements. As a linguist he was distinguished, and edited two or three ancient authors. He was therefore a competent judge of general and particular grammar, more so than any that preceded or followed him, with the exception, perhaps, of Dr. Priestley, who agreed with him, and Dr. Lowth, who wrote his Grammar, as he avows, for the special purpose of helping some of his family to study Latin and Greek.

In the preface to his Grammar, nearly two hundred years ago, Dr. Wallis says: —

" Many foreigners who wish to learn our language, complain of its difficulty; and even some of our own countrymen think it can not be subjected to any grammatical rules. These evils I have undertaken to remedy, in order that a language, in itself very easy of acquisition, may be so explained that foreigners may more easily learn it, and natives more thoroughly understand its true structure. I am aware that others before me have attempted this, amongst whom are Dr. Gill in Latin, Ben Johnson in English, and Henry Hexham in Belgic; but no one of them, as I think, has adopted the method best adapted to this design, for, *all of them, by forcing our language to conform to the Latin model, have given many useless rules about the cases, genders, and declensions of nouns, the tenses, modes, and conjugations of verbs, and other similar things, which are entirely foreign to our language, and obscure and confuse, rather than explain it.* On this account, I have adopted a different method, which aims not so much to exhibit the usages of the Latin tongue, as the peculiarities of our own; for, what causes much trouble in other languages,

is made a light affair in ours, by the aid of prepositions and auxiliaries."

How, then, does Dr. Wallis construct his True English Grammar? I will show, in as few words as possible.

1. He has eight parts of speech,—the noun, adjective, pronoun, verb, adverb, preposition, conjunction, and interjection.

2. The articles he calls adjectives.

3. He has no cases to nouns; for the possessive case, he says, is a mere adjective, and not, like nouns, the *name* of any thing.

4. All adjective pronouns, and possessive cases of personal pronouns, he calls adjectives.

5. Personal pronouns, he says, ought to be called nouns. He keeps them in a separate class, however, probably because they seem to have two cases, which he calls two states or conditions.

6. He has no active and passive voice, no moods, and only two tenses,—the two that Murray calls the present and imperfect.

7. Of the two participles, which he calls active and passive, he says, "They are clearly adjectives, and, in every respect, like other adjectives."

8. What Murray calls auxiliaries, he calls so, because, he says, they have no auxiliaries themselves, and no participles. As this is not true of *be*, *have*, *do*, and *will*, and, since Dr. W. treats them all as principal verbs, the utility of calling them auxiliaries is not very apparent.

9. He treats the other four parts of speech very much as Murray does.

This is a brief summary of the plan; and who does not see that it is founded in nature and reason, and is more simple than the grammar that prevails?

I am not aware that, in the Common School Grammar, I have departed in any important respect from the great principles laid down by Dr. Wallis; but I know that these principles, simple as they are, will not be received without great reluctance, and I shall, at the risk of being tedious, say a few words upon each of the nine points above noticed. It would be a shorter way, perhaps, to refer the teacher at once to my Grammar; but as that is intended for children, I have not discussed any disputed question, because this could only perplex the learner, and the teacher should be convinced without obliging the child to pay for the argument.

1. In regard to the parts of speech. As we have names of things that exist, and of those also "of which we have any notion," we must have names for *actions;* but we have no such names, unless the infinitive mode of Mr. Murray, and the present participle, when not used as an adjective, are called nouns. This may seem a startling position, but it does no violence even to the Grammar of Mr. Murray; for he always governs the infinitive as he would a noun, and makes a nominative of it in the same manner; nay, he even allows an adjective to qualify it, as in the sentence, "To see the sun is pleasant." He does the same thing with the present participle, and why then should not these *names* of action at once be called nouns. If it be said, "the infinitive must be a verb, because the other modes and tenses are formed from it," the answer is, that, granting that they are so formed, the consequence does not follow. *A head* is a noun, *to head* is an infinitive, *I headed* is an undoubted verb; now, if *to head* is a verb because *I headed* is formed from it, then *a head* is a verb because *to head* is formed from that. What is the difference between *I love reading*, and *I love to read; writing is useful*, and *to write is useful;* and why should they be parsed differently? It is, therefore, no departure from even Murray himself to call infinitives and present participles nouns; but, if it were, I could bring authority for doing so, with which Mr. Murray and his followers may not be compared.

I shall content myself with only one extract from Dr. Crombie's justly celebrated Grammar, cited with approbation by Bosworth, in his valuable Anglo-Saxon Grammar. Dr. Crombie says, "In what light are we to consider the phrase *to love*, generally termed an infinitive; or to what class of words is it reducible? It cannot be a verb, for it does not affirm any thing. It expresses merely an action or state abstractedly. Hence, many grammarians have justly considered it no part of the verb; and, in the languages of Greece and Rome, the infinitive was employed like a common substantive, having frequently an adjective joined with it, and subject to the government of verbs and prepositions. I decidedly concur with those grammarians who exclude the infinitive from the appellation of verb The ancient Latin grammarians, as Priscian informs us, termed it, properly enough, "*nomen verbi*, the *noun*, or *name of the verb*." In the Common School Grammar, it is called a *verbal noun*.

2. The Article, also, is struck from the list of parts of speech.

It may seem unnecessary to say a word in defence of this act, for some of the Latino-English grammarians, and W. H. W., of the Common School Journal, among them, yield this point; and yet, not many days ago, a gentleman, of some reputation as a scholar and a teacher, undertook, at one of the Normal schools, to expose my folly in uttering such a notion, and, therefore, it may be well to waste a word upon his arguments, which have been reported me.

"The articles have a peculiar *meaning* and *use*, different from adjectives," says my reviewer. When I say, Give me *an* orange, then, what do I *mean*, but that I wish for *one* orange? When I say, Give me *one* orange, what do I *mean*, but that I wish for *an* orange? So much for the peculiar *meaning;* and who can tell in what respect *an* is *used* differently from *one?* If it be still objected, that this similarity of *meaning* and *use* proves not that *an* is an adjective, for *one* is an indefinite adjective pronoun, I may grant this, and be contented, for the present, to call *a*, *an*, and *the* indefinite adjective pronouns; and the similarity of meaning and use between the expressions, Give me *a* book to read, Give me *some* book to read, and, Give me *any* book to read, may help to fix the articles among the pronouns. We shall see what adjective pronouns are, presently.

The must go into the same class also for the present, if give me *the* book you are reading, and give me *that* book you are reading, *mean* the same thing, and *the* and *that* are *used* in a similar manner. So "I saw *the* strangers you described," I saw *those* strangers you described. "I will keep *the* book that I hold in my hand," I will keep *this* book that I hold in my hand, &c., &c. It is unnecessary to multiply examples.

The fact is, that *the*, although separated from *this*, *that*, *these*, and *those*, and called a *definite* article, is not so well entitled to this distinction as they are; for, if *the* can be used for any one of the four, and they cannot be used for each other, it necessarily follows that the meaning of *the* is more general or comprehensive, and, of course, less definite than theirs.

But, says my reviewer, "It is well to have a name and a definition for the articles, to call attention to them, and fix their meaning in the mind, which is the only object of making and defining any distinctions." Well, then, what is his *definition* of the article? "*An article is a word prefixed to substantives to point them out, and show how far their significa-*

tion extends." Let us test this definition, which my reviewer thinks so very important. "*The scholars who hear me,*" is a good sentence for this purpose. *The*, we are told, points out the scholars, and shows how far their signification extends. But, I am inclined to think, the signification would be just as limited if *the* were entirely omitted, and the sentence were, "*Scholars, who hear me.*" Does not the clause, "*who hear me,*" though not prefixed to the substantive, point it out, and show how far its signification extends? and is not this *clause*, therefore, a better article than the word *the*, which is so *indefinite* that it may be omitted?

Again, in the sentence, "Normal scholars, listen to me!" is not *Normal* prefixed to the substantive? and does it not show how far the signification extends? Why is not *Normal* a good article then?—Normal scholars are, we all know.

Again, in the name, John Smith, John is prefixed to Smith to point the particular Smith out, and show how far the signification of Smith extends. John, then, must be a good article. So with *wind* mill, *elm* tree, *barn* door, &c., where *wind*, *elm*, and *barn* answer perfectly to his definition of the article. So even the verbs *grind* and *tell* become similar articles, when prefixed to the substantives *stone* and *tale*; as, *grind-stone*, *tell-tale*. So the pronouns in "*my* child," "*his* child," "*her* child," become the best of articles, by fulfilling all the conditions of the definition that my reviewer thinks so essential to show what a true article is.

I have already shown how my pupil applied the definition of the preposition to a verb, and I hesitate not to say, that no definition of any part of speech in Murray's Grammar is a whit more definite than that. To prove this, let us amuse ourselves with an experiment on Mr. Murray's definitions of the adverb, preposition and conjunction.

"An *adverb* is a part of speech joined to a verb, an adjective, and sometimes to another adverb, to express some quality or circumstance respecting it;" as,—

He reads *correctly*.	*Correctly* expresses *some* circumstance of the verb reads, viz., *its quality*.
He reads *to* me.	*To* expresses a circumstance of reads, viz., *its direction*.
He reads *as* I do.	*As* expresses a circumstance of reads, viz., its resemblance to my reading.

"*Prepositions* serve to connect words with one another and to show the relation between them."

He wished *for* a coach	It is not my business to say whether *for* connects *he* or *wished* with *coach*, but I am inclined to think the connection and relation would be just as apparent if *for* were entirely omitted.
He wished *but* a coach.	*But* connects words as much as *for* does, and it shows the relation between wished and the object of the wish, viz., the relation of *restriction.*
He wished *then* a coach.	*Then* connects *of course*, though it may be left out as *for* may, and it shows the relation of *time* between the wish and the thing wished.

"A *conjunction* is a part of speech that is chiefly used to connect sentences; it sometimes connects only words."

Two *and* three are five.	*And* connects two and three.
Two *with* three are five.	*With* connects the same words.
Two *more* three are five,	That is, $2+3=5$.

But enough of this; the definitions are all wrong, and I should ask pardon for this attempt to expose what is so manifestly absurd.

3. Next comes the subject of *Cases.* We have seen that several of the old grammarians, noticed by W. H. W., allowed no cases, and others allowed but two,—the nominative and possessive. Some English grammarians allow but one case, and some claim six, not because we vary the noun, as the Latins can, in six* different ways, but because, by the aid of certain prepositions, we can translate their cases into English. Thus the Latins say:

	SINGULAR.			
Nominative,	*Homo,*	which	means	Man.
Genitive,	*Hominis,*	"	"	of Man.
Dative,	*Homini,*	"	"	to Man.
Accusative,	*Hominem,*	"	"	Man.
Vocative,	*Homo,*	"	"	O Man!
Ablative,	*Homine,*	"	"	with Man.

* Latin nouns have usually five variations in the singular, and four in the

PLURAL.			
Nominative,	*Homines*,	which means	Men.
Genitive,	*Hominum*,	" "	of Men.
Dative,	*Hominibus*,	" "	to Men.
Accusative,	*Homines*,	" "	Men.
Vocative,	*Homines*,	" "	O Men!
Ablative,	*Hominibus*,	" "	with Men.

Now, if the Latins have six cases, and we can translate them by *a phrase* in English, we have as good a right to say that we have six cases, as we have to say that we have four or five moods, and forty or more tenses; because, forsooth, we can, *by phrases*, express what they express by only altering the termination of single words.

Dr. Crombie, by far the most judicious of modern grammarians, says, "If we confine the term *noun* to the *name* of an object, we shall exclude the possessive from all right to this appellation. This is, indeed, an inconsistency, which can in no way be removed, unless by adopting the opinion of Wallis, who assigns no cases to English nouns, and considers *man's*, *king's* &c., mere adjectives."

It is clear that, if "a substantive or noun is the *name* of any thing," *man's*, and *king's*, and *John's*, can not be nouns; for who ever saw such a thing as a *man's*, a *king's*, or such a boy as *John's?* It is amusing to see those who do not hesitate to place even the nominative or the objective case unchanged before another noun, and call it an adjective, as *town* clerk, *city* government, *head* ornament, are afraid or unwilling to call the possessive case an adjective, although there is no difference of meaning or use between *town* clerk and *town's* clerk; the *city* government, and the *city's* government; *head* ornament, or the *head's* ornament, &c.

The fact is, that, when we use a possessive case before a noun, we do so to distinguish that object from others of the same name; and all words used for this purpose are adjectives. If I see several hats in a row, and wish to describe or distinguish them from each other, I call one *new*, and another *old*, to distinguish their *age;* one *black*, and another *white*, to distinguish them by *color;* one *fine*, and another *coarse*, to distinguish their *quality;* one near, and another *distant*, to distinguish their *place;* one John's, and another Henry's, to

plural. The nominative and vocative, in both numbers, and the dative and ablative, in the plural, are generally alike.

distinguish their *possessors.* Whatever word I use to distinguish them becomes an adjective; and, if this is true when a verb, as, *tell* tale; a noun, as, *tale* bearer; or an adverb, as, the *very* man, are used unaltered, how much rather is it the case when a change is made in the termination, for the very purpose of making an adjective of the noun, as the termination *ly* makes an adverb of an adjective.

4. Adjective pronouns are called so because they have the nature of adjectives, and are used, like adjectives, to distinguish nouns. The best grammarians call them adjectives at once; but some pretend to have discovered that some of them —not all—are occasionally used *without* a noun, and therefore are said to stand *instead of* a noun, and so come under the definition of a pronoun, which is said to be, " A word used instead of a noun to prevent its too frequent repetition." If standing without its noun makes a pronoun of an adjective, it may reasonably be suspected that every adjective occasionally becomes a pronoun. In the sentence, " The *wise* and *good* are scarce," are *wise* and *good* pronouns, because their noun is understood?

But, says a shrewd philologist, " It does not follow that the words called pronouns stand *instead* of nouns, any more than it can be truly said, that those words which remain in any elliptic or abridged sentence stand instead of the words omitted." Such words refer to some noun that is understood, and point it out, but they no more stand instead of what they point at, than a guide-board stands instead of a town, to which it only directs the traveller.

The greatest grammarians of other languages, as well as of the English, have classed *all* the pronouns among the adjectives, but I have been contented with giving this name to the adjective pronouns, and the possessive case of the personal and relative pronouns.

Some, however, may say, " We grant that all the adjective pronouns may be used as adjectives, and may have nouns understood, which may be easily supplied, but it is not so with the possessive cases of personal pronouns, for when, in speaking of two books, we say, " This is *mine* and that is *yours*," although the word *book* is evidently understood, we cannot supply it, for it will not do to say, " This is *mine book* and that is *yours book*." This is all true, but the time was when *mine* was spelled *me-en*, as yours was *your-en*, or, contracted, *yourn*, and this termination *en* marked an adjective as much as *ly* now does an adverb. *Yours* is only *your's*, the possessive termination, which, it has been shown, marks an adjective.

But, what do *mine* and *yours* stand instead of? If the conversation is between William and John, *mine* means *William's*, and *yours* means *John's*. It has been shown that William's and John's, not being names of persons, are not nouns, and, consequently, if *mine* and *yours* stand instead of those words, they cannot be pronouns, for pronouns, the grammar says, are words that stand instead of *nouns*, and not instead of adjectives.

Again; if *mine* and *thine*, *hers*, *ours*, *yours* and *theirs*, are used without, or instead of, nouns that can not be supplied, this is not the case with the possessives *his* and *its*, for the noun may be introduced by the side of these, and this may lead one to doubt whether the use of the words *mine*, *yours*, &c., precludes the introduction of the noun. We find, therefore, that although, in the case above mentioned, it may not be graceful to say, "This is *mine book* and that is *yours book*," yet it is perfectly correct to place the word *book* elsewhere, and say, "This *book* is *mine* and that *book* is *yours*," in which sentences *mine* and *yours* qualify *book* as much as *new* and *old* would in the sentence, "This book is *new* and that is *old*," it being ungraceful to say, "This is *new* book and that is *old* book."

But, if the English nouns have no change of termination entitling them to the distinction of cases, they can express all the Latin cases, and many more, by the help of prepositions, or, often, without their aid. If a noun does any thing, it is an *agent;* if something is done to it, it is an *object*. The two words, *agent* and *object*, are the only new ones, I believe, that have been introduced into the Common School Grammar, and whether they can be better explained than the terms *nominative case* and *objective case*, the teacher will soon discover by trial.

5. Personal pronouns were called *nouns* by Dr. Wallis, and by several succeeding grammarians, and it would be much easier to prove them to be so than to prove that they are pronouns. They do, however, have this peculiarity, that the nominative case or agent is a different word from the objective case or object. Then, it may be asked, why not call the variations of personal pronouns cases at once, since there is really a difference in the words? *Case* is derived

14

from *casus*, a Latin word, which, some say, means an accident, the change of termination being considered an accident; or, as others say, because the cases *fall off* from the nominative. Now, in neither sense, is the objective of the pronoun of the first person a case; for *me* and *us* are not produced by a change of termination, nor by any such *accident* as happens to Latin nouns. It is safer, therefore, to say that *I* is an agent, and *me* an object, and to leave the word *case* until the child learns some language to whose nouns the term is applicable. Any one who will take the trouble to read Mr. Murray's remarks under the term *case*, will see enough, I think, to sicken him of this propensity to ape the classic languages.

6. But the great point of difference between Dr. Wallis, Dr. Priestley, Dr. Crombie, &c., and Mr. Murray and his imitators, is in the manner of treating the *verb*. This difference is so essential that it must not be lightly disregarded; and the teacher is bound in conscience to weigh well the question, "What is the verb in English, and in what manner shall it be presented to the mind of a child?" It is generally granted that the English verbs have really no great variety of termination, and yet we are told that there is a propriety and a convenience in giving the name of *tense* to certain English *phrases*, because they are translations of Latin tenses.

The example of a Latin and English verb that I have given on pages 144–5, must go far, I think, towards showing that there is no propriety in giving the name of *tense* to certain English *phrases*, which are like hundreds of other phrases, and have no better right than they to this distinction. Why not take other languages than Latin, and translate the tenses of their verbs, and say we have those tenses, also? Who can tell where we shall stop? *

But, say the old school grammarians, "We certainly have three divisions of time, present, past and future, and these are subdivided." No one will deny that all nations have an idea of past time, and of this, as of the present, history treats. They have an idea of future time, also, and this is the province of prophecy or imagination; but, because the idea of these three divisions of time is common to all nations, it by no means follows that all nations have the same manner of

* We need go no further than the Greek to find an *Optative* mood, of which the *present* tense of the verb *go* would be equivalent to "I wish to go."

expressing their ideas. The English, as has been shown by the best authority, have but two tenses, the present and the past; but the English is not so singular in this respect as some other languages. Michaelis, in his Syriac Grammar, says, "The Syrians, *like the rest of the Orientals*, have but two tenses, the *past* and the *future;*" but, he adds, "by the help of the verb or pronoun, they can express the five tenses of the Latins, and even a sixth tense; and they have a sort of present formed by the coalescence of the pronoun and verb into one word; but I have not given these tenses a place in my paradigm, lest I should cumber it uselessly." What a pity that Mr. Murray, and those who, with him, have "cumbered the English grammar uselessly," had not been blessed with some portion of the great German's judgment and discretion!

There is no *propriety*, therefore, in thrusting so many miscalled tenses into our grammar; and, *as there is no good authority for any such abuse*, let us see if there is any *convenience* in it. It may be *convenient* for a child who is going to study Latin to learn the phrases that correspond to the Latin tenses; but is it fair to impose this task upon every child? The number of children in the public schools of Massachusetts is about 175,000; the whole number of graduates annually from our three colleges falls short of two hundred. A few study Latin without going to college, but such do not make any extensive acquaintance with it, and an allowance of 300 per annum will be liberal. At this rate, one child in about six hundred of those who go to school studies Latin, and to accommodate this one, five hundred and ninety-nine are compelled to learn what is of no use to them, and what really is an insurmountable stumbling-block in their way. Can any thing be more unjust?

But it is *convenient*, say some, to have our grammar conform to other languages, that foreigners may learn it more easily. This must be a mistake altogether. Grammars constructed for the use of foreigners, are differently composed from the common grammar. They are compared with the language to be learned, and our terms are translated into the terms used by the other. Cobbett, who made a good grammar for Englishmen, made a very different one for Frenchmen to learn English But, grant that the making of our grammar on a foreign model helps the foreigner, the proportion of foreigners who study English is as nothing to our own children, especially when it is considered that we can adapt our language to only one foreign idiom, and just as far as it is forced to resemble one, it is made unlike the rest.

But in spite of the unnatural form of the common English grammars, some say there is a convenience in having the moods and tenses and the passive voice, and we can teach the use of the language better with them than without them. We have seen that, from the year 1653, almost till Mr. Murray's day, certainly for more than a century, no such thing as moods, and only two tenses, were allowed in the grammars, but who will pretend that the English language was written with less purity and power in what has been called its Augustan age, than at any time before or since? Addison, Swift, Steel, Pope, Johnson, Horne Tooke, and Junius, were educated in this period, and it is very clear that the English language did not suffer in their hands. It is clear that no such thing as moods and tenses would have been dreamed of, had there been no such thing in Latin; that is, had the English never known that there was any other language than their own.

I regret the necessity, but my plan requires that I should examine this matter of *convenience* more thoroughly. If it is an object to teach children this mixed grammar, the advantages should more than balance the disadvantages, not to the few, but to the million, whose only object is to learn English. It certainly is less difficult to teach a child two tenses only, than to teach him the common system of voices, moods and tenses. Let us contrast them by a paradigm.

PAST TENSE.
PRESENT TENSE.

The present tense, being the root of the past, is placed below it. The name of the verb being a noun, and the participles being mere adjectives, the English verb has but the two forms above given, and these are all it needs. Compare this simplicity with the common system, as displayed in the following paradigm.

Compound Perfect.	Compound Perfect.
Perfect Participle.	Perfect Participle.
Present Participle.	Present Participle.
PARTICIPLES.	PARTICIPLES.
Perfect Tense.	Perfect Tense.
Present Tense.	Present Tense.
INFINITIVE MOOD.	INFINITIVE MOOD.
Second Future Tense.	Second Future Tense.
First Future Tense.	First Future Tense.
Pluperfect Tense.	Pluperfect Tense
Perfect Tense.	Perfect Tense.
Imperfect Tense.	Imperfect Tense.
Present Tense.	Present Tense.
SUBJUNCTIVE MOOD.	SUBJUNCTIVE MOOD.
Pluperfect Tense.	Pluperfect Tense.
Perfect Tense.	Perfect Tense.
Imperfect Tense.	Imperfect Tense.
Present Tense.	Present Tense.
POTENTIAL MOOD.	POTENTIAL MOOD.
Present Tense.	Present Tense.
IMPERATIVE MOOD.	IMPERATIVE MOOD.
Second Future Tense.	Second Future Tense.
First Future Tense.	First Future Tense.
Pluperfect Tense.	Pluperfect Tense.
Perfect Tense.	Perfect Tense.
Imperfect Tense.	Imperfect Tense.
Present Tense.	Present Tense.
INDICATIVE MOOD.	INDICATIVE MOOD.
ACTIVE VOICE.	PASSIVE VOICE.

In teaching what resembles a certain tower of old times, and what, from the confusion it produces, may also not improperly be called Bab-el, it is expected that the child should learn not only the names of the voices, moods and tenses, but the distinctions that are said to exist between them. But this must be impossible, for the builders of the tower do not always agree in their definitions and explanations, and when they happen to agree, they cannot always make themselves understood. I shall not attempt to reconcile them, but shall endeavor to show the absurdity of the whole structure

14*

The bases of the two towers are the two voices. Let us look at them. The whole passive voice owes its existence to the fact that, in Latin, there is something of the kind, as has been shown on page 145. This voice is formed by adding the perfect participle of any verb to some tense or combination of the verb *Be;* as, *I am diseased; she was concerned,* &c. It has been shown that the perfect participle is an adjective qualifying nouns or pronouns, as other adjectives do. And in this case, we might say I am *sick,* instead of I am *diseased,* and she was *anxious,* for she was *concerned.* No one denies that *diseased* and *concerned* qualify the nominatives *I* and *she,* as *sick* and *anxious* do; then why not call them adjectives at once? and as the child is supposed to know how to conjugate the verb *to be,* and knows what an adjective is, why compel him to learn five moods, twenty tenses, and a hundred and twenty persons, for the sake of a mere notion called a passive voice? Many perfect participles have adjectives nearly synonymous; and what reason is there for restricting the passive voice to participles, when they are *situated* and *used* like the adjectives, and in some cases *mean* the same thing? If the child knows the forms of the verb *Be,* he can place after them any participle or adjective that expresses his thought, without knowing or caring whether the phrase is a passive verb or not.

Some grammar-makers, and many teachers, have had the good sense to reject the passive voice, but several authors still retain it, and, useless as it is, it will not be dropped without a struggle. Dr. Crombie, one of the best modern grammarians, rejects the passive voice, and Bosworth, whose Anglo-Saxon Grammar is also a precious English grammar, says, "If these cases be rejected by common consent from English nouns, why may not the passive voice, and all the moods and tenses formed by auxiliaries? We shall then see this language in its primitive simplicity. Dr. Wallis, one of our oldest and best grammarians, has divested the English of its Latinized forms, and, when speaking of his predecessors, says" — and here he quotes the sentence already given on page 149.

Dr. Webster, who preceded Murray, and, notwithstanding all his learning and good sense, was superseded by him, says in the first edition of his Grammar, "As to *passive verbs,* we have no such thing in our language. I cannot better express my ideas on this subject than in the words of Dr. Ash, who observes that, 'Properly speaking there is no *passive verb* in the English language; for though *I am loved* is commonly called a passive verb, yet *loved* is no part of the verb, but a participle or *adjective*, derived from the verb *love*.' "

Let us leave the passive voice, then, with but one remark, to show how carelessly *the verb* has been defined by Murray and his followers. They say, " A verb is *a word* that signifies to be, to do, or to suffer; as, *I am*, *I rule*, *I am ruled*." The child, of course, concludes that *I-am-ruled* is a word, for it is a verb, and Murray says a verb is *a word*, and *a* word is but *one* word. If the definition be correct, no passive verb conforms to it, but the passive voice furnishes some frightful *words*, as I-might-have-been-loved; If-I-shall-have-been-loved, &c. &c. The definition should read, "A verb is a *phrase* that signifies, — according to its meaning!"

Having despatched the *voices*, let us look at the *moods*. Of these, as we have seen, the earlier and better grammarians had none; for, allowing but two tenses to English verbs, they had nothing to make moods of. Murray found four in the old British Grammar, and he added a fifth, which he separated from the subjunctive of the Latin and of the British Grammar, and called the potential. This was the greatest departure of Mr. Murray from the model he followed, and it is rather amusing to see that one of his followers has transferred the whole potential mood of Murray, not back to the subjunctive, whence it was taken, but to the indicative! If such transfers can be made, there certainly cannot be a very definite line between the several moods, — no line that a child can ever discover; and will not the absurdity of such distinctions cause all the moods to coalesce at last into one, as it was at the beginning?

The infinitive mood we have shown to be a mere noun. The imperative differs no more from the indicative than every verb that asks a question does. *Depart ye*, is the imperative if it have a period or note of admiration after it, and the indicative if it have a mark of interrogation. " Depart ye, and begone!" " Depart ye so soon?" This may not prove that there is no imperative, but it does prove that if we have an imperative, we ought, for the same reason, to have an interrogative mood.

Murray says, " The nature of a mood may be more intelligibly explained to the scholar by observing, that it consists in the change which the *verb* undergoes to signify various intentions of the mind, and various modifications and circumstances of action." Let us try this *explanation*, which Murray says is so much better than his *definition*. "*Love ye*," says he, "is the second person plural of the imperative mood. *Ye love*," he says, "is the second person plural of the indicative mood, present tense, and *If ye love* is the subjunctive present, second person plural." As no one will pretend, I trust, that the pronoun *ye*, or the conjunction *if*, is any part of the verb, the scholar may reasonably ask, "What change does the *verb* undergo to signify various intentions of the mind," &c.? It does no such thing. The *verb* undergoes no change.

If *mood* denotes "the manner in which the verb is employed," as Murray and his followers say, then who is to determine how many forms of speech, or manners of using the verb, there are in English. Mr. Murray says, "The indicative mood simply indicates or declares a thing, or asks a question." Here are two forms of expression as different as two can be, for when a man asks a question, he does not indicate or declare anything, and he generally changes the place of the nominative. Mr. Murray seems to have had a notion that he was embarking on an ocean without a shore when he promulgated his system of moods, for he says, after making five moods, "It is necessary to set proper bounds to this business. Instead, therefore, of making a separate mood for every auxiliary verb, and introducing moods *interrogative*, *optative*, *promissive*, *hortative*, *precative*, &c., we have exhibited such only as are obviously distinct," &c. He certainly is economical, when, under the imperative mood, he includes all verbs that command, exhort, entreat, or permit, that is, the *imperative*, *hortative*, *precative* and *permissive* moods.

I have sometimes thought that, when I was myself in the right mood, and had leisure, I would carry out Mr. Murray's suggestion, and see how many moods can be made, as good as his specimens. There would be the *progressive mood*, as, *I am trying*, *I was learning*; *emphatic mood*, as, *I do love*, *I did love*; the *optative mood*, which omits the nominative, "*Would it were so!*" The *regrettive mood*, "*O that I were* as in days past!" for, why is not *O* as much entitled to create a mood, as *if* or *though*? — The *expostulatory mood*, "What! *kill me* for doing my duty!" &c. &c. As these moods would have a due variety of tenses, if the tower of Babel is not already "in the clouds," it may easily be raised there, though I should be ashamed to have Him who gave us the noble faculty of speech, "come down to see what folly the sons of men had builded."

The whole system of moods seems to me sufficiently

ridiculous to authorize this treatment of it; but I must proceed to examine the claims of what are called the *tenses*.

Dr. Wallis, Dr. Priestley, Dr. Crombie, and other learned men, could see but two tenses in our language; for they considered *tense* to have the same meaning in English as in Latin, viz., not *time*, but *extension*, from the Latin word *tensus*, the tenses in Latin being *extensions* of the simple roots, an addition to them, or merely by a change of termination. Dr. Lowth could not conceive of a language without a verb to express future time, and he added a future tense to the present and past of his predecessors. He used a phrase, however, to supply what he supposed to be a defect, and set an example that was pregnant with mischief; for, from that time to this, the number has gone on increasing, until it has doubled, and more than doubled, if the *hypothetical* tense of a late author is to be accepted by the faithful, and duly canonized by authority.

We allow, then, two forms, which, in the proper sense of the word, we are willing to call tenses, and we call them present and past, not because they actually denote any division of time, but because they appear to do so. The authors of our Latinized grammars seem to have thought that we could not speak of the future and other divisions of time, without setting apart some phrase for the purpose, although our ancestors contrived to do this without any grammars. But while they were about it, they should either have given us all the modes of expressing future time, or none of them. They no doubt singled out *shall* and *will* as signs of this tense, because the word *to* is omitted after them; but we have other phrases in which the *to* is omitted, and a great variety of ways in which future time is as well expressed. Indeed, I should not be at all afraid to assert that no verb ever expresses *time*, and of all tenses, that which is supposed to be the most exact in this respect is really the most indefinite. *I love*, for instance, is said to denote the *present* time; but it does no such thing. When I say, "I love every good man that I see," do I mean that I only do so at this moment? Far from it; I mean to say that *I have loved* them, *do* love them, and *shall love* them. *Hold* and *do* are said to be *present* tenses, but when Hamlet says to Horatio, "*Hold* you the watch to-night?" and Horatio says, "We *do*, my Lord," what are *hold* and *do* but future tenses, since the watch was not yet set? *Go*, is a present tense in good repute, but when Peter says, "I *go* a fishing," and his companions say, "We also *go* with thee," *go*, without any auxiliary, makes an excellent future. *I am*, of course, is the pattern of present tenses, and yet we constantly say, *I am* to be punished, *I am* to die, &c. &c., in which sentences *am* is as good a future as any in the world. Henry Martin, in a letter to a friend, says, "One thing I have found, that there are but two tenses in Persian and English. In the sentence, 'I will go,' the principal verb is *I will*, which is the present tense. In '*I would have gone*,' the principal verb is *I would* or *I willed*. *Should*, also, is a preterite, namely, *shalled*, from *to shall*." [See Martin's Life, p. 312.] Bosworth, after making the above extract from Martin, adds, "He might have added that *go* and *have*, after *will* and *should*, were verbs in the infinitive mood." The excellent Martin probably had never seen any English grammar but Murray's, and no doubt thought he had made a great discovery when he made the declaration I have quoted. If it took the gifted Martin so long to see his error, how long will it take the less gifted millions, who are in the same darkness, to grope their way into the same degree of light?

Will not the very general belief that the verb expresses *time* excuse me for dwelling a moment longer on this subject? Mr. Murray says, I *may* go, I *can* go, I *must* go, are present tenses, but it would be difficult to find any phrases in which the time is more indefinite. I may go *now* or *next year;* I can go *next year*, but not *to-day;* I must go *then*, if I do not *now*. What is called the present tense seems to speak of *all time*, or without reference to any time, and hence we use it to express propositions that are true at all times; as, "Two and two *are* four." "The wicked *flee* when no man *pursueth*." "The poor work for the rich." If the English language, therefore, possesses any tense capable *in itself* of expressing futurity, that tense is what Murray and his followers call the present! Nothing, too, is more common than to use this *present* tense, when we are speaking of *past* occurrences. Any preacher would think it right to say, "Jesus *sends* away the multitude and *retires* apart to pray." The historian says, "Alfred, encouraged, *takes* a harp and *enters* the camp of the enemy." If it be said, this is figurative language, I grant it; but it is said of *past* events, and it is not ungrammatical.

Mr. Murray places *shall* and *will* among the defective verbs, because, he says, they lack some forms of a regular verb. He calls *shall* and *will* present tenses, and gives *should* and *would* as their past or imperfect tenses. But, if *shall* and *will* are never used without an infinitive after them, if they make that infinitive future, and are never used except to denote future time, how can he consistently call *shall* and *will* present tenses? And if he allows, as he does, that they are always signs of the future, how can they have the *past* tenses *should* and *would?* But *should* and *would* are as much future as *shall* and *will;* for, when I say, "I *should* go next week, if he would let me," in what does the *futurity* of the expression differ from that of "I *shall* go next week, if he will let me." So, "I *would* play to-morrow, if I *could*," and, "I *will* play to-morrow, if I *can*."

If I *will* my property to my son, no one doubts that *will* is a present tense; but, if I *will* an action instead, the will, forsooth, is no longer present, but future! And yet, *I will go*, expresses a present act of the mind, as much as *I will my houses and lands.* This has generally been conceded to me by teachers, but they say they cannot get over *shall* so easily. Let us see what Dr. Crombie says of this auxiliary. "*Shall* is unquestionably a derivative from the Saxon *sceal*, *I owe or I ought*, and was originally of the same import. I *shall* denoted *It is my duty*, and was precisely synonymous with *debeo* in Latin. Chaucer says, "The faith I shall to God," that is, "The faith I owe to God." "Thou shalt not kill," that is, "Thou oughtest not to kill." In this sense, *shall* is a present tense, and denotes present duty or obligation. But as all duties and all commands, though present in respect to their obligation, must be future in regard to their execution, so, by a natural transition, observable in most languages, this word, significant of present duty, came to be a note of future time. I have considered it, therefore, as a *present* tense, because, 1st, it originally denoted present tense; 2d, because it still retains the form of the present; and, 3d, because it is no singular thing to have a verb in the present tense expressive of future time." p. 140.

When, therefore, we say, "I *will* go," we only express a *present* determination to do an action, which may never be done; but which, if done, must necessarily be subsequent to the act of the will. So when we say, "I *shall* go," we express a present obligation so imperative, that it amounts to a determination, to go. It is just so with all words that express any act of volition. "I wish to go," is as good a future tense as I will go; and "I determine to go," is as good a future as either "I will go," or "I shall go." "I hope to go," "I expect to go," "I propose to go," "I intend to go," "I desire to go," &c., &c., &c., are situated exactly like "I will go," the only difference being the omission of *to* before the following infinitive, an accident common to the verbs bid, dare, let, and others, as well as to these mystified auxiliaries.

But many who yield that the passive voice is unnecessary, that the moods are of doubtful character, and that the future tense expresses no futurity, make a stand at the perfect and pluperfect tenses, and refuse to give them up. It was behind this tense that my friend at the Normal School, to whom I have before alluded, entrenched himself; for he could not allow, that, in the sentence, "I have learned my lesson," *have* could be the principal verb; for, says he, "I have learned my lesson," is as different in meaning from "I have my lesson learned," as *sorrel horse* is from *horse sorrel.* Now, it is not pretended that, when the participle is placed before the noun, its meaning is exactly the same as when it is placed after it, but only that it is still a participle qualifying the noun. When I say "I have learned a lesson," it is clear that I have it in the condition which is called *learn'd.* So it has been said it is absurd to say, "I have my purse lost," for "I have lost my purse," because, says the objector, "I cannot have what is lost." This reasoning amounts to nothing; for *lost* expresses the condition of the purse, and modifies the meaning of *have*, very much as the negative *not* does in the sentence, "I have *not* my purse;" and who will pretend that this latter phrase is not good English, because it is somewhat paradoxical?

This objection appears with more force in the perfect tense of verbs that are said to be intransitive; as, "I have gone," "I have been," "I have sinned." I have no doubt that these participles are mere adjectives, and qualify the nominative to the verb, as if the verb were what is called passive; for *I have gone* is equivalent to *I am gone; been* expresses the condition of *I*, for the objector will not admit that *be* expresses any action; and "I have sinned," is equivalent to "I am a sinner;" in which case, sinner qualifies the nominative before the verb, as every nominative after a neuter verb qualifies the nominative before it.

Dr. Crombie had a right idea of this tense when he said, "It is compounded of the *present* tense of the verb denoting possession and a perfect participle. It clearly refers to *present* time; this, indeed, the composition of the tense manifestly evinces." If *I have*, then, is the present tense, and *written* is a participle, they must be called by their right names and treated accordingly, whether we can tell what the participial adjective qualifies or not.

I suspect that if participles and adjectives in English were varied by gender and number, as they are in French and Latin, we should soon see what they agreed with in these respects, and, of course, what they qualified.

The participle *amatus*, is not only varied in connection with the verb *sum* to express the two numbers, but also to express the three genders. Thus the Latins say:

Amat*us* est,	He	(a man)	has been loved.
Amat*a* est,	She	(a woman)	has been loved.
Amatu*m* est,	It	(a thing)	has been loved.
Amat*i* sumus,	We	(men)	have been loved.
Amat*æ* sumus,	We	(women)	have been loved.
Amat*a* sumus,	We	(things)	have been loved.

The French say:

L'homme que j'ai *vu;*
The man that I have *seen.*
La femme que j'ai *vue;*
The woman that I have *seen.*
Les hommes que j'ai *vus;*
The men that I have *seen.*
Les femmes que j'ai *vues;*
The women that I have *seen.*

In these sentences, the French participle is varied to agree with the noun, or with its relative *que*.

In Latin, the phrase *I have seen* is expressed by one word, *vidi*. But in the indicative, perfect, pluperfect and future tense of their passive voice, *amatus sum*, *amatus eram*, *amatus ero*, *sum* is the only Latin for *I am*, *eram* for *I was*, *ero* for *I shall be;* and yet these tenses are always translated, I *have* been loved, I *had* been loved, I *shall have* been loved; and not, I *am* loved, I *was* loved, I *shall be* loved. The French have a similar idiom, and say, "Je me *suis* blessé," which we translate "I *have* hurt myself;" and yet *suis* is the French for *am*, and not for *have*. As there was a time when French was more fashionable in England than English itself, it is not to be wondered at if some idioms have become common to both languages. When, therefore, these classical cavillers account for *sum's* meaning *I have* in French, or *I have been* in Latin, it will be time enough for them to complain of the obscurity that seems to hang over the English use of *have* for *am*, or of *had* for *was*.

Whenever I have repeated what all the philosophers have asserted, that the verb is a word expressing what is done, the grammatikins have always thrown the verb *to be* at me, and demanded whether that expressed any action. If, as is pretended, it expresses abstract being, without the idea of action, it would only be one exception to the most extensive rule in our language; and if the existence of a single exception be good ground for rejecting a rule or a principle, less would be left of Murray's Grammar than remained of the two feline combatants on the field of Kilkenny. I cannot consent to argue this question at length, for, if the teacher thinks that *be* never expresses any kind of action, *he* can consider it an exception, although I do not. I shall, therefore, content myself with only asking how a person can *be active* if *be* does not express any action? When God said, "Let light *be*," who supposes that light *was*, and nothing was *done?* When the Creator called himself the Great I AM, did he mean to call himself the *Great Inactive?* When I tell a coward to stand and *be* a man, do I merely tell him to continue to exist a noun of the masculine gender? When I add *be* to a noun, whence comes the activity expressed by the compound? Is there no action in *be*-fool, *be*-friend, *be*-head, *be*-siege? *Numb* is an adjective, but is Jack Frost idle when he *be*-numbs us? When a learned teacher once told me that he could do nothing with a class of teachers after I had *be*-grammared them, did he mean that my teaching produced no effect?

So with the division of verbs into active, passive, and neuter; I see no necessity, and less propriety, in any such distinction. I have shown that I am *sick*, he is *dead*, &c., are as good *passive* verbs as I am *diseased*, he is *deceased*, &c. Murray says, "A verb passive expresses a passion or a suffering, or the receiving of an action, and necessarily implies an object acted upon, and an agent by which it is acted upon; as, Penelope is loved by me." *Me* is the *agent*, then, intended by Mr. Murray. An agent necessarily implies action, and the action must be expressed by the help of the verb *is*, if not solely by it. Suppose the sentence were, "Penelope is offended with me, notwithstanding I love her;" me, I suppose, is the agent implied, and Penelope is only the nominative, or, as Murray and his followers say, the *subject* of the verb. This is the same, as if, in regard to the sentence, "Penelope hates me," I should say, I do the hating, and Penelope is the subject of it. I may not have a distinct idea of nonsense, but this comes up to my poor idea of it. How simple, compared with such absurdity, is the grammar of Dr. Wallis, which would say that Penelope is the agent of *is*, and *loved* or *offended*, like *sick* or *mad*, are only the adjectives qualifying Penelope, or expressing the condition of her mind.

This theory of the passive voice obliges those who adopt it, to give up the true definition of a nominative, and to say that it is the *subject*, and not the *agent* of the verb; a most unfortunate result, if only the confusion arising from a new use of a well-established expression be considered; for, if it be true that, in the sentence, "I love Penelope," or "I study history," I is the *subject* of love and study, then Penelope is not the subject of my tender thoughts, and history is not the subject I am studying, although I meant to say they were. When we say, Victoria governs Ireland, we of course must mean that she is the subject of the action expressed by the verb *governs!*

Again; Murray says, "A verb neuter expresses neither action nor passion, but being, or a state of being; as, I sit, he lives, they sleep." When the master tells the child to *sit*, then, he tells him to *do* nothing! *I sit*, and *I am seated*, mean the same thing; but, according to Murray's definition, the latter expresses passion or suffering, and the former does not! If any believer in such stuff were compelled to *sit* three hours on the hard and narrow seats to which children are confined in some of our district schools, without any support to their backs, or any resting place for their feet, we are inclined to think he would find *action* and *suffering* enough in the neuter verb *sit*, and if he did not get into a *passion*, also, he would be a miracle of patience.

Moreover, when I say, "He *sits* on a horse," "He *lives* upon fish," "They *sleep* in pain," these verbs, we are told, "neither express action, nor passion or suffering," but "being or a state of being." And yet, although the neuter verbs express neither *action* nor passion, Murray says, "They may properly be called *intransitive*, because the *effect* is confined within the subject, and does not pass over to any object."

The *effect*, then, of sitting on a horse is confined to the rider, and the horse never feels any effect from his load!! The *effect* of living upon fish is confined to the eater, and not felt by the fish! When the watchman *sleeps*, the effect is confined to himself, and nobody else suffers! The fact is, the action of every neuter verb may he conveyed to an object by a preposition, and, although there may be a difference between such objects and those of active verbs, they are objects still. If I send a child to school, *school* is just as much an object of the mission as *child* is. Prepositions, says Mr. Murray, serve to connect words and show the relation between them. If this means any thing, it means that prepositions connect verbs with objects, and show the direction of the action expressed by the verb.

I hope these remarks upon the common definition of verbs will not be set down as unimportant cavils, for they are serious objections; no system liable to such cavils being fitted for the use of children, or capable of being explained to the satisfaction of any mature, unbiased mind; for, "what reason never dictated, reason can never explain."

My list of *adverbs*, and my use of them, do not differ materially from Murray's. *Prepositions* I define to be words showing the direction of some action or tendency previously expressed, and this is strictly true of all real prepositions, except *of*, which, since it dropped an *f*, seems to express the relation of possession, unlike its original, *off*. Concerning, touching, during, pending, and such words, are participles, or, as I call them, adjectives, and not prepositions.

I allow Murray's list of *conjunctions* to keep the name, but I do not divide them into copulative and disjunctive, because if a conjunction *connects*, it is idle to call it copulative, and absurd to call it disjunctive. *But* and *or* connect sentences as much as *and* does, and the sentences are none the less connected because there seems to be "an opposition of meaning." I say *seems*, for it admits of question whether, in the example of opposition given by Mr. Murray, "They came with her, *but* they went away without her," there is any other "opposition of meaning" than in any two sentences connected by *and;* as, "He preached peace, and practised war." Nay, in the sentence selected as an example by Mr. Murray, *and* may be substituted for *but* without altering the sense; "They came with her, *and* went away without her."

As it regards *interjections*, none are allowed to be such,

but those natural sounds, which can hardly be considered a part of arbitrary language. Silence! Hail! Hush! and such words, belong to other parts of speech. There seems to be no doubt that the interjection was the first part of speech formed; for man, like the lower animals, has a natural language, which he uses before he learns that which is purely conventional. The infant makes its wants known long before it can talk. That the first man, when created, resembled an infant in this respect, there seems to be no reason to doubt; for the first notice we have of his uttering any words, is when the animals were presented to him to see what he would call them. And what did he call them? By some name, undoubtedly, that expressed some peculiarity; as, in English, we have a few significant words, buzz, hum, hiss, rush, bawl, blow, &c., &c. This would indicate that, next to his natural language, he must have used nouns; and infants do the same. The young being says, "Ma, baby, bread," and the mother understands him as well as if he used a verb, and was familiar with its hundred variations. If it be said that we are told that God spoke to Adam before he named the animals, it can hardly be supposed that he did this literally; and, if he did, we are not told that Adam answered. The child often understands what is said to him long before he can utter a word in reply. Men make words only as fast as they need them to express ideas, and nations having the fewest ideas, have the fewest words. This simple and natural theory is not contradicted by Scripture or human experience. I should have preferred the name *exclamations* for such words as are called *interjections*, but I have thought it prudent to continue the terms in common use, and, except in calling the nominative case an agent and the objective an object, I do not know that I have altered a single term, although the necessity of using many has been done away, such as the names of the moods and tenses, participles, auxiliaries, articles, adjective pronouns, possessives, &c.

Many private teachers have candidly confessed to me that the reformation I proposed was very desirable, and would greatly reduce the labor of the teacher, while it enabled the pupil better to understand and use the language; but an acquaintance with other grammars was a prerequisite for admission into high schools and colleges; and a pupil would not be supposed to know any thing, if he did not know the popular system, although familiar with the works of all the great philologers, who, to a man, reject it. Why is it that reform so generally commences at the foot of the educational ladder? One would think that, where there is the most learning there would be the most enterprise, the most independence; but I fear that those who accuse the higher seminaries of proverbial attachment to old forms and fixed abuses, do them no injustice.

In my visits to the Institutes of New York and Massachusetts, I became acquainted with more than a thousand teachers, and I am not aware that I met with one who felt satisfied with any grammar that he had seen, and very few had ever been able to make the study of grammar an agreeable exercise to their pupils. The reason is obvious; the teachers, not one in five hundred of whom had studied Latin, did not understand the mixed Latino-English grammar they were called upon to teach, and how could they explain it to their pupils? But, give them the pure English grammar I have endeavored to describe, and let them require their pupils to write English as soon as they begin to read and speak it, and no exercise will be so agreeable to the child, and so useful to him in all his other studies.

May I be excused, if, after all I have said on the subject of grammar, I say a few words more, by way of caution, to teachers. Perhaps there never was a time when there was so much need of care and activity as now, to prevent the corruption and decline of our excellent language. The press has deluged the land with a flood of books, some of which are worthy of the best age of English literature, but the mass of which are to be shunned for their faults of style, as much as for their emptiness, or positively demoralizing tendency. The teacher who wishes to make a selection of passages containing false grammar, or faulty construction, to be corrected by his pupils, may readily find abundant materials in the *light* literature, as the *heavy* trash is called, of the present day. He will find novels, tales and romances, written in a style often inferior to the sentimental effusions of a boarding-school girl; nay, he will even find many volumes written with the perverse intention of disregarding every rule of English grammar and orthography. Works of the Jack Downing school, witty as some may be, have done more mischief to young and old, in a literary point of view, than a regiment of well qualified teachers can undo in half a century. Our newspapers, too, which, without pretending to do so, exercise a powerful influence over the popular style of writing and speaking, have, with few exceptions, stooped to cater to the vulgar taste for cant expressions and slang phrases; and writers who aim at pure and elevated English, bear no proportion to those who study to adulterate and destroy our noble tongue.

Teachers, therefore, must set their faces sternly against this evil tendency of the times. They must guard against the use of corrupt expressions, and rigidly prohibit the use of them in the conversation and compositions of their pupils. They must be careful to associate more with persons whose conversation is correct and refined. They must set a watch over themselves, as well as hold one over their pupils. It was my custom for some time, until I had established a sort of public standard of conversation in my school, to reward any pupil who detected another in using an ungrammatical or vulgar expression, or even in pronouncing a word improperly, by giving her what was called a merit or good mark; and if she detected me in any such misdemeanor, she was entitled to five such merits. Every expression or word so reported was recorded on a sheet kept for the purpose in a conspicuous place, and the consequence was, that, in less than a year, the record sheet was laid aside, because we had no materials to augment it. A sheet of this sort, kept without any promise of reward, will be found highly beneficial to both teacher and pupils, and will do more to banish bad language and bad pronunciation, than all the set grammar lessons that can be given.

I have gone more at length into the subject of grammar, because I think that, in teaching it, we have departed further from the truth than in any other study; and we have done this without any reason or justice. Hundreds of enterprising teachers, who allow the justice of my positions, and have been desirous to attempt the reform I have proposed, assure me that they have been unable to do so, because the committees are not enlightened on the subject, or are unwilling to assume the responsibility of taking the lead. In this exposure of the prevalent system of English grammar, therefore, I have had the committees as well as the teachers in view, and I do earnestly entreat them to take the subject into the most serious consideration. If they complain of my radicalism, let them remember, that I only ask them to eradicate foreign weeds, that have been scattered amongst our wheat, and have well-nigh choked it. Many who have allowed that I have told the truth in regard to the matter of geography, and the manner of teaching it, are afraid of my ultraism in English grammar; but let such be assured that I have proposed nothing so radical in grammar as they have approved in my remarks on geography. Finally, if any accuse me of a want of modesty in so often referring to my own grammar, let such remember that there is no similar grammar to which I can refer; the grammars in common use being based mainly on the abuses introduced by Mr. Murray, and the truly philosophical works, on whose authority I rely for all I have asserted, not being accessible to one teacher in a thousand. Indeed, in referring to my grammar, I, in fact, refer to Dr. Wallis and other men, whose opinions and works I have studied with ever increasing wonder at the perversity, which, for so long a season, has preferred darkness to light, falsehood to truth, mystery to simplicity.

Some of the sternest opponents of this proposed restoration of English grammar to its original simplicity, look with favor upon the new science of phonography, and are ready to introduce it into common use; and yet this new science proposes a revolution immeasurably greater than the proposed change of grammar. The friends of phonography, it is true, propose to discard the foreign alphabet, as I do the foreign grammatical terms; but their success will render the external form of our language a dead letter, and send every scholar to learn his *a, b, c*, again. The restored system of English grammar requires no study, for he who knows Murray's Grammar, knows too much already, and has only to drop a portion of what he has acquired. A person, for instance, who has studied the popular grammar, knows what an article is, and what an adjective; and when he is told to class the articles with adjectives, it costs him no effort. He knows what a possessive case is, and by what noun it is governed; and when told to call it an adjective qualifying the same noun that is falsely said to govern it, he finds no difficulty. He knows what is meant by auxiliary verbs; and he has only to call them all principal verbs, followed by a participle, which he must call an adjective, or by an infinitive mood, which he must call a noun, governed by the auxiliary, or rather, the object of it. My system alters not the construction of any sentence, or the orthography of any word; it only removes what does not belong to our grammar, and by so doing reduces the labor of teaching it more than one half; and, by making it more intelligible, makes it more pleasant to the learner. Having full faith in the practical good sense of my countrymen, I have full faith in the final success of the system of English that I would restore, and I mistake greatly the signs of the times if the restoration is not speedily to be accomplished

COMPOSITION.

I HAVE already said that every step in English grammar should be a step in English composition, and my grammar provides for this union of the two. I have said, also, that every step in reading and spelling should be made an exercise in English grammar also. But little remains, therefore, for me to say on the subject of composition.

The orthographical exercises contained in the Companion to Spelling-Books, the copying of short pieces of prose and verse, and the writing of easy sentences from dictation, made my pupils early acquainted with the mechanical part of composition, syllabication, the use of capitals, the division of sentences, punctuation, &c. As soon, however, as the child seemed to require some higher exercise, I was accustomed to call up the little class, and tell them a short story or anecdote, and then require them to write the same story in their own language. As I continued this course for many years, suitable stories became scarce, and at last I was obliged to make them as they were wanted. This labor was forced upon me also by the fact, that the pupils read more story-books than I did, and, too often, some one of the class was not a stranger to the source of the story that I had selected. In this way I prepared a vast number of suitable lessons, of which I published several in my Primary Reader, to which the young teacher may refer for materials, until he finds it for his interest himself to make such lessons for his pupils.

About this period of their education, my pupils generally began to study some other language than their own, and this afforded me a fine opportunity to forward them in English composition. I required most of their translations to be *written*, and I corrected them as carefully as if this were the primary object of the new study. Children, who are required to write a translation, are more likely to examine the idioms of both languages; and as they are only to supply language to clothe the ideas of the foreign author, this exercise may be required much earlier than a set composition.

My next step was to select a subject, and write under it

such notes or questions as would guide the thoughts of the children, and suggest, perhaps, a few of the leading ideas connected with the subject. The subject, with notes, written fairly on a sheet of paper, was posted up in the school-room, so that no pupil could plead ignorance of what was required.

When the pupil had but a small stock of ideas, and was prepared to express them, I was accustomed to call the class around me, and after stating the subject of their next composition, I conversed with them about it, allowing them to ask questions or discuss each others' opinions, until their minds were awake to the bearings of the subject, and then I sent them away to write what they had gathered from the conversation. I am inclined to think that the children were benefited, in more ways than one, by this free interchange of thoughts; and were I again to become a teacher, I think I should make conversation a regular exercise of the school.

Finally, I gave a subject to the highest class, and left them to write upon it as best they could, without any assistance. If the pupils were studying Rhetoric, I found full employment for them by requiring original as well as selected examples of the different figures, or of the different kinds of style. If they were studying Prosody, exercises in the composition of verse were frequently required. I found the translation of short poems from some foreign language a valuable exercise, and the poetical part of my "French First Class Book" contains a hundred or more suitable poems for this purpose.

Another method by which the pupils were encouraged to exert themselves, was the recording of all praiseworthy compositions in a neat book kept for the purpose. I have several volumes that were filled in this way by my pupils; and on winter evenings, it was not uncommon for the parents to assemble at the school-room and listen to the reading of selections from this record.

Besides these set exercises in composition, I occasionally called the classes around a black-board, and taught them punctuation by writing sentences for them to punctuate and correct. Of course, there may be some difference of opinion in regard to some points, but the rules of punctuation are about as well settled as those of grammar, and yet on no one subject, perhaps, are young teachers so much at a loss. May I be excused, then, if I say a few words to them for their guidance and encouragement.

The comma is the main stop, and, of late, it has almost

superseded the semicolon, colon and parenthesis. A correct knowledge of the use of the comma is, in fact, one half of the whole science of punctuation. The following rules, perhaps, embrace the greater number of occasions when the comma must be used.

1. Two verbs, nouns, or other parts of speech, following each other, and not connected by *and*, must be separated by a comma; as, "That wise, good and great man lived, labored and died for his fellow-creatures."

2. The word *and* is equivalent to a comma, and, when it is understood, a comma must be supplied; as, "Wise, good, great men live, labor, die for their fellow-creatures."

3. Nouns in apposition are separated by a comma; as, "John, king of England."

4. The name or epithet by which a person is addressed must have a comma after it; as, "John, come here!" "My good friend, forgive me!"

5. The phrase that includes a case absolute with a participle, as Murray calls it, must be preceded and followed by a comma; as, "They, all hope being lost, surrendered."

6. Certain adverbs are generally preceded and followed by a comma; as, indeed, perhaps, moreover, therefore. Nay, besides, firstly, secondly, &c., at the *beginning* of sentences or phrases, require a comma after them.

7. When the exact words of another are quoted, the quotation must begin with a capital and follow at least a comma. The quotation marks must not include words not borrowed; as, "Go," said she, "but return soon;" and not, "Go, said she, but return soon."

8. A comma marks the omission of a verb; as, "To err is human; to forgive, divine."

9. All parenthetical clauses or words, that is, all words that may be omitted and not destroy the sentence, must be preceded and followed by commas; as, "Grammar, properly understood, is a simple affair; but, unfortunately, it has not been so understood."

The ancients made no use of punctuation, and this has led to many mistakes, and much difference of opinion among critics. It is probable that to the absence of these points the ancient oracles owed much of their renown; for the response was generally given so that it would be true whatever was the event. It is said that a Grecian king, doubtful about the policy of invading a neighboring kingdom, sent to Delphos to ask the opinion of the oracle. The answer was not punctuated, and they read it, "He shall go, return, not be slain in battle." He went and was slain; and when his friends reproached the oracle with want of truth, they were told that they had read the answer wrong; its meaning being, "He shall go, return not, be slain in battle."

The *semicolon* must be used when a comma does not seem to be sufficient, that is, when more than the smallest pause is needed; but it should not be used instead of a period, as is too often the case. It is difficult to give any invariable rules for its use.

1. It generally separates clauses rather than words; as, "He may become the victim of misfortune; he is incapable of crime."

2. A comma followed by *and*, *or*, *but*, *for*, *because*, *yet* seems to be equivalent to a semicolon; as, "He may become the victim of misfortune, but he is incapable of crime."

Many writers, when in doubt as to the proper stop, make free use of the *dash*, but this is a bad practice, and teachers must not tolerate it in their pupils.

The *colon* is rarely used, and, perhaps, is never necessary Usage places it still after the words, *to wit: as follows: thus*. and after the abbreviation, *viz:* but, in other cases, it had better be avoided.

The *period* marks the end of a complete sentence, and the teacher must be careful not to let his pupils string together several sentences. They must be encouraged to write short sentences at first, and should always be required to cut up such as are too long to be easily managed. Thus the following sentence may be cut into two, at the semicolon. "To live is pleasant, and to die may be gain, but, as there is some doubt of the gain, most men desire to live; let them not, however, forget, that death cannot always be put off, and he whose life is lengthened only to be misspent, will gain little by the extension."

It is a common thing for makers of spelling-books to say that a comma requires a pause long enough to count one; a semicolon, two; a colon, three, and a period, four. Some, who have felt wise, have ridiculed this rule, and said, that some commas require a longer pause than merely to count one. As the books do not say how fast a person must count, it is but fair to conclude that the authors meant that every reader should count to please himself, making the semicolon twice as long as the comma, &c., after the length of the comma is agreed upon. Some say, also, that, at a comma and semicolon, the voice must be kept up, and others mock at this. Yet, it is a safe rule for children, who have little judgment or discretion, and I should so teach them at least one generation longer.

The *exclamation* point sometimes seems to conflict with the note of *interrogation;* as, "What is more amiable than virtue?" If no answer is expected, the exclamation may be used, although the sentence has the form of a question.

Every question must have the interrogation mark after it, but it must not be placed after words that are no part of the question; as, "Did you call me? sir," and not, "Did you call me, sir?" which has a very different meaning.

As many teachers are at a loss whether the voice should rise or fall at the end of a question, I may be excused for giving them the almost invariable rule, that, "If the question can be answered by yes or no, the voice must be raised, and, in all other cases, it must be allowed to fall."

The *parenthesis*, ( ), and *brackets*, [ ], are less employed than formerly, and are often misused. For this reason, I never allowed my younger pupils to use the parenthesis, but required commas instead. The correct rule is, to use the parenthesis when what it encloses is a sort of comment upon the rest of the sentence; and to use the brackets when what they enclose, though useful information, is no part of the sentiment; as, "An eccentric clergyman, preaching against the fashions, selected the text (and a ridiculous conceit it was) 'Top not, come down!' [Matt. xxiv. 17.]"

The *dash*, placed after a comma, semicolon, colon or period, lengthens the pause. Sometimes it only marks a broken sentence. If the teacher allows it to be used to lengthen pauses, he must not allow it to be used *instead* of them by children.

The *hyphen* must never be used at the beginning of a line when a word is divided, and no word must be divided except at the end of a syllable. No monosyllable can be divided by a hyphen.

The *apostrophe* marks the Possessive Case, as Mr. Murray calls the adjective that is formed from every noun by adding the apostrophe and s, or the apostrophe alone. In other cases, it marks the omission of one or more letters. Nothing can be more loose than the prevalent custom of using the apostrophe.

For a general rule, it must never be used to omit a letter in prose, and never, even in poetry, if the omission does not alter the pronunciation of the word. In the Companion to Spelling-Books, I have given many rules and exercises on this subject.

As the (.) is used to mark the end of a sentence, an abbreviation, and the place between units and decimal fractions, the teacher will do well in the first case to call it a *period;* in the second, a *dot;* and in the third, a *point.*

Every word abbreviated, unless it be by an apostrophe, must have a dot placed after it. This rule is so little regarded, that teachers cannot too carefully look to it. At every Teachers' Institute the Secretary of the Board of Education required the young teachers to write a letter, and the result was, that not one in twenty knew how to begin and end one, in every respect, correctly. I shall do a favor, then, by giving a form, which they may follow with safety.

Boston, Oct. 14, 1846.

John Smith, Esq.,

My dear Sir,

I herewith send you a copy of the "Teachers' Institute," which has been written in great haste, but with great good will. Of course, all descriptions must be dull compared with an actual lesson, but, if this volume shall enable you to profit, however little, by my long experience, I shall be well rewarded for my trouble in writing it.

Yours, very respectfully,
Wm. B. Fowle.

If more epithets are used at the end, let each occupy a different line, thus:

Very respectfully,
Your humble servant,
Wm. B. Fowle.

Recollect that no dot of abbreviation must ever be placed after an entire word. The address of the person for whom the letter is intended, should always be written on the inside of the letter, and it is safer to begin with the name than to place it, as some do, at the end, on the left hand side; for, if left to the last, it may be forgotten; and if placed first, should the letter be misdirected on the outside, the direction on the inside will first strike the eye, and induce any honorable person to close it at once, and consider it a sacred trust, to be kept in charge for the real owner. It is safer, too, to put the date where I have placed it, lest it should be forgotten. I generally omit the *place* after the name of my correspondent, but some careful merchants always insert it, that, if the letter falls into the wrong hands, the error may be rectified. When I insert the *place*, I direct the letter at the end, for the sake of appearances. May I be excused if I warn my young female friends of the besetting fault of their sex, the entire omission of dates, especially in what they consider unimportant billets. May I also caution all writers of letters to superscribe them as fast as they are written. I have twice received letters from gentlemen, who, in writing to me and to their wives, at the same sitting, sealed both letters, and then directed them to the wrong persons. Few persons fold a letter well, and seal it neatly, and none can be too careful in directing it to write a fair hand. The name of the person should be much larger than the common hand of the writer, and the name of the place, larger still. If directed to a town of the state in which the writer resides, it is not customary to place the name of the county, as well as that of the state, after the name of the town. Some omit both county and state, and the postmasters understand that a town so left is in the state where the letter is mailed. But, where the town is in another state, the town, county, and state, if known, should all be plainly designated. My position, as publisher of the Common School Journal, has led me to notice the great inattention of teachers to these forms, or I should not feel authorized to allude to what seems so obviously proper.

THE MONITORIAL SYSTEM;

A Lecture delivered before the Teachers' Institutes at Andover and elsewhere, in Oct., 1846, *by* William B. Fowle.

My fellow-teachers, I think you will bear me out in the assertion, that one of the most difficult parts of a teacher's duty is the keeping of every pupil usefully employed all the time. The number of children in our schools is often so large, that, if divided into few classes, the class is so large that it must embrace many who are unfit to work together; and if the classes are numerous, some must be neglected, because it requires as much time to hear the recitation of a small class as of a large one, the length of the lesson being the same.

I know not that I can enforce this point more clearly, and more effectually, than by quoting the words of the first President of the Essex County Convention of Teachers, the Hon. David Choate, who, while chairman of the Committee of Education in our Legislature, is reported to have said, "I am confident, from my own observation, that nearly all occasion for severe discipline in schools is owing to the fact, that most children at school really have nothing to do for a very large part of the time. In a school of fifty scholars, no one is entitled to more than three minutes and a half of the teacher's time in half a day. The child must sit still, if he can, nearly three long hours, and a teacher is held to be no teacher, and his school, no school, if children so situated — play. Innocent creatures, the hope of parents, and the hope of the state, are whipped from one end of the commonwealth to the other, for no earthly reason than because they have nothing to do that they know how to do. Now, sir, what is the remedy? It is, clearly, to employ so many assistants as to occupy the whole time of the pupil. It is sometimes said that a child's time is not worth any thing, and if they are out of the way, no matter if they do not learn. That parent makes a wretched bargain who gains relief from the presence of his child by sending him into a large and idle school. He may learn nothing there that is valuable, but it by no means follows that he learns nothing. Idleness is the hotbed of mischief, the nurse of vice and crime, and how many owe their distaste for study, their irritable tempers, their diseased bodies, to the constrained idleness of the school-room. There is but one remedy,—*we must have more teachers.*"

So the Examining Committee of the Boston schools, in their memorable Report of 1845, say,—"It will be found upon examination that, in most cases where severe injury has followed corporal punishment in our schools, the offence was very trifling, and no great severity intended when the master *began* to strike. Moreover, it is beyond all question that, in the majority of cases of corporal punishment, and other kinds of punishment, in our schools, it is inflicted for violations of arbitrary rules of discipline, for whispering, for disorderly conduct arising from bodily uneasiness, the fault as much of the school as of the scholar. Whoever will go into our schools, at any hour of the day, will find a large portion of the scholars unoccupied by any study; they may have a book before them, but as its contents are insipid, or, perhaps, incomprehensible, yet, nevertheless, to be committed to memory; and as there is no master immediately over them, *they do not study.* Now, to expect boys, full of young life and pent-up vigor, to remain motionless, is to expect that which is impossible; oftentimes, the best boys, those who will make the ablest and best men, will manifest their uneasiness in such a way as to bring down punishment. *Something is wrong.*"

"*We must, then, have more teachers.*" But who does not know that, much as the Board of Education have done to improve the character of teachers, and augment the number of good ones, so far from increasing the number employed in our large schools, the expense of even one teacher is more carefully calculated than any other item of public expenditure. Much is said about the *incalculable* value of general education, but the highest expenditures are still within the reach of very limited arithmeticians. I hesitate not to say that, compared with the importance of its object, no appropriation is so small as that usually made by our towns for the support of public schools. What should be expended in education, that is, in prevention, is generally expended in the support of prisons and poor-houses; for the public have not yet learned that, to pay the great and accumulating debt incurred for supporting paupers and restraining or punishing criminals, there is but one adequate sinking-fund,—a good education of children in knowledge and virtue.

But, as our schools are now constituted, the natural increase of pupils involves a proportionate increase of expense, and unless the constitution of the schools is altered, we cannot, in the present state of public feeling, expect to see any important reform. He, therefore, who can propose a plan, by which all the additional teachers that we need may be obtained without any additional expense, must be esteemed a benefactor, and this is the improvement that I now intend to propose for your consideration.

So far as I can learn, there never was a time when the teachers of our New England schools were not accustomed, in one way or another, to call in the assistance of their pupils. When I was at school, the highest class boys were often employed to hear the lower classes recite English grammar; and this they could do as well as the master, for the recitation consisted in merely saying a few lines of the text-book by rote, without any explanation of terms, or application of principles. So every large boy was required to take a small one and set his copy. And, worse than all, certain boys were constantly employed to call out or name talkers and other offenders, and he was a bold fellow who dared to remonstrate against such a nomination, the master seldom if ever inquiring into the truth of the accusation.

Parents and School Committees knew that this was the practice, but I never heard that any objection was made to it, until it was proposed avowedly and systematically to use the pupils as assistants to the teacher. Then, forsooth, it was fraught with danger, and violently denounced; although, at the worst, it could be no more than a benevolent experiment to remove an acknowledged defect in our system of instruction.

The Lancasterian method was a charitable invention, applied at first to the education of the utterly ignorant millions of England, in the merest rudiments of a common English education. Had the English government patronized the schools, they would have done all that was expected from them; but it has never comported with the plans of that government to educate the people; and even at this moment, the whole amount appropriated by Parliament to educate the twenty-seven millions of Great Britain and Ireland, is less than is appropriated by the city of Boston alone. A few choice Lancasterian schools in England and Scotland were completely successful, but they depended upon individual enterprise, and not upon the patronage of government. In France, the system of Mutual Instruction, as that allowing the use of pupils as assistants was called, was adopted as the national system under Napoleon, and it was working wonders, when the restoration of the Bourbons revived the old parish schools, taught gratuitously by the priests, for the sake of the influence it gave them over the politics, as well as the religion, of the people. Lancaster came to this country, but he was out of his element here; and so little did he know of our wants, and of the expansive capabilities of his own system, that he spoke of New England as if it were old England, and denounced every deviation from his plan as a damning error. Lest, in my remarks upon the use I make of monitors, I should be suspected of using the plan as taught by Lancaster, it may be well for me to say, that, when he visited my school in Boston, he refused to acknowledge it as a legitimate branch of his system. I had retained the great principle of requiring pupils to teach as well as learn, but I had rejected all the machinery and tactics that he had used in teaching the uneducated and uncivilized masses of England.

In this country, the system was first tried at New York, by a benevolent association, who established schools like those of England, for the destitute poor, and for the merest elements of learning. For twenty years or more, those schools, in which four or five hundred were taught by one teacher, were the boast of that city. In imitation of the metropolis, the whole state adopted the plan, and the reports, for some years, spoke of the experiment as completely successful. Why it has become so entirely disused in that great state, I could never discover; but from my acquaintance with the teachers and schools of New York, and many inquiries of the superintendents, I am satisfied that it was not from any fault inherent in the system, but from its mismanagement by inexperienced or incompetent teachers.

In the city of New York, the Monitorial System is still continued, and lately they have established normal schools for the instruction of monitors as well as teachers. Let it be remembered, however, that these schools have always been charity schools, managed by a society; the pupils are of the poorest and least permanent portion of the population, and little more than the merest rudiments of knowledge are required to be taught in them. Their 34 large schools now average 300 pupils each, under one teacher and one assistant; and the 13 primary schools average 300 also, with but one teacher and one assistant. As the pupils belong to a class seldom if ever seen in even the large towns of New England, the failure of such schools can prove nothing here, and their success and lengthened existence are almost miraculous. When there was a proposition to introduce the Monitorial Plan into the Boston schools, a comparison was instituted between the schools of the two cities, and it being evident that the Boston children had advanced further than the others, this was at once concluded to be the consequence of the different systems, and no change was made. At the same time it was true, that the greater part of our children attended the public schools from 4 to 10 years, while the average attendance at the New York schools did not exceed one year. The first time I visited those schools, a young teacher was shown to me as a prodigy, and the wonder arose from the circumstance, that he was the only teacher that had ever been trained in their own schools! Had the comparison been confined, as it should have been, to the *discipline* of the rival schools; or had proper allowance been made for the different quality of the pupils, the New York system would not have suffered. Philadelphia also took up the system, and the following extract from the Report of the Controllers of the Public Schools will show their present condition. "It will be remembered," say they, "that, at the introduction of the Monitorial System here, one teacher, aided by monitors taken from his own pupils, was considered sufficient for the care, and government, and instruction of 300 children. * * * The effort now made is to furnish, even at considerable increase of expense, an adequate number of well-qualified teachers, so as to secure to each child a due share of instruction from his teacher." This is merely making the monitors what they ought to be, *assistants* and not *substitutes* for teachers. At first, the merest elements were taught, and one master sufficed; but, just in proportion to the new branches introduced, must be the increase of teachers or the diminution of pupils.

The plan was never generally adopted in any part of New England. New Haven has maintained one popular school more than a quarter of a century, and it is still prospering under the original teacher. Portsmouth* followed next, and

* In the summer of 1845, at a meeting of many friends of Education at Concord, N. H., the Governor and both branches of the Legislature being present, Levi Woodbury, late Secretary of State, and now Judge of the

for many years its Monitorial School was the best school of any kind in that state. Two public schools at Newburyport followed, and did much to raise the standard of their schools. But the plan was unluckily supposed to be only fitted for teaching the elements, and for enforcing good discipline, and when this was done, the system was discontinued, instead of being adapted to the improved condition of the children. Nantucket tried the system, and liked it for some years, but she has gone back to the old plan. Providence once had an excellent private school on this plan, but has none at present. Springfield tried the plan in one large school with entire success, but after two years, a change of masters put an end to the experiment. Portland bought off the excellent teacher of the Portsmouth school, but in time the system was disused, and the teacher was shorn of his strength, when his favorite system departed. The only monitorial school extant in Massachusetts is one at Boston for boys. It has been in operation about eighteen years, and has annually sent forth as thoroughly instructed youths as any in the city. The number of pupils has never been large enough to make the use of monitors a matter of necessity, but the teacher has always used them from choice, and teaching every pupil as much as any other faithful master does, all the practice obtained by this mutual instruction is clear gain.

It fell to my lot to make the first experiment on this plan in Boston. In 1821, the Primary School Committee, of which I was a member, collected about ninety girls and ninety boys who went to no school, being thought too old for the primary schools, and too ignorant to be admitted into the grammar schools. The grant to support a temporary school for the instruction of these neglected children was very small, and we adopted the monitorial plan because we had not money enough for any other, the whole grant being but 1000 dollars, of which more than half was expended in fitting up the schoolroom. We borrowed a teacher from Albany, who was recalled in a few weeks; but, rather than let the experiment

Supreme Court of the United States, being prevailed on to address the very respectable audience, remarked that in his opinion there had been but one invention in the art of teaching for more than half a century, and this was, "*the employment of the pupils as assistants to the teacher.*" The excellent school at Portsmouth, of which he had been overseer, was one of the facts on which his discerning judgment was based; the great success of Dr. Arnold in England, whose improvements in school discipline depended upon the use of his pupils as assistants, was another.

fail, I assumed the office of teacher, and carried on the school two years. Nothing could have been more unpropitious than this commencement, whether we consider the want of funds, the character of the pupils, or the inexperience of the teacher, who had never seen a monitorial school, nor taught any school on any plan.

The first difficulty arose from the fact that none of the unfortunate pupils knew enough to teach their companions, and the best of them were supposed to be unworthy of trust for a moment. The superior committee ordered the teacher of a regular grammar school in the same building to lend me a dozen boys, and he sent me the worst he could select; remarking that, "if the experiment succeeded, it should not owe its success to his scholars." Fortunately, a few girls, who had become discontented at some grammar school, were allowed to enter mine, and these I employed as my assistants, sending back all the boys that had been so *generously* loaned. As many of my boys were large, and as all, boys and girls, were unaccustomed to order or subordination, it is an interesting fact, that, for two years, that school was mainly taught by female monitors, and instances of disobedience and misconduct were as unusual, to say the least, as in any other school. When the school was publicly declared by the mayor to be second to no grammar school in the city, I felt that my duty was done, and I immediately resigned. The children were all transferred to the grammar schools, for which they were all fitted, and the "School of Mutual Instruction," as it was called, was discontinued.

A few days after my resignation, some members of the School Committee, with other gentlemen who had watched my experiment, proposed a school on the same plan for their own children, and made me such a liberal offer, that I relinquished the business to which I had been trained, and which I had carried on while teaching the other school, and thenceforth devoted myself exclusively to the work of instruction. I taught this second school more than seventeen years, having, on an average, over a hundred pupils, without any limit in regard to age. In addition to the common branches, I taught Latin, French and Spanish; natural history and natural philosophy in all their departments; astronomy, book-keeping, &c. &c., without any assistance except what was afforded by my own unpaid pupils. This plan enabled the trustees to reduce the rates of tuition to about half those of other schools where the same branches were taught, and yet the surplus income, beyond all expenses, enabled the trustees to purchase a choice library of 600 volumes, a better apparatus, and more of it, than any academy or school in the state possessed, besides paying for the instruction of all our pupils in vocal music, dancing, drawing, painting and needlework, branches that I did not attempt to teach.

This experiment was not entirely lost upon Boston, for, four or five years after I commenced, the city established a High School for girls, entirely on the monitorial plan, and this school enjoyed a high reputation the two years that it continued. In fact, the immediate cause of its discontinuance was its popularity, for the applicants for admission were so numerous, that not half could be received; and, as the parents of the rejected ones clamored for more high schools, the question arose whether several such should be established, or such alterations made in the grammar schools as would afford the highest class of girls all the advantages of a high school. The latter course was adopted; the girls were allowed to stay at the grammar schools two years longer than the boys, who had a high school; the masters of the grammar schools were required to teach all that had been attempted in the high school, and then the monitorial high school was discontinued. The experiment, however, was considered perfectly successful, and had new schools been established, they would undoubtedly have been on the same plan.

Again, in 1831, the School Committee, believing that some radical change in the city schools was necessary, voted, unanimously, I believe, to introduce what they considered a monitorial plan into all the grammar schools. Our buildings had two rooms, in each of which was a master and usher. Half the pupils were in each room alternately; in one, learning writing and arithmetic, and in the other, reading, grammar and geography. The masters were equal in rank and independent of each other, and the same system, called the "double-headed system," is now in force in most of this class of schools. The new plan proposed to have but one master, one adult assistant subordinate to him, and six paid assistants, young persons, but not pupils. The old grammar masters were made the new principals, and they, from motives of friendship made the old writing masters their assistants, who were willing to serve at very reduced salaries. All the ushers were dismissed, and three young assistants appointed instead of each of them. As the principals were known to be opposed to the change, and as the adult assistants, the old writing masters, were interested in having the old order of things restored, it would require no great discernment to foresee the result of the experiment in such unfriendly hands. At the end of two years, it was declared a failure; the double-headed system was restored, and has continued, with one or two exceptions of new schools, until this day. Two circumstances, however, should be mentioned in connection with this experiment. The teacher of the Boylston School, one of the largest and best, having lost his usher, requested permission to use monitors taken from his pupils, and conducted his school, with no other assistance, more than a year before the experiment I have just described. His success had been so complete, and the economy so evident, that the committee voted him extra compensation for his services. When the schools were put back, his school went with the rest. Another teacher, finding that the *paid* assistants did not work well, freely employed his pupils, and from being the poorest school, his had become second to none, — his second class reading and pursuing all the studies of the first class, — when, to the great regret of this eminent teacher, the double-headed system was reëstablished. It has always been a source of regret to me that my friends, the Boston teachers, were so afraid of the system that I loved, because, knowing how arduous are their duties, I wish them to be furnished with the only means that, in my opinion, can afford them any substantial relief.

The city of Boston has had four successful trials of the system in her public schools, and two in private hands. Five or six different teachers have been found competent to conduct these difficult experiments, and probably every master in the public service is equally competent, and yet the schools are going on in the old way, at double the expense that would be required if the use of pupils as assistants was allowed.

I have entered into these details, although somewhat tedious, because I sincerely believe, as I have before said, that the failure of attempts to teach on the Monitorial Plan has not arisen from any defect in the system, and ignorance of this fact is leading us to reject an instrument, which, if judiciously used, may be of incalculable advantage. I have thought this sketch of the history of monitorial instruction necessary also to a full understanding of the further remarks which I may make upon some theoretical objections to the plan, and upon its advantages over the old system.

In the first place, then, a prejudice has always existed against the Monitorial Plan, especially as Lancaster taught it, because at first it only aimed at humble attainments. Its first object was to teach the ignorant poor, and it has been called, by way of derision, the *pauper* system. If I thought this objection could have any weight with an intelligent person, I would attempt to refute it, but it is idle to argue against prejudice.

A more specious objection is, that children have not judgment enough to govern children. This objection has probably arisen from the teacher's entrusting too much to his monitors. Require too much of an adult, and he will fail to do it well. Give an adult too much power, without proper checks and restrictions, and the chance is a hundred to one that he will abuse it. Children do not differ from adults in this respect; but they may surely be trusted to a certain extent, and are as faithful, as honest, and as anxious to do well as we are. Can we expect them to do better than their elders? The objection goes upon the assumption that monitors are to be allowed to reward and punish, and to make rules and affix penalties, without being accountable for their conduct; but, in every case that can possibly be anticipated, the power and duty of a monitor should be defined, and appeals to the teacher should always be respectfully considered. But if it be insisted that the young are less sincere, less docile, less teachable, less just, less anxious to do right, and less pure in heart, than adults, I solemnly deny the charge; and, if my twenty-one years' experience with monitors, as well as with children, does not give weight enough to the denial, I will ask, why a certain great Teacher, to whom we all bow, once selected a little child and set him up as an example to men, whom he had just sent forth to teach the world.

I have no doubt that monitors may occasionally have been unfaithful to their trust, but not oftener than adults; the failure is an exception to the general conduct. A monitor who has to teach a child of inferior ability, may become tired, and may slight a lesson; a child, whose judgment is exercised by a perverse little class, may sometimes err; such a one may sometimes be partial to the good and harsh to the disagreeable; but when this little one is arraigned, who is the teacher that will not stoop and write his accusation in the sand, that it may be erased and forgiven, rather than rise up and cast the stone that will condemn himself as well as the little offender? The child who is exposed to no such trial, but who is only required to have no intercourse with his fellows; the perfection of whose conduct is to keep silence and sit immovable, possibly may not err, but the hermit who retired from the world that he might not sin, blasphemed when he accidentally overturned his only furniture, a pitcher of water. Indeed, it is a fair question for the moralist, whether a system that tries the character in youth, and develops traits that would otherwise have grown with the growth, and strengthened with the strength of the child, and thus have become an incurable defect in the adult character, is not to be preferred on this very account. The moral character, the moral sentiments, must be educated, as well as the intellectual faculties; but how is a moral sentiment to be instructed unless it can act, can manifest itself? He is a man who regulates his faculties, and not he who never uses them. The child who commits to memory, as many do, a whole moral class book, or every chapter in the Bible, knows not his own strength or weakness, and in the hour of trial or temptation, will be as helpless as the drowning child that has only learned to swim on the parlor floor.

I could detain you for hours with the detail of cases in which I have seen the better feelings of the heart, and the most delicate moral sensibility, exhibited as a consequence of the relations between monitor and pupil, but I will only allude to one or two classes of such cases. It was not unusual in my school, when a pupil was inclined to talk, or otherwise habitually to offend, for two pupils who never offended, to ask that she might sit between them, to be out of temptation. It was no uncommon thing, when a very young pupil was often reprimanded, and yet continued to offend, for some older pupil, of excellent character, to become bound for her good behavior; in which case, the little one was allowed to sit next to her, where she could be separated from companions whose influence was unfavorable. The child generally became so attached to her patron that I had no more trouble with her. I had monitors, therefore, for moral training, as well as in the comparatively unimportant matters of reading, writing, grammar, &c., the knowledge of all which, without a cultivated moral sense, is a curse oftener than a blessing. Dr. Arnold, of England, perhaps the most remarkable teacher of the present century, who reduced one of the most vicious and ungovernable schools not only to order, but to Christian sobriety, did this through the medium of monitors. He rarely, if ever, used them as assistants in teaching the various branches of knowledge; but in reclaiming the school from vice, and governing it afterwards, the point in which monitors are said to be especially unqualified, he found their aid indispensable. "I could do nothing without my Sixth Class," said he. "When I have confidence in the Sixth," was the end of one of his farewell addresses, "there is no post in England that I would exchange for this; but if they do not support me, I must go." When fears were expressed that mischief would ensue from the method he pursued, his memorable reply was, "The victory of fallen man lies not in innocence, but in *tried* virtue." "I hold fast to the great truth," said he, that "Blessed is he that overcometh."

If, therefore, the employment of monitors, under the eye and direction of the teacher, will afford them opportunities of cultivating the judgment, the conscience, the kind affections; if it will strengthen those who are right, but weak in moral courage; if it will expose those who are defective in morals, and thus lead to their timely correction, this plan is the very touchstone we need. The best disciplined minds are often found in those children, who, by what the world terms a misfortune, are thrown upon their own resources, and early accustomed to the exercise of their moral and intellectual faculties; and do I err when I say, that no good opportunity for such exercise is afforded in common schools, where each is required to hoard up knowledge, and is forbidden to impart it to others; where intercourse is prohibited, and whispering is high treason; where change of place, if not of position, is punished as depravity; where implicit obedience is the divine right of the teacher, and the divine wrong of the pupil; where, in fact, the best pupil is he who most nearly resembles an automaton?

It has been objected, too, that the employment of pupils as monitors increases that love of domination, which is already too active in the youthful breast. I believe this charge to be unjust, even when the delegated power is not under proper restraint; and it certainly is unjust, when the teacher does his duty as a watchful overseer. It must be recollected, that the monitors in every branch are the best pupils in that particular branch, and every monitor may also be a pupil of his fellow-scholar, as he is of the master; and though, one hour, he may govern his class according to fixed laws enacted by the master, and well understood by every pupil; the very next hour, he may be subject to one of the very pupils that he had just directed. The monitorial plan, as I used it, is the true democratic one; the children all had a chance at the offices, though only the qualified and the deserving were appointed. Being sometimes governed, children are less likely to become imperious; and sometimes commanding, they will not too easily become servile.

About the worst pupil in my first school was reformed by being made a monitor. One day, a class of eight or ten small boys, who only wanted age to be as bad as himself, entered school while I was at my wit's end to know what to do with the large offender. "Do you know those boys?" said I. "I believe I do," said he. "Bad fellows, are they not?" said I. "I guess you 'll find them all that," said he. "Well, now," said I, "you know better than I how to manage such fellows; why can't you be their monitor, and teach them how to behave? You may teach them what you can, but the main thing is to bring them to order. Will you try to help me?" He was evidently moved by my confidence in him, and yet seemed to doubt my sincerity. When convinced of this by being introduced to the new comers as their monitor, he arranged them in order, and prepared, as well as he knew how, to teach them. Soon he came up to me and said, "That boy won't mind me, sir; what shall I do to him?" "Well," said I, "*you* do not mind *me* sometimes, and perhaps the best rule is for you to do as you would like to be done unto. Shall I flog him?" He thought a moment— "No, sir," said he; "I guess I will try him once more." As he learned what it was reasonable to require of them, he grew more and more ready to do what I required of him. One day, his father came to the school-room to inquire what I had done to his son. I was alarmed at first, but he soon relieved me by saying that, a few weeks ago, his son had given him much trouble by being out every evening, and getting into difficulty; but of late he staid at home and studied his lessons, and behaved so much better, that he had determined to come and ask what I had done to him. I told him what had taken place, and being curious to know what lessons he studied, since I had excused him from saying any to me, I called the boy up, and asked what lessons he studied at home. He blushed, but gave no answer. "Tell me," said I, "because your father says you study at home, and I wish to reward you for your industry." "I study the lessons of my class," said he, "but father need not have told of it." "O," said I, "this is very honorable to you, and while you continue to do as well as you have done, you will find a good friend in me and in your father, who has come here to tell me how well you behave at home." That boy gave me no further trouble afterwards, and he trained his class better, probably, than I could have done, had I done nothing else. Bad as he was, one spark of virtue remained unextinguished, and this one instance of unexpected and undeserved confidence kindled it into an enduring flame.

Another common objection against the use of children as assistants is, that their knowledge is imperfect, and of course their teaching must be of the same character. A judicious teacher would not set a child to teach what he did not know; but, if a child may not teach what he does know to one who knows less, because his knowledge is limited, I do not see out all teaching must cease; for, oftentimes, there is not more difference between the attainments of the teacher and those of his best pupils, than between those of the latter and of the poorest scholars. The wisest and best of us go to church, and to lectures, without repugnance, although we know that the preacher or the lecturer is only a monitor, who knows, perhaps, a little more than we do of the subject under consideration, but who would perhaps come to us for information on many other subjects. The art of teaching depends more upon adapting the explanation to the capacity of the learner, than upon the amount of knowledge accumulated by the teacher. Is it unreasonable, then, to suppose that the explanations of children may sometimes be better suited to the understanding of children, than those of adults would be? I am not ashamed to own that I often called on my monitors to explain what I had failed to make a little scholar apprehend. When I began to teach, I was for a long time obliged to study in the evening what I was to teach the next morning; and I believe I succeeded better then in explaining those lessons, than I did afterwards when the subject had become familiar to me. What was I but a monitor; and what else was I ever afterwards?

It is also objected against Monitorial Schools, that they are necessarily noisy. Now, there are two kinds of noise, that of disorder, which is useless, and that of business, which is sometimes unavoidable. If several classes are reciting at once, more noise may be made than where only one is reciting in the old mode; but this is not necessarily the case, for, in small classes it is not necessary to speak loud, and as all are employed, there are no idlers to make the noise that often interrupts the single recitation of common schools, and furnishes victims for the rod. To my ear, however, the hum of business is much more agreeable than the stillness of inactivity and idleness. If I owned a cotton factory, I should be glad to be rid of the noise, but I should be rather simple to stop all the spindles but one to procure silence. I would not tolerate any noise that was unaccompanied with work, but, after I had perfected the machinery, and oiled all the wheels, I would keep up the steam, and get used to the noise as busy workmen easily do. The sacrifice, therefore, of industry, and often of happiness and humanity, to the god of silence, is an idolatry, which, if not paid to stocks and stones, has a tendency to make stocks and stones of the worshippers. "You may play, if you will make no noise," said a teacher to her pupils. "Thank you, ma'am," said they; "such play would be too much like work."

Finally, it is objected, that, if teaching helps a monitor, only a few are helped, and as the monitors are taught exclusively by the master, and the rest have only his occasional care, those who are not monitors must suffer. In schools on every plan, the teacher bestows more personal attention upon the best scholars than upon the lower classes. But, if the teacher bestows more time upon the monitor of the present season, the next year, when those who are pupils now have become monitors, they will have the same exclusive care, and the aggregate of personal attention will be about the same. If it be urged that some pupils will never be fit for monitors, then my experience tells me that great practice under monitors is better for such, than the slight attention that teachers can pay to dull scholars. Besides, it must be borne in mind, that the teacher is always active, and will give such children as much of his time as they would have had, if no monitors had been employed. The mischief most to be feared is that the masters will use the monitors as substitutes, and not as mere assistants; and will look on, when they should be at work. The great wheel that moves all the little wheels in a factory might as well stop to see how the others get on.

But I shall not be satisfied with replying to *objections* for there are positive *advantages* in the Monitorial Plan when properly employed, and I must briefly notice a few of them. I have already hinted that one of the greatest evils inseparable from the common plan, is the defective classification. If the teacher makes many classes, he must slight them all; for the more classes he has, the less time he can bestow upon each. The teacher, therefore, of a large school, makes as few classes as possible, and, of course, brings together children whose capacities are very unequal; and then, if he sets a lesson to give full employment to the brightest pupils, he oppresses the poorer scholars; and how often are they punished for imperfect recitations, when the teacher only is to blame for overtasking their capacities. On the other hand, if the humane teacher sets the large class a short lesson, in mercy to the feeble intellects, he represses the ardor of the brighter scholars, and by keeping them only half employed exposes them to the temptations of idleness.

Again, in these large classes, children are brought together with little or no regard to their peculiar talents. One may be a good reader but a poor arithmetician; another may be a good arithmetician but a bad geographer; a third may be a good geographer but a bad grammarian, and so on; and few will be found to excel in every branch. No matter, all must work together, however unlike, and this defect seems to be inseparable from the classification of our large schools.

Now the evils arising from imperfect classification are all remedied by the Monitorial Plan, for the teacher can make as many classes as are necessary to bring all scholars of equal attainments or capacity together. No class, perhaps, except his own, contains more than six or eight, and, if necessary, a single child may have a separate monitor, if she needs extraordinary care, or is unfit to go with any other in the school. The teacher takes whichsoever class needs him most; the monitors, all under his eye, take the rest, and, generally, all are reciting at the same time. These small classes get an immense amount of practice, and every child may easily be made to recite the whole lesson, and not merely one or two questions of it. I always required the whole lesson to be recited by every pupil.

But the classification is different in every branch of study, and every child who has any talent has a chance to rise and improve it. It is no great stretch of credulity to believe, as I do, that a monitor, selected in this way for his skill in one branch, and required only to teach that branch, may succeed as well in teaching his single study to beginners, as the teacher will, who is required to teach many branches, who, perhaps, excels in none of them, and can hardly be expected to excel in all.

Again; in common schools, it is difficult for a teacher to keep alive in the minds of his pupils what he has taught them. It is necessary to drop the lower branches, or even the elementary part of the same branch, as the pupil advances; and a review of past studies, to which some good teachers resort, rarely goes further back than the last branch studied, and not only interrupts business, but generally is equivalent to teaching the whole matter over again. No exercise is so often dropped in this way as spelling; and I have often known a first class, who had thrown aside the spelling-book, unable to spell decently. In answering fourteen questions in grammar, the first division of the first classes in the Boston grammar schools, averaging about fourteen years of age, misspelled 924 words, and some of these the easiest in the language. I do not believe, however, that these pupils were worse than pupils elsewhere.

Now the Monitorial Plan effectually meets this evil. By teaching the younger children, the more advanced are constantly reviewing their studies, not by learning merely, but by the surer method of teaching what they have learned to others. In reality, the children never drop any study till they drop the school, and never need to do so. If it be objected, that only monitors enjoy this privilege, it may be answered, that monitors only need it, their pupils not yet having any study to drop. But the fact is, the ingenious teacher will, at times, make monitors of all his pupils, and thus give them practice, if they do not need any review. I often employed my second class in showing beginners how to study their lessons; a duty that teachers themselves are too apt to neglect, and to lay upon the parents, although it is often far more difficult and important than the hearing of the recitation afterwards. No child, but the very lowest, was so low that she could not teach something, and that something I always required her to teach if possible. Once, when I made this remark to a visiter, he pointed to a little girl, not yet four years old, and who had only been taught a few of the letters, and asked, "Can you make a monitor of her?" "To be sure," said I; and knowing that she had a large rag-baby in her desk, I asked her if her dolly knew her A, B, C. "No, thir," said she. "Can you teach them to her?" said I.

"Yeth thir," said she. I gave her a piece of chalk, led her before the black-board, and told her to do as the monitor did. She at once chalked A upon the board, and held her doll up before it; but finding it difficult to get the idea into her pupil's head, she adopted an expedient that, I will venture to say, not one adult in a thousand would have thought of,—she rubbed the letters into the doll's head by rubbing them out with it.

There is a common notion that knowledge easily acquired is as easily lost; and, therefore, learning should be made somewhat difficult, that the labor of acquisition may prevent too rapid progress, and impress the words or the ideas more deeply on the mind. But this principle will apply as justly to the repair of roads, and prove the impolicy of a highway tax; since the worse the road the more careful will be the driver, and the more attentive the passengers; and the longer the journey is, the more pleasant will its end be, and the aching bones will more powerfully come to the aid of memory. There is no royal road to knowledge which the privileged only may travel; but there may be a rail-road, nay, there must be one, or all progress must cease. I am not like the honest Scotch schoolmaster, who, when asked why he did not teach his pupils a certain part of mathematics by a new process which shortened it amazingly, replied, "Ye dinna think I 'd teach the blackguards in a week, what it cost me a year or twa to learn!" For my part, I had rather travel a road two or three times over in a comfortable way, if once going over it is not enough, than receive any of those deeper impressions of a more painful route. I consider an idea like a town, and am content to reach it by the shortest and easiest road.

But the most crying evil in our common schools is that alluded to at the commencement of this lecture,—*the want of constant employment.* One class only can recite to the master at a time, and, of that class, but one child at a time. It is true that the rest are expected to attend, but they do not, and it is useless to deny the fact. Now, if there is idleness and inattention in the very class that is reciting to the teacher, what may we expect to find in the rest of the school? What do we find there? Idleness and all its fruits, from innocent sleep up to active mischief. It is true, that classes not reciting are expected to study their lessons; and some children, no doubt, do this; but the majority do no such thing. Now, just in proportion as the Monitorial Plan diminishes the number of pupils in a class, and increases the number of teachers, it diminishes the opportunities for idleness and mischief. By the judicious employment of monitors, and the proper selection and change of studies, the children can be all usefully employed, and employed all the time.

Again; on the old plan, as the children of a large school cannot be classed so that they can work advantageously together, an attempt has been made to remove the evil by having several grades of schools, as the infant, the primary, the intermediate, the grammar, and the high school. This arrangement, no doubt, is a great improvement, and diminishes the difficulty of classing the pupils; but it does not remove idleness,—it does not reduce the number in a class,—it does not produce equality of talents or attainments; for the schools are classed by age generally, and classing them by age will do no more towards bringing equals together, than will classing them by the number of feet and inches that they measure. The Monitorial Plan renders all this separation of ages unnecessary; for the charm of a school on this plan is the gradation of ages,—the presence of the little ones always having a kindly influence upon the benevolent feelings of the older pupils, while the example of the latter assists the example of the teacher, and gives to him a sort of ubiquity. I generally found, too, that little children, who witnessed the exercises of the more advanced pupils, learned so much, that, when promoted to a new study, they were half acquainted with it. In schools that are classed, the primaries see nothing of what the grammar scholars do, and these are ignorant of what is done in the high school. This classification of schools sometimes separates the older children of a family from the younger, when their protection is almost indispensable. The proportion of ages in a common district school is favorable to the use of monitors; and, if two or three districts unite, so much the better; for they may employ a first-rate teacher, who, with the aid of his pupils, will do more in the united school than three poor teachers could do in their separate districts, and do it three times as well; for a good monitor, under a good teacher, is worth more than a poor teacher alone. When the schools are classed, the child who leaves the primary school leaves the teacher also, who has laid the foundation of his education, and goes to another, who builds upon a foundation that he did not lay, and, after a while, leaves the work to be completed by a third. How this plan would operate in the building of a temple, any one can guess; and yet the comparison of the material with the intellectual temple, shows a perfect parallel.

I shall name but one advantage more, and this is of immense importance. *Every pupil educated in a monitorial school becomes a teacher.* This is important even in a pecuniary point of view; but it has higher claims than merely affording a respectable means of support. If it be said, as it has been, by parents, "I do not expect my child ever to become a teacher," it may be asked, "Do you never expect him or her to become a parent?" And is it of no advantage to a parent to be able to educate his own children, or to know how to superintend this all-important concern? Many of my pupils, with no other preparation than they obtained from acting as monitors, have become teachers of excellent schools, without feeling at all embarrassed. Once, when the trustees of my school had tried several adult teachers in the needle-work and drawing department, which was conducted when I was not present, and had concluded to abandon the enterprise, from the inability of the teachers to conduct so large a school, I proposed that one of my monitors, then only seventeen years of age, should be allowed to try her skill; and although the pupils were all her fellow-scholars, and some nearly as old as herself, she conducted the school to the entire satisfaction of all concerned, until she was married, four years afterwards.

The want of competent teachers is felt and acknowledged throughout our land, and great efforts are making to furnish an adequate supply. Although I believe teaching to be a natural gift, as much as poetry or music, still, like them, it is an art that must be studied and cultivated, and one that, perhaps, will be hidden, unless an opportunity is afforded for its exercise. Acquiring knowledge is not acquiring the art of teaching, any more than accumulating money is the same as active beneficence. Not one learned man in a thousand is able to communicate what he knows, clearly and simply, to a child. Practice is necessary; but few have this, until they are called on to instruct. How different is the case where children, as fast as they learn, are required to impart what they have learned to others. The truth is, that a well-conducted Monitorial School is the best normal school in the world; for practice goes with precept every step of the way. If our common schools were conducted, even in part, on the monitorial plan, those children who have any tact, any peculiar love or aptness for teaching, would soon show it; and who does not see that pupils thus brought out would furnish the very best stock for normal schools, and the demand for teachers would not only be supplied, but would be supplied with teachers of the true birth, born and bred to their business? Our normal schools have done immense good under every disadvantage; but many of the pupils who have entered them have lacked the necessary degree of knowledge, as well as the true spirit of teaching; and this must continue to be the case until preparatory schools, in which the Monitorial Plan is used, are connected with the normals; or until the common schools are so generally conducted on this plan, that a full supply of suitable teachers can be selected from them.

The precept of our great Teacher, that, "It is more blessed to give than to receive," is true in intellectual as well as in material things. Teaching is learning, and learning of the very best kind. I appeal to teachers of common, private and high schools, and ask, whether every faithful attempt to teach the children under their care does not increase and improve their own knowledge? I appeal to parents, and ask, if every attempt to educate their own children does not also educate themselves? I appeal to all lecturers, preachers, and others, who try to instruct their fellow-men, and I ask whether teaching is not learning? I appeal to all the young teachers in our Sunday schools, many of whom are but monitors, and yet are safely intrusted to teach those mysteries which angels cannot fathom, although in the district school they are not allowed to teach reading, spelling, and arithmetic,—I appeal to these young coädjutors of our divine Master, and ask them, if, when they are pointing out to their young pupils the path to heaven, they are not compelled to advance therein themselves?

We need more good teachers, and must have them. He who thinks otherwise, must be blind to the signs of the times; to that bigotry, which hopes to thrive in the general ignorance; to that selfish pride, which looks with coldness upon all attempts to raise the mass by the agency of common schools; to that infidelity, which, half instructed, fancies itself to be the only true wisdom; to that disregard of law, which blindly claims to be the only true liberty; and to that restless love of novelty, which rejects the most solemn lessons of experience. Impressed with the necessity of creating a higher race of teachers, and of providing surer and better methods of instruction, I have ventured to plead the cause of a system which has few acquaintances, and, of course, fewer friends. I have no private interest to subserve, for I am no longer a teacher, and I have made no book that is better fitted for instruction on this plan than on any other. I believe that the prevalent mode of instruction is defective in some vital points, which the mode I advocate seems to be eminently fitted to remedy. I do not conceal the fact that the system has been tried somewhat extensively and laid aside, but the same thing once happened to the greatest of all improvements, or Luther was no reformer. I am aware that many obstacles will arise, and some experiments may fail, in making the change of systems that I propose, but the schools have less to fear from this than from remaining as they are. "Let well enough alone," is high treason in these days, when the perfection of our schools is to our institutions the only hope of salvation. Nor do I speak as a mere theorist. I have taught on this system more than twenty years; I have taught large numbers of the rich and of the poor—the cared-for and the neglected; I have taught the elements and the advanced studies, and all this in a community boasting of its schools, and sternly opposed to innovation; I know what the system can do, and I am ready to stake the welfare of the coming generation upon a fair experiment.

Perhaps few teachers will be safe in introducing the entire system at once; a wiser plan will be to employ only a few monitors, and these with caution, until practice gives confidence, and success removes the existing prejudice. But in recommending this system to teachers, I ought not to conceal the fact that they who employ monitors must be more vigilant, more active, more industrious than those on the old plan; for, what the teacher is, the monitors will most assuredly be. Remember, however, that the labor, though doubled, will be less fatiguing to both pupils and teacher; for there will be a life in the instruction, a charm in the intercourse of teacher, monitor and pupil, which no labor can weary, and no ordinary vexations disturb. You will, for a time at least, be troubled by the fears of parents and the incredulity, perhaps, of committees, who, naturally, will lack faith until you give them experience; and therefore you must possess your souls in patience, and persevere in meekness. When told, as you will be, of the importance of silence *in school;* speak of the greater importance of industry *every where.*—If the system is stigmatized as a pauper system; comfort yourselves with the reflection that your blessed religion is a religion for the poor; not to keep them so, but to make them rich. — If told that your monitors are imperfect; acknowledge with unfeigned humility that you are imperfect also. — If told that your monitors do not govern wisely; acknowledge frankly, what will no doubt be the truth, that you have not shown them how. — If told that, once in a while, a monitor is partial or unfaithful; you may whisper a suspicion, that, once in a while, teachers, too, are partial and unfaithful. — If told that the knowledge of your monitors is imperfect; you may hint, for the sake of argument, that that of teachers is not *always* perfect. — If told that, in exercising their judgment, monitors sometimes err; do not be so rash as to assert that teachers also sometimes err, but ask, if children had not better sometimes err than never exercise their judgment? — If told that a monitorial school is more noisy than others; express a quiet hope that there will be less chance to sleep in it. — If told that children cannot, in the nature of things, teach children; allow that this is strange, since children can often teach adults. — If your classes are too large; cut them up, in the full belief that, with them, as with the polypus, the more pieces the more vitality. — If told that one hour under a teacher is better than ten under a monitor; be sure to ask who that teacher is. — If told that it is better to recite one or two questions to a master than the whole lesson to a monitor; ask, inquiringly, which are the healthiest children, those who get a few mouthfuls of dainty food, or those who get as much as they can eat of plain but wholesome fare. — If told that monitors must spend a *portion* of their time in teaching what they know already; you may insinuate that teachers spend *all* theirs in the same manner. — If told that the monitorial plan mixes old and young together; hint that, in the great school of the world, the Almighty does the very same thing. — Finally, if told that the use of monitors is an innovation unknown to our fathers; after doubting the fact, you must, in justice to those farsighted men, say, that the very establishment of public free schools by them was also an innovation, a most glorious innovation, which their children are called upon to cherish and perfect, without prejudice and without fear.

THE USE OF MONITORS.

I do not know that I need to say any more on this subject. for, besides the lecture, I have, in this volume, frequently alluded to the use of pupils as assistants to the teacher. It has given me pleasure to hear that many of the teachers who attended the Institutes last autumn, have made successful use of monitors since, and have never been so well satisfied that they did their duty towards their employers. I have not heard that any one, parent or committee-man, has objected to the improvement; and, if the teachers are judicious, I presume they will not be interfered with, and checked in their progress towards a thorough reform. From every quarter I hear indications of a better feeling toward this "only invention of the nineteenth century," and the very natural hostility of teachers and schools who have no enterprise, and whom the world has gone by, cannot prevent the general adoption of a plan, which gives us more and better instruction at half the expense, and which is the only remedy for most of the evils under which our schools have groaned for at least a century, viz.. want of teachers, want of practice, want of employment, want of discipline, want of interest, want of almost every-thing.

Just twenty years ago, at the request of William Russell, that most excellent of men and most judicious of teachers, I prepared some directions for the introduction of the system of mutual instruction into the common schools of Massachusetts, and he published them in a small manual. The book is not now to be found, and I may be excused for making a few extracts from it touching the arrangement of a school-room.

"Mutual instruction was first introduced to save the expense of teachers in large schools; but experience has discovered in it a far greater benefit, which is, the more thorough and practical education acquired by those children who are required to *teach* as well as learn; and, in a well ordered school on the monitorial plan, *every* child, before he leaves the school, is employed as a teacher. In schools, therefore, of only twenty or thirty scholars, although the master may feel perfectly competent to teach them all personally, still it is desirable that they should learn the use of his instructions by transmitting them to the younger scholars.

"It is to be regretted that, in our common school-rooms, so little regard has been paid to the convenience of the master and pupils.

The bench of one desk is often fastened to the front of the next desk, so as to allow no passage behind the scholar, and to oblige him to disturb the whole row when he wishes to leave his seat. This arrangement also effectually prevents the master from passing between the desks to examine the books of the writers. Another fault of construction in our school-rooms is, that the forms or desks do not all face the master's desk. This prevents his having a commanding view of the whole, and the scholars' having a convenient view of him, and what he wishes to show them. Besides, it enables the children to look at each other, — a serious evil, were one sex only present, but much more serious, when, as in most of our country schools, both sexes are in the same room, and placed opposite to each other. These are the two greatest defects in the construction of our school-rooms, and it is desirable that they should be remedied before the new system is introduced; but let it be understood, that the new system may be tried in a room of any construction, although its advantages cannot be so fully appreciated as when the room is more conveniently arranged.

" The annexed diagram will give some idea of the most simple and convenient form of a school-room; and school committees who are about to erect new schoolhouses, may be assured that the arrangement we propose will be found as convenient for the *old* system of instruction, as for the *new*, besides the economy of room, which will be evident. The size of the room is about 30 by 24 feet, and will accommodate 60 children with ease, but, the larger the room the better for the pupils, the teacher, the discipline, the neatness, and other important points of a good school. Black-boards should surround the room, or at least be behind every reciting station, and behind the master's desk, which latter should be ruled as I have directed under the head of Writing.

" The diagram represents the *interior* of a school-room only. An anteroom, or wide entrance, should be built at the end where the door is, and should be well lighted. If divided in the centre, so that the girls may have a separate room for their garments, so much the better; and in this case, a door may be cut at A. If the sexes have different yards, so that they can take recess apart, but at the same time, some minutes will be saved, and the teacher will not be obliged to stay in the room to look after those who are not taking recess. It will not cost much to dig a small cellar under the school-room, that the wood may not be covered with snow or look unneat in winter; and, if a small furnace is placed there, by which fresh-heated air may be sent into the room, many a life will be saved. The school-room should not be less than 12 feet high, and should be ventilated at the top and bottom.

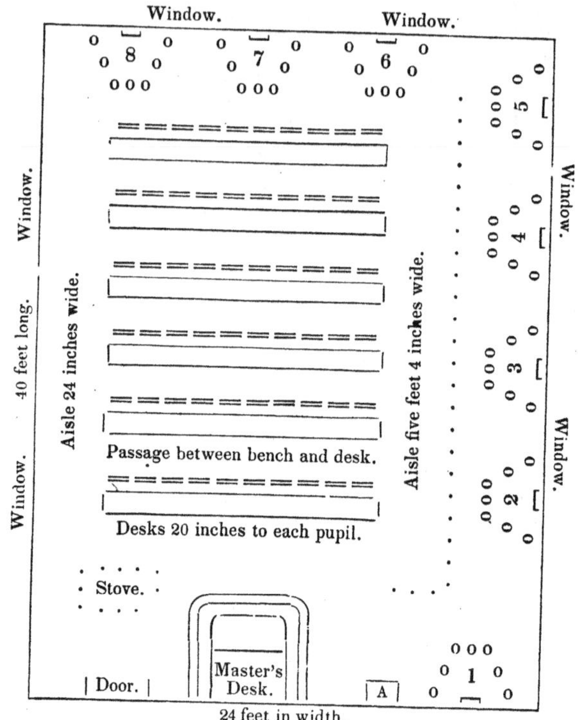

"The semicircles, as they are called, are not perfectly so, for it is found that the shape here given takes up less room and is more convenient for the class. These are the reciting stations, in the centre of which is a seat for the monitor. This seat may be a permanent one, a desk, or a chair; or the monitor may be required to stand, which is the preferable mode.

"There should not be less than eighteen inches between the ends of the semicircles, so that children standing at each may not touch one another.

"From the wall to the front of the semicircles may be about four feet; and then there must be room between the front of the semicircles and the desks, to allow of a person's passing down the aisle, while the children are standing at the stations. One foot will be sufficient, thus making the aisle five feet wide.

"The master's desk had better be semicircular, that classes may occasionally form around it, and recite to him. It should be elevated about eighteen inches above the floor, and have two circular steps, ten inches wide, around it. Its front should be five feet from the wall.

"The narrow aisle on the left side of the school will be found convenient, but may be dispensed with if the other aisle is a wide one.

"The nearest form should be about eight feet from the master's desk. The seats for the scholars may be separate stools, nailed to the floor, or single benches strongly made and fastened.* The desk should have a shelf under it, to hold the slate and books of the children.

"Between the seats and the front of the next row, should be a passage way of fifteen inches width, that master and monitors may pass freely behind the scholars.

"The reading stations, 6, 7 and 8, behind the desks, may be dispensed with, if there are enough elsewhere, and, perhaps, one or two may be made by the door. These stations should be marked by grooves in the floor, cut or scratched. Paint is sometimes used, but is soon effaced.

"The desks nearest the master's should be somewhat lower than the others, to suit the smallest children. In arranging the relative height of the seats and desks or forms, the best plan is to set a child upon the seat, and place the form *just high enough for him to write and keep his elbow at his side, and let it slope just so that a slate will not slide off from it.* Always recollect that both desk and seat had better be too low than too high.

"Such is the arrangement we should propose, and a judicious teacher will come as near to it as circumstances will allow. If he can get more room, so much the better. He may adopt the whole, or a part, or none; for it *is* possible to do without reading stations; the monitor sitting at the end of a bench, and the children standing in a semicircle around him. It is better, however, for the classes to read towards the wall than towards the centre of the room, for less noise is made, and there is less to distract the attention.

"In regard to the system of Mutual Instruction, it should be understood that there are various modifications of it, caused by a greater or less deviation from the old method of saying things by rote, without exercising the judgment or proving the knowledge of the pupil by requiring him to apply it to some practical purpose. In some schools on the new plan, monitors are used, but lessons are recited in the old way, without explanation. In others, the children are allowed to ask an explanation of the monitor; and the monitor is required to give it. We mention this circumstance because many good old-fashioned ears are shocked with the noise necessarily made

*JOSEPH W. INGRAHAM, ESQ., of Boston, has invented an excellent chair for Primary Schools. It is *easy, strong* and *cheap*, and is manufactured by WILLIAM G. SHATTUCK, No. 86, Commercial Street, Boston. Mr. S. also manufactures a Grammar School chair, having the same excellent qualities. Specimens can be examined at the Publisher's Book-store, as well as at the manufactory.

in a school of the *explanatory* kind, and may judge of the comparative merit of schools by their comparative silence and *orderly inaction*. No instructor can teach a class without frequently speaking to them; and the same indulgence should be allowed to monitors; the only point is, to check unnecessary conversation. It is easy to keep a silent and still school; but the free interchange of ideas amongst the pupils, when conducted in an orderly manner, is productive of much good, and should be encouraged. Noise is only injurious when it obstructs business; and in monitorial schools, *well-regulated noise* is rather an indication of industry than of disorder. It should be recollected also that those who make a noise are not those most offended by it. The tin kettle discourses excellent music to the child who beats it; the cotton factory stuns all but the workmen.

"We shall conclude with one word of advice to school-committees. As the success of any system depends upon an impartial exercise of it, and as the system proposed in this manual requires more exercise of the judgment of children than any other, it must be your endeavor to second the exertions of the master. Encourage him to deal impartially with all. Submit your own children entirely to his guidance; allow them no distinction to which their merit does not entitle them. The aristocracy of cities is proverbial; but you must have seen that few country schools are free from family influence. Frown upon all such distinctions; and recollect that undeserved promotion will not excite your own children to exertion, but will discourage those who have nothing beside their own exertions to depend upon, and who, keenly feeling their wrongs, will entertain but a poor opinion of your justice. Be generous towards the teachers you employ. Be careful to select a man of mild temper and pure morals; and when you have found such a one, let not the whole term of his service be embittered by the reflection that his services are undervalued. How can you expect a man to devote himself to the school under such circumstances? Depend upon it he will give you only the money's worth of his time and exertions; and this is all you can reasonably expect. We mention the subject of salaries, because we believe they are generally too low to induce a gentleman of talents to undertake the charge of a village school, and because to this circumstance, more than to any other, (if we except the short term for which a male teacher is employed,) may be attributed the low standard of education in our common schools. If you cannot afford any additional expense, let a small piece of ground be cultivated annually by the boys for the benefit of the school; or let the clergyman and selectmen see that those who have nothing to spare to educate their children, spare nothing for the indulgence of some useless or pernicious habit."

The following letter, from one of the most intelligent and experienced female teachers of Barnstable county, may serve to show what evils exist, and may furnish the text for a few remarks on classification

B———, Nov. 19, 1846.

MR. FOWLE,

Dear Sir,

In less than two weeks from this time, I shall, probably, find myself surrounded by some fifty or sixty pupils of all ages, and of various attainments. In view of this responsibility, and wishing to secure the greatest amount of good to every member of my school, I often ask myself, *how shall I classify my school?* During my past teaching, I have tried, by way of experiment, several modes of classification, but have never been fully satisfied with any of them. The question comes up renewedly, since the Institute in our county, and I have said to myself, I wish I could see Mr. F., and avail myself of his suggestions.

You are aware, sir, of the increased difficulties to be surmounted in schools like ours, compared with those of your city, and that a teacher's plans must be graduated, not according to his views of what a school should be, or to what it may become at some future time, but according to what it is NOW. I must descend to a level with the present system of school discipline and classification, bad as it is, as a starting point, and endeavor to raise the whole *en masse* to a higher degree of excellence. * * * *

I should like to know, in particular, if some general method of classification might not be adopted, by which the whole school, or the greater part of it, may be exercised at once. For instance, might not an hour be given to arithmetic, exclusively; another to grammar; a third to reading; a fourth to spelling, and so on. The idea to me is a new one, but it strikes me that some arrangement of this kind might be made, that would be much better than any I have adopted heretofore; and which, by directing the attention of the whole to the same subject, would diminish idleness. Such a course would require a thorough acquaintance with the subjects taught, on the part of the teacher, to enable him to supply the place of textbooks to his pupils; and would have a tendency to make a teacher what he should always aim to be, "A workman that needeth not to be ashamed, thoroughly furnished unto every good work."

Wishing you success in all your efforts to elevate the condition of our public schools, I am, sir, yours, &c. &c.

This enterprising teacher, if allowed to follow the bent of her mind, would, I think, soon settle down upon the Monitorial System; for this, and nothing else, will enable her to carry out the rational classification of which she has, through suffering, obtained a glimpse. Let me say, then, in a few words, how I should manage such a school, if called on to teach it, and allowed to do as I thought best.

On the day appointed for opening the school, I should require every child who intended to be a pupil, to bring his last writing-book, which I should ask permission to keep till the end of the term. I should ask the children to stand in alphabetical order, and then I should take a list of the names. Having ruled several columns at the right hand of the list, I should begin to examine the pupils in the several branches, recording the result opposite each name, as I advanced. Let all stand in a line, according to age or size, and if any do not know their letters. separate them into the first class, send them to a black-board, and let a large pupil teach them in the method I have described under the head of Reading. As these little ones are well employed, they will not trouble me while classing the rest.

I now take a reading-book, say my Primary Reader, or Swan's Second Part, and, as each of the remaining pupils reads in turn, I mark against his name 1, 2, 3, or 4, as he reads well or ill, the best readers having the highest numbers. This trial will probably enable me to pick out such as can hardly read the lowest class-books, and these I can send away to read under one who has read better than the rest. I let the class read again, in a higher book, say Swan's Grammar School Reader, marking the quality of their reading as before and I keep them reading, until I have separated them into classes of 6, 8 or 10, to my satisfaction. Suppose that there are 60 pupils, of whom 6 are in the alphabet, 8 in Swan's First Book, 8 in the Primary Reader, 6 in Swan's Third Part, 8 in Swan's Grammar School Reader, 10 in the same book, and 14 in the District School Reader. From this highest class, I should select my monitors of reading. I could detach six of them to hear the other classes read, while I heard the rest of the highest class, say 15 or 20 minutes. Then I could detach six of those who had read to me, to take the place of the monitors, and let them have a chance to read to me. If I am faithful to my highest class, it will only be necessary for me occasionally to take the other classes, and this I can easily do by giving my class some useful occupation at their seats, while I take the fifth or any lower class. Every book should be read through *in course*, that every one may know the place;

but, on stormy days, when many are absent, the monitor may allow the class to choose pieces, as a sort of reward for punctual attendance. I always made it a point to allow some privilege on such days, and not unfrequently allowed any two or three to select dialogues, and read them before the whole school. Indeed, I would often take part in a dialogue myself, and then the pupils were sure to be more attentive to do their best. The whole school would catch the spirit, and, when alone, would practise, and improve themselves.

Such was the arrangement in the school I taught so many years. All but the highest class were all engaged in the same branch at the same time, and such an arrangement seems to meet the idea of the writer of the letter; but it would be so completely monitorial, that the teacher might be forbidden to employ it, by parents who would not believe, until they had seen, as I have, that little children so taught by monitors will learn faster than when taught exclusively by the master,—the great amount of practice more than making up for the difference of quality. It will be necessary, therefore, to modify the system; and it may be done in this manner.

I may hear the first class read, and let the rest be employed in drawing the map of the geography lesson; or in writing the spelling lesson; or in any thing that is better than committing books to memory. But, as soon as any one gives a sign that his lesson is learned, let him be sent out to read, or cipher, or write, or draw; or, if he is fit to teach, let him keep others out of idleness by teaching them. As soon as the highest class have read, let the second come up to the teacher, and so on, till all have read to him. If my books are used, there will be nothing to commit to memory, and the books contain directions for their use, so that the teacher will seldom be troubled by questions as to how the monitors or children must proceed.

The teacher must recollect that, to keep the pupils who are not reciting to him employed, he has the writing of copies on the black-board over his desk; the writing of spelling lessons from dictation on the ruled slates; the drawing of maps relating to the lesson in geography on slate, black-board or paper; ciphering on the slate or on the black-board, with or without speaking; orthographical exercises from the Companion, a never-failing source of employment; the writing of sentences from dictation, or set grammatical exercises; and, if he has one or two good monitors to inspect or direct, while he is busy with a class, there will be no noise or trouble, at least, not half so much as if the children are left idle.

But I have only examined the children in one branch; it must be done in all the other branches, for a thorough examination is an indispensable step at the commencement of a school. Select 50 words or more from the spelling-book, and let each child spell them all separately, and without hearing each other, or knowing what the words are. As it will take too long for the teacher to hear all, he must hear a few of the best first, and let these copy the words, and help him hear the others. After he has shown them how to pronounce, they will put out the words as fairly as he does. As fast as one has spelled, let the number he has missed be put against his name. Try even the smallest, for those who miss every word should be classed together. The eight, or ten, or twenty, who spell next best, may go together in a class, according to the number of classes needed. It is unimportant whether the same readers are in the same spelling class or not.

In Arithmetic, let all stand up and first write the figures. Those who can not do this, form the lowest class. Give a short single column in addition to those who can make figures, and if any can not add this, let them form a second class. Try the rest in a long column, or in numeration, and as soon as any fail, stop them for another class. Go on with subtraction, multiplication, simple and then long; division, simple and long, and so on, until you find the limit of every scholar's knowledge, and have classed him accordingly, recording his doings on the list, writing the name of the rule over the column, and making + if he understood it, and — if he did not. Let the following represent the list after the trial.

	Figs.			Ad.			Num.			Subt.			S. Mult.			L. Mult.			S. Div.			L. Div.		
A.	+	+	+	+	+	+	+	+	+	—	—	—												
B.	—	—	—																					
C.	+	+	+	+	+	+	+	+	+	+	+	+	+	+	+	+	+	+	+	—	—			
D.	+	+	+	+	+	+	+	+	+	+	—	—												
E.	—	—	—																					
F.	+	+	—	+	+	—	+	—	+	+	+	+	+	+	+	+	+	+	—	—	—			
G.	+	+	+	+	+	+	+	+	+	—	+	+	+	+	—	+	+	+	+	+	+	—	+	+
H.	+	+	+	+	+	+	+	—	+	+	—	—												
I.	—	—	—																					
J.	+	+	+	+	+	+	+	+	+	—	—	+												
K.	+	+	+	+	+	+	—	+	+	+	+	+	—	+	+	+	—	+	—	—	—			
L.	+	+	+	+	+	+	+	+	+	+	+	+	+	+	+	+	+	+	+	+	+	+	—	—
M.	+	+	+	+	+	+	+	+	+	—	+	+	+	+	—	+	+	+	—	—	—			
N.	+	+	+	+	+	+	+	+	+	+	+	—	+	+	+	+	+	+	+	+	+	+	+	—
O.	+	+	—	+	+	—	+	+	+	—	—	—												
P.	+	+	+	+	+	+	—	+	+	+	+	+	—	+	+	+	—	+	+	+	+	—	+	—
Q.	+	+	+	+	+	+	—	+	+	—	+	+	+	+	+	+	+	+	—	+	—			
R.	+	+	+	—	+	+	+	+	+	—	—	—												
S.	+	+	+	+	—	+	+	+	+	—	+	+	—	+	+	+	+	+	—	—	—			
T.	+	+	+	+	+	+	+	+	+	+	+	+	+	—	+	+	+	+	+	+	+	+	+	—
U.	+	+	+	+	+	+	+	+	+	+	+	+	—	+	+	+	+	+	—	+	+	+	+	+
V.	+	+	+	+	+	+	+	+	+	—	+	+	+	+	+	+	—	+	+	+	+	—	+	+

The result will be that
B, E, I, form the 1st class, and make figures.
A, D, H, J, O, R, form the 2d, or subtraction class.
C, F, K, M, Q, S, the 3d, or simple division class.
L, N, P, T, the 4th, or long division class.
G, U, V, must be tried in more advanced rules.

This list should be preserved, not only to show what the children knew at the beginning, but what progress they made during the term. I think this method better than written questions in the elementary rules. Three sums should be given in each rule, and if two are done correctly, the child may be passed to the next rule, but not otherwise. In my school, at the beginning of every term, every pupil, whatever had been her standing in arithmetic, was examined in this way; for the practice was useful, and it was important that I should know their comparative skill.

In Mental Arithmetic, I took a similar list of names, put out six fair questions in every Part of the Child's Arithmetic, and recorded the answers as before. These answers were given in the *quiet* method before described, only, instead of numbering in order, as fast as correct answers were given, those right were all marked +, and those wrong, —. If any children answered readily in the Child's Arithmetic, I gave them three fair questions in every section of Colburn's First Lessons, which I have reason to believe is still *first* in more senses than one. In this way, I easily ascertained which pupils could work together, and which I could use upon occasion for monitors.

In Geography, if you use the Common School Geography, select five questions on each map, and write them on a black-board, requiring each pupil to write answers on paper while you are looking at them. Number your questions on the board, that they may save time by placing the number only before their answers. If a scholar, who has advanced far, misses in the beginning of a book, it may not always be prudent or necessary to send him back to a lower class, but he should be required to review that map in extra lessons, under a faithful monitor, if the teacher has not time to attend to him. Make a record of the answers of each pupil, as before.

In Grammar, select fifteen or twenty questions, write them on the black-board, and require written answers. Record these answers.

Then count the errors made by the pupils in writing their

answers, and record these under the heads of Grammar, Spelling Punctuation and Capitals.

Select ten or twenty words to be parsed, and require each, unheard by the rest, to parse every one. If this takes too much time, you can teach the best who have parsed how to help you hear the rest.

If you have The Companion to Spelling-Books, select a good lesson or two, and let every scholar write it from your copy on the black-board, if they have not the book; or from dictation, which is better, because then they must attend to the orthography of *every* word.

Finally, give them a subject, and require all who can to write upon it what they can in 15 minutes or half an hour. This trial, more than any other, showed how unused many of the young teachers at the Institutes were to expressing their thoughts on paper. In such cases, the record may be made by figures 1, 2, 3, &c., the highest numbers denoting the best exercises.

When his scholars are thus classed in every branch, and he knows which his best pupils are, the good teacher can always find employment for all; and, whether it is his general rule or not, he can occasionally set all at work on one branch at the same time. For instance, to give variety to the exercises he could order the five classes described on page 217, to form around the black-boards, or to take their slates, if black-boards unfortunately are scarce. Let him go to the first class, and make the nine figures and zero, requiring each pupil to do the same before he comes to them again. Let him then proceed to the 2d class, and set them a sum in Subtraction, to be done before he returns; and to secure order and attention, let him place G, of the 5th class, over them as monitor. Then, going to the 3d class, let him give them a sum in Simple Division, and set U over them as monitor. Next, let him give a sum in Long Division to the 4th class, and set V over them as monitor. By this time the first class will have written their figures, and he must examine them, and order a new copy. Then, proceeding to class 2, he examines their work, hears the remarks of the monitor, if he has any to make, sets a new sum in Subtraction, and goes to class 3. He does the same by 3 and 4, and keeps going the rounds as long as he thinks proper. An immense deal of work may be done in this way, especially if the monitor is active, and sets a new sum for the class, if the master does not come in time to do it.

Of course, there will be some friction when the wheels first move, but every day it will be diminished, and the activity of teacher and pupils will make the hours pass pleasantly, usefully, imperceptibly.

How different this from my experience at school. The rule then was, that any boy who came to school early enough to make the fires, or who staid after school long enough to sweep the school-room, should be allowed to go home fifteen minutes before the rest. So irksome were school hours, that we used to contend for the privilege of working an hour, to have fifteen minutes cut off from the last hour of school-time. When I was a teacher, I was obliged to impose a heavy penalty against tarrying after school; for the tendency to unpunctuality was at the end, and not, as usual, at the commencement of the school; in going home, and not in coming to school.

I hope I have made it sufficiently clear that it is not my wish to spare the master. He must work as hard as the hardest; but, in addition to this, he can be sure that the children are all employed when not reciting to him. By the aid of monitors, he can give the pupils ten times the practice they can ever get otherwise, and give them as much personal attention as he would have done on the old system.

For the encouragement of those teachers who feel the insufficiency of the prevalent system, and yet are afraid to try the gradual use of monitors, I will add that, during the past year, and especially during the past winter, more than a hundred teachers, male and female, who had the care of large schools, have used monitors, with all the good results that I have promised. I have many letters and other communications from them; and even since I copied the letter from Barnstable county, on page 213, I have received another from the same teacher, which says, "I received your letter of November 11, and am much obliged to you. It is just what I needed. Perhaps I owe an apology for writing to you, but, in the prospect of having a large school, one that has been noted for insubordination, having been repeatedly broken up heretofore, and in which a female teacher has never before been employed during the winter term, you will excuse me, sir, for wishing to avail myself of all the assistance I can obtain. It is now three weeks since I entered upon my duties, and my success has been beyond my expectation thus far."

A pleasing incident occurred at the Bridgewater Institute

in November, 1845. After I had delivered the preceding lecture on the Monitorial System, many of the young teachers asked why I could not show them a specimen of a school on that system. The superintendent, who was the principal of the Normal School, seconded the application; and although entirely unprepared for such an experiment, in about five minutes, I turned the whole Institute, consisting of more than a hundred teachers, half of them normalites, into a Monitorial School, and set the whole at work, in about 12 or 15 classes, under monitors. We first tried arithmetic, and then spelling, orally, and by writing; and the perfect readiness of the teachers to submit to whatever arrangements I proposed, showed that they possessed one great accomplishment of a true teacher, the docility of pupils. Since that, I have been told by the able assistant of the principal, who was also present at the experiment, they have regularly employed some of the pupils in the Normal School, as monitors, and have found great benefit from it. I know that many members of the Institute went forth, and, from that moment, used the system to good advantage.

At Harwich, in November, 1846, a County Convention of teachers and friends of education met during the session of the Institute, and while it was under my care. The Convention repeatedly honored the Institute by attending its meetings, and patiently witnessing its exercises for nearly two whole days and evenings. I delivered no lecture on the system under consideration, and only incidentally showed, after a lesson or two in the common method, how the power and usefulness of the teacher could be increased, by the occasional use of monitors. To my surprise, before the Convention adjourned, they unanimously passed a resolve recommending to the teachers of the county the use of monitors. Among the members present, were two members of the Board of Education—several clergymen, distinguished for their talents and exertions in favor of general education, three of whom gave most excellent lectures on important points of instruction—several principals of flourishing academies—and several intelligent physicians. I know not who offered the vote, for I was not aware of the intention; it was a free-will offering to truth, and intended, no doubt, to encourage me in my honest endeavors to improve the common schools. Every one of nine other Institutes that I attended and taught, passed unanimous votes of thanks, without the least reservation in regard to monitorial instruction.

There is no lack of authority, therefore, nor of encouragement, for the use of assistants selected from the pupils; and, if the teacher is judicious in the selection and management of his assistants, there is no reason to fear that the committee or the parents will interpose any obstacle. One thing is certain; there must either be more adult teachers in our schools, or the pupils must be employed as I propose. Every new principle and every new rule should be explained by the teacher, but after this is done to one class, and the teacher is called to another, there is nothing to prevent the former class from practising, under one or more monitors, upon the principle just explained. This want of practice in every department of a common school education was, perhaps, the most striking deficiency of the teachers at the several Institutes; and several of the best of those teachers have thanked me for the hint which has enabled them not only to double the amount of labor actually done by their pupils, but also to double the amount done under the teacher himself, because of the greater celerity with which many operations are performed, in consequence of the practice acquired under monitors.

The limits of my book will not allow me to go further into the subject, and I must leave it to the good sense of teachers and school-committees, advising the latter to dismiss a teacher the moment he relaxes his own exertions, and throws upon his monitors any duty that he can perform himself.

NEATNESS.

I SHOULD not feel that I had done justice to the cause, if I omitted to say a few words on the subject of neatness. Perhaps in no one particular can a teacher be more useful to his pupils, than by inculcating a habit of neatness; and in no one thing, perhaps, will the importance of his own example be so distinctly felt. The superiority of female teachers in this respect is, perhaps, one of the strongest reasons for the growing preference which is given to them. At every Institute, I saw young gentlemen, who, in manners and personal appearance, were all that could be wished; but I saw, also, many who, in these respects, were far better fitted to be warnings, than models for the imitation of youth.

If any one will think for a moment with what awe he looked up to the example of his teacher, he will have some idea of the influence which he may exert over his youthful charge. I do not wish the young teacher to expend all he earns in dress, for no one who knows me will suspect me of estimating men by the skill of their tailors; but I do wish to see every teacher careful in regard to his external appearance.

His clothes may always be neat and whole, however coarse. His boots may always be cleaned. His beard may be always kept invisible. His hair may always be neatly combed, his teeth always perfectly white, his finger-nails cut, his hat and clothes brushed, and his hands, eyes, nose and ears, always perfectly clean. Frequent ablutions of his whole person, as well as of his face and hands, are indispensable. He must have a care to his breath, that it be not offensive to those whom he is obliged to face so often. He must never be seen to spit, if he can possibly help it, and at any rate he must never spit upon the floor, or any where else where any eye can be offended. Above all, he must never be guilty of the abominable practice of blowing his nose with his fingers, even if he wipes them, and it, afterwards, on a handkerchief. How many who pretend to be gentlemen indulge in this beastly habit, even in the presence of ladies! I do not hesitate to say, that, if I were on a school-committee, no man who used tobacco in any form, who spit on the floor, or was guilty of that other enormity, which I dare not name again, should ever have my vote, if he applied for a school, and would teach for nothing.

The teacher's desk, too, should always be in order, his books arranged, his papers filed, and just what he requires of his pupils. In his positions, whether sitting or standing, he should be decent, if he can not always be graceful. I have seen a fat teacher leaning backward on the hinder legs of his chair, with his feet not only up as high as his head, but up against the front of a form occupied by female pupils. I speak plainly, because I wish by plainness of speech more distinctly to show the offences that I would prevent.

In purity of language, also, the teacher must be free from every taint. Not only no indelicate word or allusion must ever escape from his lips, but he must avoid every expression that approaches to vulgarity. He should freely converse with his pupils, and the more he does so the better, if his words are fitly spoken; but nothing will so completely destroy his influence as an oath, or an indecent word. If any man is bound to set a double watch over his mouth, it is the teacher, and he can not too resolutely say,

"I will take heed to my ways, that I sin not with my tongue;
I will keep my mouth with a bridle, while the" *innocent* "are before me."

If the teacher is thus mindful of himself, he may with propriety require his pupils to be neat and orderly, to at least the same degree.

Every schoolhouse should be furnished with a wash-stand, basin, towel, and plenty of soap and water; and the teacher should see that every child's hands and face are clean. I know it will be said that children will slop the water, and waste the soap, and dirt the towels; but I know, by experience, that if the teacher looks after these things, the children will soon use them well, nay, will seldom need to use them at all. When I saw how many of the children of my first school were neglected at home, I procured a tin basin and dipper, and a few coarse towels, for the boys and for the girls, and I placed at the doors a large boy and a large girl, whose duty it was to see that all faces and hands were clean, before the pupils came into the school-room. The inspector's office was no sinecure for two or three weeks; but, after that, we had no trouble. Near the wash-stand was a comb also, and all unkempt heads were introduced to this by the monitors of neatness, as the inspectors were called; and, as they sometimes plied the comb for the pupils, when it required unusual vigor to clear a snarl, it was not long before the children found it for their comfort to use a comb before coming to school. While on this subject, it may be well to mention, that the reason why very neat parents send their children to select or private schools, is more frequently the fear of contact with uncared-for children, than from any aristocratic feeling. The teacher must not shrink from recommending the fine-tooth comb occasionally, if he wishes to keep children of neat mothers in his school; and until these children can be brought into our public schools, and educated there, these schools will only do half the good of which they are capable.

Another point to which the attention of the teacher must be turned, is the clothing of the pupils. This should be tidy and clean; and the teacher can make it so, by occasional remarks which will not offend, and which need not even be personal. Sixty or eighty of the pupils of my first school were children of Irish immigrants, neglected in almost every respect, and probably harder subjects than usually enter our district schools; but even these were civilized in a few weeks, and, let me add, that my monitors did more to effect the reform than I did. If a boy was accustomed to come with hair uncombed, or with ragged trousers, the monitor would say kindly, "Johnny, can't you ask mammy to sleek your hair before you leave home? Can't you ask her to patch your knee, when she finds time?" &c. I never knew any one to take offence, but, on the contrary, the hint was almost sure to be effectual.

But teachers are not sufficiently careful in regard to the hats, bonnets, and outer garments that are taken off on entering school. A place must be provided for these, and every child should know his place. There is a kind of double iron hook, having a knob on which to hang a cloak, and another knob above for the hat or bonnet. These hooks do not cost much, and every child should have one. My custom was to number both the children and the hooks; and the monitors of neatness saw that every garment was put upon the right hook before the child was allowed to take his seat. Most schools have a few hooks or nails, but frequently I have seen half the garments thrown into a corner on the floor; and, what is worse, I have seen them trampled upon in the passage-ways. Neat parents will not put up with such conduct, and they either dress their children in clothes that can not be injured, or withdraw them from the school. I made it an offence for a child to *pass* a garment that had fallen down, and *treading on one* was accounted a serious misdemeanor. The monitors of neatness having a list of names and numbers, and knowing most of the garments, prevented any injury to them, by a strict supervision.

There is not room in some schoolhouses for any arrangement of this sort, but I believe the teacher can often get abundance of room, if he will only show how much it is needed. The mischief is, that teachers pay too little attention to the virtue under consideration; and the committees, of course, seldom are sensible of the evil habits that are generated by his inattention. After I purchased towels for my poor scholars, the pupils would take them home when necessary, and wash them. Every little while the tin basin would be made to shine. A mat should be placed at every door, not only to keep the dirt out of the school-room, but to teach the children a habit of cleaning their feet before entering a house. No school-door should lack a scraper, also. I believe that any teacher who should make a schedule of such articles, and ask the children to get up what is called a *Bee*, at the schoolhouse, would generally get all he wished. At any rate, he should make some effort to save himself from the responsibility of helping to rear a generation of slovens and slatterns, cursed with chronic hydrophobia, and its kindred vices.

Every teacher should make it against the rules of the school to throw any thing on the floor, or to spit upon it. Every thing, whether nutshells, paper, leaves of flowers, or any thing similar, found upon the floor, should be picked up by the offender; and, if he can not be found, by the nearest neighbor. Monitors of neatness were allowed to look into the desks to see that all was in order there, but no other pupil could take this liberty without permission of the owner.

Every exercise that the pupils wrote was obliged to be filed and endorsed neatly, and for this they were as much rewarded as for writing the exercise at first. That the files might appear very neat, the pupils were instructed to do their maps, or other work, on paper of uniform size, and then to fold them exactly alike, write upon the end of each, in a uniform manner, what it was, and then tie the bundles with a neat string,—a piece of red tape usually. The effect of these little things upon the general character of the children was excellent, and their utility can not be overrated.

Most teachers are afraid to speak to their pupils about many things which really need correction. Once in a while, I made general remarks upon such subjects as the biting of finger-nails, the picking of the nose, scratching of the head, &c., &c.; and although I singled out no one, I believe that many singled out themselves, and corrected their offensive habits. No one, who knows me, will accuse me of being a *precisian* in these matters of neatness, and yet there are few things at which I have been so often offended as at the neglect of neatness that so extensively prevails, especially in old, ill-looking school-rooms.

There can be no doubt of the fact, that the better a school-room is, the better it is treated by the children; and the larger it is, the more easily it is kept in order, and the more easily the children are governed. Much allowance must be made for teachers who are condemned to teach in small, ill-furnished rooms, and no teacher, who values his reputation and his health, should ever put them in such peril. I know of few things more offensive than the atmosphere of some small district schools that I have visited. It requires some courage in a committee-man to enter such a room, and some minutes to get reconciled to breathing such impurities; and yet hundreds go through this disagreeable transition, and depart wondering how any body can live in such a medium. The ventilation of school-rooms will not be attended to, till committees and teachers are made to realize, that to breathe impure air is not less injurious than to drink dirty water, and ought not to be considered less loathsome; the lungs, which drink the air, being more delicate than the stomach, and inaccessible to medicine.

THE OPENING AND CLOSING OF SCHOOL.

While at the Institutes, I was frequently questioned as to the best method of opening and closing a school. The *daily* opening is here intended, and not the commencement of the term, which should begin with a thorough classification and record of the children in every branch, whether the branches are kept separate or not. Of this classification I have spoken under the head of Monitorial Instruction, and it only remains to show how I should open the school from day to day. I have already alluded to the simultaneous reading of the Scriptures, an exercise into which I was led after various experiments. I have said that I preferred a selection of passages to the reading of the Bible in course, not because one portion of Scripture is of higher authority, or more obligatory upon us, than another, but because some portions are better understood by children, and are more interesting to them. The Board of Education have uniformly recommended the use of the *whole* Bible; but when the whole Bible is used, selections only are read, and surely a selection made with care and judgment is preferable to one made in haste. I prefer reading in concert, for reasons given under the head of Reading; and I am glad to learn that many teachers, who practised with me at the Institutes, have adopted my plan, with profit to themselves and to their pupils.

Before reading a portion of Scripture, which exercise should not average more than five minutes, it is desirable to have a hymn sung by the children. I am no singer, but I never found any difficulty in obtaining a choir for this exercise. The pupils of my second school were instructed by a professional singer, and, knowing which could lead, I had only to propose the hymn, and they would take care of the rest. As it was desirable that all should sing, I confined the tunes to a small number, and rarely sung new tunes until old ones were familiar to all. Every school has some child in it that can lead in this exercise, and in every district the teacher can find some person who would occasionally teach the children a new tune. No one needs to despair of doing this himself, if he is earnest in his desire to learn.

Besides a hymn, and the reading of Scripture, some committees require that prayer should be offered. This exercise is more difficult than the others, and it is rarely performed so as to engage the attention of children. I am satisfied that, unless the teacher is a prayerful man, accustomed to commune with his Maker, and able, moreover, to express his thoughts with simplicity, and to condense all he should say into a few words, he had better not attempt to pray in school. Children dislike long prayers; they disregard cold ones, and they are not benefited by those they do not understand. The method which appeared to me best to command attention, was that of requiring the whole school to repeat my words. Sometimes I wrote a form for every day in the week, and continued the course for several weeks. Sometimes I tried extempore prayer, and required the whole to join; and sometimes I prayed alone. This change of form procured attention, and as the prayer was always short, not exceeding one or two minutes, it was not irksome, to say the least. It requires about half a minute to repeat the Lord's Prayer distinctly, and the teacher should be contented with four times that space at the most. He should confine his petition to such matters as concern the children, and relate to their wants at the moment. If he wanders beyond this limit, he will be more likely to induce the children to hate the exercise than to join in it.

As it has always been a leading object with the Board of Education to encourage the reading of the Scriptures in our common schools, to inculcate reverence for God and all sacred things, and in every way to impress upon the minds of the young that piety towards God which is the only security for their fidelity in every social relation, I felt it my duty, at the various Institutes, often to call the attention of teachers to the importance of religious instruction, and to urge upon them the duty and necessity of personal holiness, that they may feel the responsibility that rests upon them, and be enabled heartily to undertake the work of educating the affections and the consciences of their pupils. It is a pity that school-committees, in their examination of teachers, pay so little regard to their religious character, and in their examination of schools, make few or no inquiries after the moral and religious progress of the pupils. I hope I shall not be misunderstood; I do not wish the committee to pry into the peculiar doctrinal belief of a candidate, but I do think they should be certain that he is a man fearing God and loving his fellow-creatures, and with a deep sense of his obligation to God and man, endeavoring to make every child under his care, as far as his agency is concerned, a child of heaven. This part of the teacher's character is far more important than his attainments in any science; and while calling the attention of committees to this subject, the author feels bound to testify to the fact, that, in all his intercourse with the teachers at the Institutes, he never saw any action, or heard any expression, that would lead him to doubt their strong sense of religious obligation. All he would urge, then, is more earnestness, more activity, more interest in the present and eternal welfare of their pupils.

The author has already prepared suitable selections from the Scriptures, which teachers can use as he has printed them, or as a guide in making their selections, if the whole Bible is preferred. He hopes to be excused if he also gives a few forms of prayer, and a few hymns suitable to be used at the opening of school. The prayers are broken into lines of suitable length to be repeated by the pupils, if that method is adopted; or they may be used by the teacher alone, or by the pupils and teacher at the same time, or even by the pupils alone, under a monitor. I never heard more solemn prayers than have been offered in this latter way.

The teacher, in this exercise of prayer, may often find a good opportunity to explain its nature and obligation; and, if he thinks as I do, he will see that it is always performed with solemnity and reverence. It is to be hoped that the custom, which was unknown to our fathers, of *sitting* while in the act of addressing the Lord of Heaven and Earth, will never prevail in our schools. The most reverent position should be preferred, and if, as is generally the case, it is impossible to kneel, the petitioners should stand. Nothing seems to me more inconsistent, also, than for the preacher or leader in the prayer to stand while the audience sit; and nothing seems so distinctly to imply that the audience are only listeners to the performance of another. We should not dare to sit while addressing an earthly king, and how shall we be less respectful to the great King of kings?

PRAYER FOR MONDAY MORNING.

We thank thee, Lord of the Sabbath,
For its holy rest, and heavenly influence.
We thank thee for preserving us from harm,
And bringing us again together in safety.

Bless us all in our various exercises;
May the spirit of wisdom guide our teacher,
And may we be obedient to his commands.
Forgive the sins and follies of our youth,
And make us truly penitent for them.
Bless our parents and benefactors,
And teach us to forgive our enemies.
Guard us from the dangers that surround us,
And keep us from the evil that is in the world;
From lying, deceit and profaneness;
From impure words, and thoughts, and actions;
From disregard of holy things,
And from forgetfulness of thee, our Maker.
And the praise shall be thine forever,
Through thy beloved Son, our Lord.
Amen.

If it be thought advisable to have a prayer at the close of school in the afternoon, let the *Lord's Prayer* be repeated by the children together, standing, and then let them sing the closing hymn. I have broken the prayers into lines, that they may be repeated in unison. A pleasing variation may be made by chanting the Lord's Prayer, as directed in the American School Song Book, page 157.

Our Father, which art in heaven,
Hallowed be thy name.
Thy kingdom come;
Thy will be done on earth,
As it is done in heaven.
Give us, this day, our daily bread,
And forgive us our trespasses,
As we forgive those who trespass against us.
And lead us not into temptation,
But deliver us from evil;
For thine is the kingdom,
The power, and the glory,
Forever,—Amen.

TUESDAY.

Our Father, who art in heaven,
We have again risen together,
To thank Thee for preserving our lives,
And giving us strength to worship Thee

We humbly ask Thee to meet with us,
And to fill us with thy Holy Spirit,
That whatever we may now do
May be done in thy fear and love,
And be followed by thy blessing.
Give to the pupils, attentive minds,
And obedient and thankful hearts.
Give to the teachers, a deep sense
Of their responsibility to Thee,
And crown their labors with success.
Teach us all the value of time,
The certainty of death and judgment;
And enable us so to live,
That we may not fail of thy grace
Revealed to us in the gospel of thy Son.
Amen.

WEDNESDAY.

Our Maker and our Preserver,
We thank Thee for thy protecting care,
And for all the blessings we enjoy.
Give us hearts sensible to thy goodness,
And obedient to thy commandments.
Forgive our many transgressions,
And teach us to forgive those who offend us.
Enable us to learn thy holy will,
And strengthen all our good resolutions.
Help us to remember Thee in our youth,
Before those evil days draw nigh,
Which have no pleasure and no hope in them.
Bless our parents and friends,
And save them and us,
Through faith in thy beloved Son.
Amen

THURSDAY.

O Thou, who seest our hearts,
And knowest all our thoughts,
We beseech Thee to be with us, and bless us.
Make us willing to receive instruction,
And fearful to offend against our God.
May what we shall learn here
Help us onward, by thy blessing,

Towards that world of peace and love,
Where we shall see Thee as thou art,
And no longer offend Thee as we do.
God of mercy! forgive our sins;
God of love! keep us from evil,
Through Jesus Christ, our Saviour.
Amen.

FRIDAY.

Our heavenly Father, and our Friend,
Now that we have risen to worship Thee,
May we feel how solemn is the service,
And may we perform it with reverence.
Fill our hearts with that fear of Thee
Which is the beginning of wisdom,
That we may early learn to love Thee,
And may always dread thy displeasure.
Give us confidence in thy providence,
And cheerful submission to thy will,
That, like the young Redeemer,
We may grow in wisdom as in stature,
And in favor with God and man.
Bless our parents, and all who watch over us;
Bless all the exercises of the school;
May we not offend in thought or word or action,
And thus may we become heirs of that hope
Which came by Jesus Christ, our Lord.
Amen.

SATURDAY.

O thou Giver of every good gift,
We pray that thy most Holy Spirit
May fill our hearts, and form our lives.
Grant that these, our imperfect lessons,
May be given in thy fear, and in thy love,
And be blessed to the eternal good
Of those who give and those who receive them.
Watch over us, and guard us from danger,
And keep us away from temptation;
That, whether we live to grow up,
Or fall like the early flowers,
We may go to those mansions in heaven
Which Jesus has gone to prepare

For those who truly love and obey him.
And thine shall be the glory, forever.
Amen

PRAYER AFTER THE DEATH OF A PUPIL OR FRIEND.

Eternal Father,
Who livest forever, though thy creatures die,
We acknowledge thy providence,
And submit without a murmur to thy will.
We thank Thee that we have been spared,
Whilst others have gone down to the grave,
And we implore Thee still to spare us.
May the death we mourn make us thoughtful,
And may we, who live, lay it deeply to heart.
May the uncertainty of our lives
Induce us to be dutiful and diligent,
That we may not die unprepared.
And when we have lived in thy fear,
And done all thy will, on earth,
May we be accepted by Thee,
Through that mercy revealed by Him
Who died that we sinners might live.
And to Thee we will ascribe the praise
Forever.
Amen.

HYMNS.

MONDAY MORNING.

(Tune, Brattle Street, or Hymn Second.)

While Thee I seek, protecting Power,
  Be my vain wishes stilled;
And may this consecrated hour
  With better hopes be filled.

Thy love the power of thought bestowed,
  To Thee my thoughts would soar;
Thy mercy o'er my life has flowed,
  That mercy I adore.

In each event of life, how clear
  Thy ruling hand I see!
Each blessing to my soul more dear,
  Because conferred by Thee.

In every joy that crowns my days,
  In every pain I bear,
My heart shall find delight in praise,
  Or seek relief in prayer.

EVENING.

(Tune, Hebron.)

Thus far the Lord has led me on,
  Thus far his power prolongs my days,
And every evening shall make known
  Some fresh memorial of his grace.

Much of my time has run to waste,
  And I forget my Father's home;
May He forgive my follies past,
  And lend me strength for days to come.

TUESDAY MORNING.

(Tune, Hamburg.)

O God, I thank Thee that the night
  In peace and rest hath passed away,
And that I see, in this fair light,
  My Father's smile, that makes it day.

Be thou my guide, and let me live
  As under thine all-seeing eye;
Supply my wants, my sins forgive,
  And make me happy when I die.

EVENING.

(Tune. Lanesborough.)

And now another day is gone,
  I 'll sing my Maker's praise;
My comforts every hour make known
  His providence and grace.

And till the night of death draws near
  O, leave me not alone,
But make my path of duty clear
  Through thy beloved Son.

WEDNESDAY MORNING.

(From The American School Song Book, page 123.)

The eastern hills are glowing
  With morning's purple ray,
Arrayed in light he 's coming,
  The glorious orb of day.
All hail, thou constant emblem
  Of Him who dwells above!
Of Him so great and glorious,
  And yet so full of love.

How nature now rejoices,
  With life and beauty new;
And every grass-blade twinkles
  With pearly drops of dew.
How good is He who made thee,
  Thou glorious orb of day!
With grateful hearts we 'll praise Him,
  In morning's earliest ray.

EVENING.

(American School Song Book, page 146.)

Softly now the light of day
  Fades upon our sight away;
Free from care, from labor free,
  Lord, we would look up to Thee.

When, for us, the light of day
  Shall forever pass away,
Then, from sin and sorrow free,
  Take us, Lord, to dwell with Thee.

THURSDAY MORNING.

(Tune, Bonny Doon. American School Song Book, page 142.)

While nature welcomes in the day,
My heart its earliest vows would pay
To Him whose care hath kindly kept
My life from danger while I slept.
O, may each day my heart improve,
Increase my faith, my hope, my love;
And may its shades around me close
More wise and holy than I rose.

EVENING.

(A. S. Song Book, p. 64.)

For a season called to part,
  Let us now ourselves commend
To the gracious eye and heart
  Of our ever-present Friend.

Father, hear our humble prayer,
  And when we retire to sleep,
Let thy mercy and thy care
  All our souls in safety keep.

What we each have now been taught,
  If of God, may we retain;
May we, in thy love, be brought
  Here to meet in peace again.

FRIDAY MORNING.

(Tune, Naomi.)

Our Father, who in heaven art,
  Thy name all hallowed be;
Thy kingdom come within my heart
  Thy will be done by me.

Give me to-day the food I need,
  And all my sins forgive,
As I forgive, in thought and deed,
  The injuries I receive.
And in temptation's dreadful hour,
  From evil keep me free,
For thine 's the kingdom, glory, power,
  Throughout eternity.

EVENING.

(Tune, Araby's Daughter. — A. S. S. Book, pp. 82, 149.)

Let us love one another,—not long may we stay
In this bleak world of mourning, so brief is life's day ;
Some fade ere 't is noon, and few linger till eve,
And there sinks not a sun but leaves some one to grieve
E'en the fondest, the purest, the truest that met,
Have still found the need to forgive and forget;
Then O, since we know not how brief is our day,
Let us love one another as long as we stay.

SATURDAY MORNING.

(A. S. S. Book, p. 128.)

How happy is the child who hears
  Instruction's warning voice,
And who celestial wisdom makes
  His early, only choice.

She guides the young with innocence
  In pleasure's path to tread;
A crown of glory she bestows
  Upon the aged head.

According as her labors rise,
  So her rewards increase;
Her ways are ways of pleasantness,
  And all her paths are peace.

EVENING.

(Tune, Sicily.)

Praise to thee, thou great Creator!
  Praise to thee from every tongue;
Join my soul with every creature,
  Join the universal song.

For ten thousand blessings given,
  For the hope of future joy,
Sound his praise through earth and heaven,
  Sound Jehovah's praise on high.

MISCELLANEOUS.

(Old Hundred.)

Be thou, O God, exalted high,
And as thy glory fills the sky,
So let it be on earth displayed,
Till thou art here as there obeyed.

(Old Hundred.)

From all who dwell below the skies,
Let the Creator's praise arise,
Let the Redeemer's name be sung
Through every land, by every tongue.

Eternal are thy mercies, Lord;
Eternal truth attends thy word;
Thy praise shall sound from shore to shore,
Till suns shall rise and set no more.

(Tune, Shirland.)

Thy name, Almighty Lord,
  Shall sound through distant lands;
Great is thy grace, and sure thy word,
  Thy truth forever stands.

Far be thine honor spread,
  And long thy praise endure,
Till morning light and evening shade
  Shall be exchanged no more.

[The author does not pretend that there is any particular merit in these forms of prayer, or any remarkable beauty in the hymns; and he would be rejoiced to learn that no such guides are needed by any young teacher.]

It is not uncommon for children to enter school in confusion and to depart with noise. I have even known them, when dismissed, to shout and howl in the school-room, and even to jump over the forms, in their eagerness to gain the door. The good teacher will see that his children enter and leave school in silence, and in order. Any rudeness should be checked; and a monitor should be placed over the garments, and at the door, to see that all is done according to the regulations of the school. If the school consists of both sexes, and they go out by the same door, the girls and boys should be alternately dismissed first, and the desire to see which can behave best will often produce most orderly behavior. If the pupils are playing around the schoolhouse, before school or in recess, at the sound of a bell, or at some other signal given, let them instantly form a line in some place appointed by the teacher, and let them enter in the order best adapted to taking their several seats. There would be no objection to their singing the multiplication table, or some suitable song, while entering, but they should sing till all are seated and a signal given to stop. If possible,—and it should always be possible,—the sexes should have different yards and different conveniences, even when they take recess at different times. Playing in the road is a bad practice, especially if the children are unruly and disrespectful to travellers. The credit of the town as well as that of the teacher is involved in any indecorum of this sort, and when it can be so easily prevented by the aid of a monitor or two, the teacher who allows it is without excuse.

I remember the time when it was the rule for children to stop playing, if a traveller was passing, and salute him with a respectful bow or courtesy, and I regret that this custom has become so unfashionable. When I pass the pupils of a village school, I generally test their manners by bowing first, and I am sorry to say that I rarely get any civil return. I know it is objected by some, that the teacher's jurisdiction over his pupils is confined to the school-room, and he is not accountable for their conduct beyond its walls. But this is a great mistake; the true teacher will endeavor to follow his pupils *wherever they go.* He will, in school, give them advice and direction in regard to their behavior in the road, at home, at church, in lecture-rooms, and everywhere else; and, if he is what he ought to be, his pupils will be distinguished for their good conduct; his school will have the credit of it, and the jurisdiction of the teacher will rarely, if ever, be called in question.

My pupils, for years, were all females, and my external regulations were, of course, adapted to their sex. They knew that it was contrary to my rules for them to talk or laugh loud in the street, to gaze at a deformed person, or to stop when there was any gathering of idlers around a drunken man; they knew that any irreverent conduct in church, or any play or whispering at lyceum lectures or other meetings, would meet with my disapprobation, and the consequence was that I could send my whole school to such meetings with perfect confidence that their behavior would do honor to the school. One winter, the lecture that I was giving to the pupils and their families was disturbed by the boys, who accompanied their sisters. I stopped at once, as every lecturer should do, and told the audience what my rule was, and declared that if I was again interrupted, no boy should be admitted again. The fault was repeated, and the boys were all excluded. After much intercession, my pupils became sureties for the good behavior of their brothers, and they were admitted, and I was never troubled again, although I gave a course of lectures every winter for twenty years. If I heard of the misconduct of a pupil anywhere, even at home, I took the liberty to let her know that I had heard of it, and as I had a perfect understanding with many parents, the pupils were often amazed at the secrets I revealed to them. The teacher, *by law*, has a right, and is under obligation, to watch over his pupils, when not under the immediate eye of their parents; and he may exercise this right, and fulfil this important obligation, without any difficulty, if he is discreet, and evidently shows that he has the good of his charge at heart. A teacher who is circumspect in his own conduct, and who is anxious for the welfare of his pupils, may be sure, I think, of the cheerful coöperation of parents and committee-men; and the more this kind of influence is exerted, the less employment will there be for the police, the less need of prisons for juvenile delinquents.

But, say some of the teachers, we have little or no intercourse with the parents, and no opportunity to coöperate with them. This shows a want of care and tact on the part of a teacher. It is not difficult to communicate with the parents through the pupils, if the teacher cannot visit them all; but if his mind is well informed, and his manners agreeable and refined, he will usually be a welcome visitor; and if he is faithful to the children, they will prepare the way for his reception at their homes. When I was a teacher, I contrived often to attract the parents and families of my pupils to the school-room, by preparing lectures or other entertainments in which they took an interest. In this way, I had constant intercourse with the parents, and the best opportunities to explain to them my modes of instruction and discipline. This was productive of another important benefit, *my own improvement;* for no man can get up as many courses of useful lectures as I did, without much study and much activity. Self-culture and constant progress is every thing to the teacher, and yet how few feel its importance!

Many inquiries of the young teachers that I met at the Institutes, convinced me that this neglect of the means of self improvement prevails to an alarming degree. Secluded as most district teachers are, it is impossible for them to become acquainted with the improved methods of instruction that are every day published, unless they read such works as are calculated to impart this information. Let me illustrate this remark by one or two examples. The Common School Journal has been published for eight years by the Secretary of the Board of Education. All the laws of the state relating to education; all the Reports of the Board, and all those of their Secretary, which are acknowledged to be unequalled by any similar papers in the world; many Reports of school-committees, and countless essays by the first teachers in the land on subjects pertaining to practical teaching, — to physical, intellectual and religious instruction, — these and similar materials fill the volumes, and render the Journal absolutely essential to the Massachusetts teacher, if not to all teachers; and yet, not one in fifty of the teachers of Massachusetts takes this Journal, or any other work on education! Not one teacher in fifty has any library that deserves the name, and how can he know what it is to study, in the true sense of the word? It will not do to say, that, if teachers do not subscribe for the Journal, they read the copy taken by their employers or neighbors; for it is a deplorable fact that only five school-committees in the state officially take the Journal, and of the 309 towns in the state about 200 do not take a single copy. I know that most of the teachers plead inability to bear the expense of one dollar a year, but they should buy the Journal to get the dollar; for the mower who has no scythe and feels too poor to buy one, will hardly grow rich. The teachers complain of low pay, but I think there is less reason than many suppose in this complaint, for the moment that a teacher increases the value of his services, he is sure to find an employer. The public will not pay him an advanced price until he has rendered himself worthy of it;

and my position enables me to say with confidence, that the demand for good teachers is fully equal to the supply.

The exertions of the Secretary of the Board of Education have done much to raise the compensation of teachers, by raising the teachers themselves; but I hesitate not to say, that had the teachers communed more with their best friend, through his writings, they would have stood much higher than they do. One or two of them have hinted to me that the Secretary aims too high, and shoots above them, and they would have him come down to their standard; but how clear it is that such a course would keep them down. Our great Master recommends to them to take the lowest seats, but I no where read that when the master of the feast says to them, "Come up higher," they must decline the invitation, and ask him to come down to them.

One other fact shows the inertness of the teachers in regard to the means of self-culture. There are six thousand teachers in the state, and yet hardly fifty of them are found at the Normal Schools, the greater part of the pupils at these schools being young persons who have never taught. I am aware that many young teachers may with justice urge the expense of *board* at these schools, — the *tuition* being free, — as a reason for not attending them; but when, with ever watchful care, the Board of Education placed almost at their doors the Teachers' Institutes, how few came forward to enjoy these advantages, compared with the number who needed instruction, and might have been accommodated.

From numerous letters received by me, and from much personal intercourse with the young teachers who did attend these important meetings, I am satisfied that, at future Institutes, there will be less ground for this complaint. The members of the ten Institutes that have been held, appear to have gone to their fields of labor encouraged and invigorated; and I know that their districts have felt the good effects of the impulse given in the short sessions of these temporary Normal Schools. Such was the satisfaction of the Barnstable Convention of the Friends of Education, who in a body attended the Institute at Harwich, and such their wonder that so few teachers attended, that they appointed two members of the Convention for each town of the county, to inform the teachers of the objects of the Institute, and to urge them by all means to attend the next that may be held in their vicinity. When their employers have to do this, it is high time for the teachers themselves to be moving.

MUSIC.

I HAVE already alluded to the utility of music as a religious exercise; and, although I have never attempted by example to teach this pleasing science, I may be excused for saying a few words in its favor as a branch of popular education. I think mine was the first school in which vocal music was regularly taught, after Mr. Mason, by a private experiment, had shown the practicability, as well as the utility, of the exercise. He was regularly employed in my school as long as the school was continued, and perhaps the success of his labors with my pupils, as much as any circumstance, gave that impulse to the science which has now made it a more general exercise than geography or grammar was half a century ago.

The observation of many years has satisfied me that children can be taught to sing as well, and as easily, as they can be taught to read. I do not mean to say that every child in a large school can be taught to sing equally well, for they can not be taught any study with this result; but I do mean to say, that enough of music may be taught to every child to afford him pleasure, and to assist the teacher in the general discipline of the school. Nor do I mean that every teacher can succeed equally well in learning and teaching his pupils to sing; but I do mean that every teacher may acquire some skill in music, and, by the aid of his more gifted pupils, he may make the exercise of singing extremely useful and agreeable to his pupils. The time has not yet come, but is fast approaching, when a competent knowledge of music will be considered an indispensable qualification in a district school teacher. In many towns, preference is already given, other things being equal, to one who can sing, and in many places a teacher who can not sing can not get employment. The effect of this preference has been, that hundreds who never imagined it among the number of possible things that they could sing, have corrected their mistake without much effort, and have acknowledged the additional power they thus acquired over the morals, the discipline, and the happiness of their pupils.

The power of imitation is so great that the youthful voice will remember sounds almost as easily as words. Much is said of the importance of teaching what is taught of music scientifically, and I know of but one professional teacher who has proceeded upon what I think the more easy as well as the more natural plan.* All children learn to talk before they learn to read; and singing by rote is to the reading of music what talking is to the reading of books. Many children learn to sing before they learn to read books, and shall such be precluded from exercising their sweet voices in harmony with those around them?

The main object of introducing music into schools may be attained as well by teaching children to sing by the ear as by a more scientific method; and why should a whole season be spent in acquiring this power, when it may be attained in a few days? I have seen the teacher to whom I have just alluded, go into a school where singing had never been attempted, and teach the majority of the pupils to sing several tunes in one hour. I have known him even to collect the children of a town in whose schools music never had been taught, and, in three or four lessons, prepare hundreds of them for a concert at which the parents and the citizens were delighted to attend. His plan was to select some simple melody, such as was, perhaps, familiar to the ear, unite it with some interesting words, and then sing it over several times with the children. Sometimes he sang a line at a time, the children repeating it after him, till the tune was finished; and then he would sing the whole tune with them, till they could sing it alone. As the model was good, the imitation had few faults, and the result confirmed me in my good opinion of that simultaneous exercise of reading after the teacher, which I have recommended under the head of Reading.

The style of the music should be adapted to the age, taste and acquirements, of the pupils. The infant or primary school should have simple music, easy of performance, and adapted to words of an infantile character. If exercises of the hands or feet, marching or other movements of the limbs, can be united with the music, so much the better. Such exercises are given in the Primary School Song Book, at pages 9 and

*Mr. Asa Fitz, the author of the American School Song Book, the Primary School Song Book, &c., whose books, I believe, are constructed on this plan the science coming last.

26; and any one who has seen the animation that these put into a school, will hardly be willing to substitute for them a a lesson of Time or Rhythm chalked upon the black-board, important as it is that such lessons be given at a future day.

The great secret of good order and discipline in school is full employment; and music enables the teacher to fill up even those moments which come between the regular recitations and are usually lost. Many good teachers practise music between every exercise. When the classes go out to recite, or when they return to their seats, a short song, or perhaps a single stanza. is sung. The multiplication table, as set to music by Mr. Fitz, is a favorite marching tune; and, besides the order which is thus introduced into the movements of the classes, much noise is covered up, and the children's tongues, being pleasantly engaged, are not employed in whispering and forbidden talk.

For the higher schools, music adapted to poetry of a higher order should be sung. It is the great fault of most school singing-books that the words are often so simple as to be silly. As the words thus committed to memory are usually retained while life lasts, they should be worthy of being thus retained. As far as my observation goes, children over eight years of age care very little for the sentimental babyisms that adults are so apt to think peculiarly adapted to them. I know no book which contains so many unexceptionable songs and hymns, and so great a variety of pleasing tunes, as the American School Song Book, to which I have before referred.

The amount of time which should be devoted to music must depend upon circumstances. If a hymn is sung at the beginning and end of school, and if the change of recitations is accompanied with a short tune, much exercise will be attained. A short tune immediately after recess often tranquillizes the spirits of the pupils, and prepares them for quiet labor after active recreation. All this may be done by rote, but if the teacher understands the science of music, he may have his regular time for instruction in this department, as in any other.

The sooner teachers take hold of this matter the better; for it is futile to expect the districts to employ a professional musician, as has been done in Boston, and one or two other large places. It would be easy for a town to employ some qualified citizen, the leader of the village choir, perhaps, to go from school to school once or twice a week, until the teachers felt competent to do without such assistance; but few, if any, towns will do this, and the teachers must act without regard to any such expectation.

In no one branch have I seen the necessity and utility of monitorial instruction so well illustrated as in music. I have known regular exercises to be given by a teacher who did not sing a word himself, but who operated by the agency of his better pupils. But monitors are more useful in another way. If the school is large, all the children usually form but one class, and practise together. Whether singing by rote or by rule, it will soon appear that some are far in advance of the rest. anxious to advance faster than others are prepared to go, and uneasy if they are detained, while what is familiar to them is explained, over and over again, to those less apt to learn. The teacher may, perhaps, form the class into two divisions, and give to each division half of the time before allotted to the whole; but the same evil will soon recur, if the school is large, and a further subdivision will soon be necessary, if justice is done to all. Now, I but describe my own experience when I say, that the very dullest singers will often learn faster under a good monitor than under the teacher, because they will feel more at ease, and will get more actual practice. The monitor, too, will be improved; and when the weather is pleasant, and a class idle, the monitor can take them into the open air, and thus reduce the number of those who are, perhaps, breathing over for the tenth time the atmosphere of the confined school-room.

It is remarkable how very generally the notion has prevailed, that few can learn how to sing; and yet, perhaps, no person can be found who does not amuse himself sometimes by singing or humming a tune, while not one mother in a hundred, who sings her infant to sleep, could tell a semibreve from a demi-semi-quaver. Once, the eminent gentleman with whom I had the pleasure to coöperate for so many years in my school, told me that he had only met with one pupil that he thought he could not teach. She had taken lessons with the class for three or four years, but made no progress, and never was in time or harmony with the rest. I afterwards called that scholar to me, and asked her if she loved to sing. She said, "Yes, indeed." "Do you find any difficulty in keeping time and according with the rest?" 'Not at all,' said she; "it comes perfectly easy to me."

"And you love to sing?" said I. "Yes, I do, dearly," said she. This singular instance shows that no great degree of natural ability or skill is necessary to enable one to take pleasure in music, while it shows how very rare it is to find a pupil unable to profit by instruction.

A case more encouraging to teachers happened at one of the Institutes. After I had made some remarks on the almost necessity of a teacher's being able to sing, I saw one of the young female teachers in tears. On inquiring the cause of her grief, she told me that she had long been endeavoring to qualify herself to be a teacher, and thought she had made some progress; but a teacher of music had told her she never could learn to sing, and I had just told her that singing was essential to her success, and she was now completely discouraged. I asked her to read to me, and finding that she had a good voice, and knew how to modulate it, I told her she might rely upon it that she could learn to sing. I then told her case to the teacher of music who accompanied me to that Institute, and in less than twenty-four hours, she was singing with the rest, and evidently taking pleasure in what so lately had caused her to despair.

EMULATION AND DISCIPLINE.

As it is unreasonable in adults to expect from children what they do not find in themselves, I have never objected to the judicious use of rewards as a source of emulation. The ordinary method, however, of distributing a few prizes,—such, for instance, as the distribution of the Franklin medals in the Grammar Schools of Boston,—I consider fraught with evil, and to be avoided. Whatever rewards are given, should be given justly; and the moral sense of the whole school should be satisfied. The reward should be more like the good gift that parents are said to know how to give to their children, unexpected, perhaps, and unpromised; not to elevate one child above his fellows, but to give a tangible expression of approbation, in which all the fellow-students will rejoice. I have long entertained the belief that, if school-committees would allow the pupils themselves to designate the most worthy, the selection would generally be more just, as well as more satisfactory to all concerned.

The first year of my pedagogical life, I adopted a plan, which, with trifling alteration, I continued for twenty years; and, as it effected all I desired in the way of emulation, and was never complained of in any one instance, to my knowledge, I will endeavor briefly to describe it. The basis of the system was, that every child should be rewarded in exact proportion to her desert, and the reward should be as small as it could be and have any value. To effect these two ends, I adopted the following method. A sort of currency, called *merits*, was established, and every exercise had its value. Every child knew exactly what she was entitled to in ordinary cases; and, in extraordinary cases, a fair valuation was made. The record of merits was in fact a class list, by which I could judge of the relative industry and good behavior of the pupils. As the allowance of an equal number of merits to every pupil, for a similar exercise, would have enabled the talented to get more than those less gifted, but equally meritorious, I always exercised the right to do justice in the case. For instance, if one child could write two orthographical exercises while another, doing her best, could write only one, the reward was the same for the one as for the two. As good behavior was more important than good scholarship in any branch of study, merits were given for this. Again, as teaching was a part of the employment of every pupil, the faithful monitor was paid as much for teaching as she would have earned at any study. In fine, the aggregate of merits obtained by each for industry, good behavior, monitorship, &c., determined her rank on the *merit roll*, at the end of every term. Now, I am persuaded that such a merit roll, even if not followed up by any prizes, would enable many teachers to govern a school without much, if any, resort to the infliction of physical pain; but I did not stop here.

Every term, it was understood that a certain sum, called the *merit fund*, would be distributed among the pupils, in proportion to the number of merits each had received. Of course, the value of a merit depended upon the whole number obtained by all the scholars. If the fund was ten dollars, and the number of merits sixty thousand, sixty merits would be equal to one cent. When I first adopted this plan, the merits were so few, that ten or twelve were worth a cent; but when I had taught ten years, the facility of doing every kind of exercise was so much greater, that it rarely took less than 70 or 80 merits to represent a cent. This, in a pecuniary point of view, was next to nothing; and yet it was sufficient to induce every pupil to take good care of her exercises, as well as to write them, and it led to a more careful attention to the school record. Besides these merits, we had also what we called *demerits*, which were given for misconduct, careless exercises, neglected lessons, &c. These were recorded, also, and, if unatoned for, were deducted from the scholar's merits at the end of the term. As I soon knew the character and capacity of every pupil, and had, moreover, the advice of my monitors, it was easy to do justice to every child; and as the pupils knew that I aimed to be just and impartial, I never heard any complaint.

At the end of the term, every child was required to bring up such exercises as had been written or drawn, or otherwise preserved, neatly filed, as vouchers for the merits she claimed. These exercises had all been examined by me, and the merits they were entitled to, awarded at the time they were corrected. Then all the class lists on which the lessons recited, mistakes made, &c., had been recorded from day to day, were added up, and merits awarded. Next, the record of conduct was attended to; that of absence and tardiness, &c. Sometimes monitors would report pupils as having made extraordinary efforts to improve; sometimes acts of kindness, forbearance, disinterestedness, &c., would be reported, inquired into, and rewarded: and the consequence was, that character became a matter of some importance, and her due rank was assigned to every pupil. After a little practice, all this required but little time; so little, indeed, that a visitor would hardly have noticed that any record was kept in the school.

This was the system by which I governed about a hundred pupils for eighteen or twenty years, without once resorting to corporal punishment of any kind. If any one has fears that other evils, worse than physical pain, were induced by this course of discipline, I can only say, that I never saw any ill effects; and whether I should have been likely to see or hear, by myself or my monitors, the reader may judge.

The district teacher may not often find a committee ready and willing to make a small grant for the purpose of carrying out this system, and he may not feel able to appropriate a small sum for this purpose from his wages; but he will do well to try the system without attaching any pecuniary value to the merits. So evident was the good effect of this system at school, that several parents adopted it at home, with similar results, in the government of their children.

It will be observed that this is a sort of medium between that system of fear which brutalizes the pupil, by treating him as one void of understanding, and that transcendental system which expects him to do well from the mere love of right and truth and goodness. It is not a mere theory, for I have tested it successfully for twenty years; it is not applicable only to one class of children, for I tried it with equal success upon the unfortunate children of my first school, and upon the middling and higher classes of my second. I believe it is fully competent, in the hands of a discreet and patient teacher, to maintain order and encourage industry in any district school, and I recommended a trial of it to the teachers at some of the Institutes. At all of these, the subject of corporal punishment was freely discussed, and I was surprised at the prevalence of the milder system. I had a good opportunity to learn the opinions and the practice of the young teachers, and I know I speak within bounds when I say, that half of them disclaimed the use of corporal punishment altogether, and all considered it the lowest and last resort of the teacher.

Can it be, as some pretend, that in introducing a milder system of discipline, one that appeals more to the reason and conscience of the pupil, and less to his physical susceptibility to pain, we are "throwing ourselves across the Word of God," "treading the Bible under foot," "rejecting the inspiration of the Scriptures," and making "infidel factories of our common schools?" If I thought there was any truth in this charge, any tendency to this terrible result, I should be the last man to persevere in the course I have recommended. The charge is absurd, but it has been often and very lately reiterated, and it is of such moment that I hope to be pardoned if I say a few words in regard to it.

All the defenders of corporal punishment have agreed in citing the precepts of Solomon, as the principal, if not the only *direct* command or authority, for the infliction of bodily pain upon children, and the passages most relied on are the following:

Prov. xiii. 24. "He that spareth his rod hateth his son; but he that loveth him chasteneth him betimes."

Prov. xix. 18. "Chasten thy son while there is hope, and let not thy soul spare for his crying."

Prov. xxii. 15. "Foolishness is bound in the heart of a child, but the rod of correction shall drive it far from him."

Prov. xxix. 15. "The rod and reproof give wisdom."

Prov. xxiii. 13. "Withhold not correction from the child; for if hou beatest him with the rod, he shall not die."

14. "Thou shalt beat him with the rod, and shalt deliver his soul from hell."

The argument assumes that these precepts, and a few others found in the Old Testament, are the commands of God, and of perpetual obligation, and any attempt to lessen their obligation, even upon those not under the Law, is impiety, if not fatal heresy. One writer, in a religious paper, went so far as to assert, that it was the duty of every man to use the rod, whether his child deserved it or not.

The milder system of discipline rests its defence upon such passages as the following, from the New Testament, but more especially upon the milder *spirit* that pervades the teachings of the Gospel.

1 Peter iii. 8. "Be ye all of one mind, having compassion one of another; love as brethren, be pitiful, be courteous; *not rendering evil for evil*, but contrariwise, blessing."

1 Thess. v. 14. "Now we exhort you, brethren, *warn* them that

are unruly; comfort the feeble-minded; support the weak; *be patient toward all.* See that none render evil for evil unto any."

Romans, xii. 17. "Recompense to no man evil for evil." 19. "Dearly beloved, avenge not yourselves, but give place unto wrath; for it is written, Vengeance is mine, I will repay, saith the Lord." 21. "Be not overcome of evil, but overcome evil with good."

Matt. v. 39. Jesus says, "I say unto you that ye resist not evil."

Matt. xviii. 21. "Peter said, Lord, how oft shall my brother sin against me and I forgive him, till seven times? Jesus saith unto him, I say not unto thee till seven times, but until seventy times seven."

Luke xvii. 3. "If thy brother trespass against thee, rebuke him; and if he repent, forgive him. And if he trespass against thee seven times in a day, and seven times in a day turn again to thee, saying, I repent; thou shalt forgive him."

Mark xi. 26. "If ye do not forgive, neither will your Father which is in heaven forgive your trespasses."

2 Tim. i. 7. "For God hath not given us the spirit of *fear;* but of power, and of *love*, and of a sound mind."

1 John iv. 16. "God is love." 18. "There is no fear in love."

Ephes. iv. 15. "Speaking the truth in love."

There is not a word in the New Testament about the literal use of the rod; and the figurative prophecy of Isaiah was literally fulfilled, when, as if contrasting the rod of the ancient system with that of the Gospel, he says, "There shall come forth a rod out of the stem of Jesse — and he shall smite the earth with the *rod of his mouth.*"

Now I do not conceive the belief in the plenary inspiration of the Scriptures to be at all affected by the entire disuse of the rod. It seems to me that St. Paul knew the bearing of his words, when he said to the Hebrews, to reconcile them to giving up the law of Moses, "God, who at sundry times, and in divers manners, spake in time past unto the fathers by the prophets, hath in these last days spoken unto us by his Son, whom he hath appointed heir of all things, by whom also he made the worlds," &c. This passage conveys to my mind the doctrine, that God spake by the prophet Moses, and gave such instruction as befitted the condition of our race at that remote period; that, by subsequent prophets, he gave more and more light, but the full revelation came not until the Son of God himself came among men. "The *law* was given by Moses, but *grace* and *truth* came by Jesus Christ."

The very fact that a second revelation was made, proves that the former one was not complete; but it does not prove that holy men did not speak as they were moved by the Holy

Spirit. Jesus, in educating his disciples, says to them, as God might have said "to them of old time," "I have many things to say unto you, but ye cannot bear them now." Paul says to Timothy, when speaking of the Old Testament, "From a child thou hast known the Holy Scriptures, [of the Old Testament,] which are able to make thee wise unto salvation," not of themselves, "but *through faith which is in Christ Jesus.*"

In accordance with this view, is that other declaration of Paul to the Galatians, iii. 23: "Before faith came, we were kept under the law, shut up unto the faith *which should afterwards be revealed.* Wherefore, the law was our schoolmaster, to bring us unto Christ; but after that faith is come, we are no longer under a schoolmaster." It by no means follows, therefore, that, because the Gospel, "in these last days," spoke more clearly or more mildly than the law had done two thousand years before, Moses was any the less inspired.

The Proverbs that I have cited are attributed to Solomon, and if he was one of the prophets alluded to by Paul, and even superior to Moses in the gift of the Holy Spirit, this would not weaken my position; for Jesus himself told the Jews that the conduct of the Queen of Sheba condemned them, for she went to hear only the wisdom of Solomon; but, added he, "*a greater than Solomon is here.*"

It seems to me that the gospel of Jesus not only revealed to us the true character of God, viz., that of a tender Father, but it revealed much in regard to the relation of parent to child, of man to man, and of man to God. Hence, Solomon tells us, what no doubt was true in his experience, that, "Foolishness is bound in the heart of a child, but the rod of correction shall drive it from him;" but our Saviour takes little children in his arms, and blesses them, and declares that "of such is the kingdom of heaven." Nay, he even sets one of the little ones up before his disciples, and tells them that unless they become such, they cannot *enter* into his kingdom.

It would be unsafe, also, as well as unnecessary, it appears to me, to assume that every precept of Solomon is binding upon those who believe the Gospel; for the consequence would be terrible indeed. For instance; Solomon, alluding to the Law of Moses, says, Prov. xx. 20, "Whoso curseth his father or his mother, his lamp shall be put out in obscure darkness." We are bound, then, to put disobedient children to death, if the Gospel has not taught us otherwise. We find no such thing under the new dispensation, but we have the mild precept, "Children, obey your parents," not through fear of being stoned to death, but for the *reason* given by the apostle, viz., "This is right," "This is well-pleasing unto the Lord." "The law and the prophets were" only "until John, and since that time, the kingdom of God is preached."

Other precepts of Solomon and Moses, seem to me to have been superseded by those of Jesus and his apostles; and, therefore, when Jesus says, that "One jot or one tittle shall in no wise pass from the law, till all be fulfilled," I am led to think that all was fulfilled, when, on the cross, the Redeemer declared that "it was finished."

The law of Moses evidently allowed retaliation, but if I understand the spirit of the Gospel, it is there expressly forbidden. "Ye have heard that it hath been said, an eye for an eye, and a tooth for a tooth; but I say unto you, that ye resist not evil." If this does not directly repeal the retaliatory clauses of the Mosaic law, I know not how to read. Again, the Jews were under the yoke of the law, and Christ says to them, "Take my yoke upon you, and learn of me; for my yoke is easy, and my burden is light." Here are two yokes, and one is to be rejected, because both cannot be worn. The masters are so different, that no man can serve them both. I will name but one other instance of many that crowd upon my memory. Solomon says, Eccles. iii. 19, that men die like the beasts. "Yea, they have all one *breath*," "so that a man hath no preëminence above a beast;" and he asks, tauntingly, "Who knoweth that the *spirit* of man goeth upward, and that the *spirit* of the beast goeth downward to the earth?" Nothing shows more clearly than such a sentence, what is meant by the glorious truth, that, "Life and Immortality are brought to light by the Gospel."

If I read my Bible aright, the human race has been educated like a child, and the divers speakings of God to it have been adapted to its state of progress. It seems to me, that the question of the plenary inspiration of Moses or Solomon is not affected by the fact that the grace of God has revealed more of his will since they were inspired to speak; but, at any rate, I feel bound to follow the teachings of the Saviour, in whom alone dwelt the fulness of the Godhead bodily.

Is it not evident, therefore, that the "sundry times" have been those of Moses, of the Prophets and of Jesus Christ;

that the "divers manners" were those of the Law, the Prophets and the Gospel? and is it not also evident, that we must receive the latest revelation as we do human laws required by the progress of civilization and humanity, to which are usually appended the provision, that "all laws or portions of laws inconsistent with the last are, by its enaction, repealed?"

I know it will be said,—for it has just been said by the editor of a new religious magazine, got up mainly to keep the rod in the schools,—that God, in his providence, inflicts physical pain, and our Saviour, once at least, made a whip and drove those who sold cattle from the temple. But if any one thing is evidently taught by our Saviour, it is, that God does not punish moral offences by inflicting physical pain. Even the ancient Scriptures assert, that sinners live and die like other men: "There is one event to the righteous and the wicked;" and who dares say that God does *not* send his rain on the unjust as well as on the just? Some physical excesses, to be sure, draw their punishment after them; but the tower of Siloam did not fall on certain men because they were sinners above all others; the man was *not* born blind because he or his parents had sinned. Those who have urged this argument have also expressed the utmost horror at that tenet of one portion of the Universalists, which asserts that sin carries its punishment with it in this world, and, this obviates the necessity of a future judgment; yet this tenet is confirmed by that which considers physical evil as the punishment of moral guilt; so true is it that extremes are most apt to meet. In regard to the alleged violence used by our Saviour, it should be known that the original Greek, and some translations, authorize no such wrong to the gentle character of the blessed Redeemer; but only assert that he made a whip of *small* cords, that is, he used small cords as a whip, to drive the *animals*, and not the men, from the temple. Even our translation may mean this; but the French protestant version reads thus: "He drove all out of the temple, both the sheep and the bulls." So says the Greek, so says the Vulgate, so says Beza, and so would our common English version say, if the word *them* were printed in Italic type, as words generally are that were inserted by the translators on their own authority, and if, as in Tindal's early and excellent version, the first *and* were rendered by *both*, according to our idiom.

Were it not so perfectly evident that the translation is at fault in regard to the conduct of the Prince of Peace, it seems to me that the whole course of his benignant teaching, the whole tenor of his patient, long-suffering and unaggressive life, should have saved him from the charge; and yet, to support a practice which the spirit of the Gospel has long been silently repudiating, some men have been willing to affix a stigma to the character of Jesus entirely at variance with every word, and with every other act of his life.

Those who have not been satisfied with the Scripture argument for corporal punishment, have urged another, that would deserve serious consideration, if the fact on which it is based were true. We are told that vice and crime are on the increase, and that this deterioration of morals can only be accounted for by the great progress of the milder system of discipline within a few years.

Now, it is by no means certain that there is any increase of crime beyond the natural increase of population, and the unusual increase of uneducated foreigners. On the contrary, the facts, that there has been great general improvement in all the schools of the state, as proved by the annual Abstracts of School Returns; that every year the number of schools broken up by the insubordination of pupils has greatly diminished; and that many hundreds, even of winter schools, have been taught, and easily managed, by females; would indicate a great improvement in the state, even if, in one or two large towns, the criminal calendar may seem to have increased. But, were we to grant that crime has increased, it would not follow that the milder discipline of the schools has been the cause of it, unless it also follows that a more direct attempt to educate the conscience, the affections, and the higher sentiments of a child, has a tendency to reduce him nearer to the level of the beasts that perish. The fact is, that vice and crime abound most where the lenient system of discipline complained of has never been approved, has never prevailed.

It should be remembered, too, that whenever the use of the rod is recommended in the ancient Scriptures, it is to be in the hands of *parents;* for there were no schools nor schoolmasters in those days. It is hardly probable that Solomon would have urged so strongly the exercise of the rod, had he not known that the natural feelings of the parent would sometimes be averse to even reasonable chastisement. I know it will be objected that the teacher stands in the parent's place; and so he does to a certain degree, and it is sometimes fortunate that he does; but he can not have the natural affection of a parent; his office was unknown in the age of Solomon, and, therefore, no precept of Solomon can, with justice, be applied to the intercourse between teacher and pupil, which is the subject under consideration.

I should not, as some do, recommend the disuse of the rod without allowing the free use of other motives. Of these, there is a choice, and the highest that will move the child should always be preferred. I do not allow the infliction of physical pain to be an intellectual motive, and, therefore, I never use it in the discipline of beings that have minds, and hearts, and consciences, and souls. If I err in this, I err on the side of humanity. I do not act contrary to what I consider to be the *spirit* of my Divine Master. I do not act, as some seem to think, from any perverse wish to go wrong, or from any disrespect to the revealed will of God.

I hope I shall be excused for attempting, less briefly than I could wish, to remove the fears of those whose tenderness of conscience may have prevented them from cultivating that tenderness of disposition which prefers long suffering, patience and kindness, to the free use of the rod. I have never maintained that there may not be good schools where the rod is applied; I have never maintained that a teacher, who did not know what else to do, might not resort to the rod till he was better informed. I am no lover of confusion, no apologist for disobedience, but one who believes sincerely that the fear of bodily pain, though producing temporary submission, rarely produces any change in the moral condition of the offender. I reason from my own experience when a pupil; from my own experience as a teacher; from the confession of other teachers, who have used the rod, and of pupils who have been subjected to it; I reason, in fine, from what, after much study, I believe to be the real instruction of the Bible on the subject; and having no interest in the question, except the love of children, the love of teachers, and the love of truth, I trust my character will not suffer because I honestly express my convictions.

THE CONCLUSION.

I HAVE thus, in great haste, given my thoughts upon such points as were agitated at the Teachers' Institutes, and I can only hope that my book will be received by the younger part of the profession with as much kindness and respect as was shown to my personal instructions. I have much more to say, but I fear that I have already exceeded the limits of a school manual. In taking leave of my young friends, I would, therefore, only add, that the faithful teacher, on every plan, has much to do and much to endure. He must be contented to labor and be ill-rewarded; he must be willing to see his pupils increase while he decreases; and even to see the world, whose movement he has accelerated, leaving him behind. No matter; — the school of life lasts not long, and its best rewards are reserved till school is over.

When Jupiter offered the prize of immortality to him who was most useful to mankind, the court of Olympus was crowded with competitors. The warrior boasted of his patriotism, but Jupiter thundered; — the rich man boasted of his munificence, and Jupiter showed him a widow's mite; — the pontiff held up the keys of heaven, and Jupiter pushed the doors wide open; — the painter boasted of his power to give life to inanimate canvass, and Jupiter breathed aloud in derision; — the sculptor boasted of making gods that contended with the Immortals for human homage; Jupiter frowned; — the orator boasted of his power to sway a nation with his voice, and Jupiter marshalled the obedient hosts of heaven with a nod; — the poet spoke of his power to move even the gods by praise; Jupiter blushed; — the musician claimed to practise the only human science that had been transported to heaven; Jupiter hesitated, — when, seeing a venerable man looking with intense interest upon the group of competitors, but presenting no claim, — "What art thou?" said the benignant monarch. "Only a spectator," said the gray-headed sage; "all these were once my pupils." "*Crown* him crown *him!*" said Jupiter; "crown the faithful *teacher* with immortality, and make room for him at my right hand!"

THE NATIONAL SERIES OF READERS.

COMPLETE IN TWO INDEPENDENT PARTS.

I.
THE NATIONAL READERS.

By PARKER & WATSON.

No. 1.—National Primer, ... *64 pp., 16mo,*
No. 2.—National First Reader, . . . *128 pp., 16mo,*
No. 3.—National Second Reader, . . *224 pp., 16mo,*
No. 4.—National Third Reader, . . *288 pp., 12mo,*
No. 5.—National Fourth Reader, . . *432 pp., 12mo,*
No. 6.—National Fifth Reader, . . *600 pp., 12mo,*

National Elementary Speller, . . . *160 pp., 16mo,*
National Pronouncing Speller, . . . *188 pp., 12mo,*

II.
THE INDEPENDENT READERS.

By J. MADISON WATSON.

The Independent First (or Primary) Reader, *80 pp., 16mo,*
The Independent Second Reader, . *160 pp., 16mo,*
The Independent Third Reader, . . *240 pp., 16mo,*
The Independent Fourth Reader, . . *264 pp., 12mo,*
The Independent Fifth Reader, . . *336 pp., 12mo,*
The Independent Sixth Reader, . . *474 pp., 12mo,*

The Independent Child's Speller (Script), *80 pp., 16mo,*
The Independent Youth's Speller (Script), *168 pp., 12mo,*
The Independent Spelling Book, . . *160 pp., 16mo,*

*** The Readers constitute two complete and entirely distinct series, either of which is adequate to every want of the best schools. The Spellers may accompany either Series.

PARKER & WATSON'S NATIONAL READERS.

The salient features of these works which have combined to render them so popular may be briefly recapitulated as follows:

1. **THE WORD-BUILDING SYSTEM.**—This famous progressive method for young children originated and was copyrighted with these books. It constitutes a process with which the beginner with *words* of one letter is gradually introduced to additional lists formed by prefixing or affixing single letters, and is thus led almost insensibly to the mastery of the more difficult constructions. This is one of the most striking modern improvements in methods of teaching.

2. **TREATMENT OF PRONUNCIATION.**—The wants of the youngest scholars in this department are not overlooked. It may be said that from the first lesson the student by this method need never be at a loss for a prompt and accurate rendering of every word encountered.

3. **ARTICULATION AND ORTHOEPY** are considered of primary importance.

4. **PUNCTUATION** is inculcated by a series of interesting *reading lessons*, the simple perusal of which suffices to fix its principles indelibly upon the mind.

5. **ELOCUTION.** Each of the higher Readers (3d, 4th and 5th) contains elaborate, scholarly, and thoroughly practical treatises on elocution. This feature alone has secured for the series many of its warmest friends.

6. **THE SELECTIONS** are the crowning glory of the series. Without exception it may be said that no volumes of the same size and character contain a collection so diversified, judicious, and artistic as this. It embraces the choicest gems of English literature, so arranged as to afford the reader ample exercise in every department of style. So acceptable has the taste of the authors in this department proved, not only to the educational public but to the reading community at large, that thousands of copies of the Fourth and Fifth Readers have found their way into public and private libraries throughout the country, where they are in constant use as manuals of literature, for reference as well as perusal.

7. **ARRANGEMENT.** The exercises are so arranged as to present constantly alternating practice in the different styles of composition, while observing a definite plan of progression or gradation throughout the whole. In the higher books the articles are placed in formal sections and classified topically, thus concentrating the interest and inculcating a principle of association likely to prove valuable in subsequent general reading.

8. **NOTES AND BIOGRAPHICAL SKETCHES.** These are full and adequate to every want. The biographical sketches present in pleasing style the history of every author laid under contribution.

9. **ILLUSTRATIONS.** These are plentiful, almost profuse, and of the highest character of art. They are found in every volume of the series as far as and including the Third Reader.

10. **THE GRADATION** is perfect. Each volume overlaps its companion preceding or following in the series, so that the scholar, in passing from one to another, is only conscious, by the presence of the new book, of the transition.

11. **THE PRICE** is reasonable. The National Readers contain more matter than any other series in the same number of volumes published. Considering their completeness and thoroughness they are much the cheapest in the market.

12. **BINDING.** By the use of a material and process known only to themselves, in common with all the publications of this house, the National Readers are warranted to outlast any with which they may be compared—the ratio of relative durability being in their favor as two to one.

WATSON'S INDEPENDENT READERS.

This Series is designed to meet a general demand for smaller and cheaper books than the National Series proper, and to serve as well for intermediate volumes of the National Readers in large graded schools requiring more books than one ordinary series will supply.

Beauty. The most casual observer is at once impressed with the unparalleled mechanical beauty of the Independent Readers. The Publishers believe that the æsthetic tastes of children may receive no small degree of cultivation from their very earliest school books, to say nothing of the importance of making study attractive by all such artificial aids that are legitimate. In accordance with this view, not less than $25,000 was expended in their preparation before publishing, with a result which entitles them to be considered "The Perfection of Common School Books."

Selections. They contain, of course, none but entirely new selections. These are arranged according to a strictly progressive and novel method of developing the elementary sounds in order in the lower numbers, and in all, with a view to topics and general literary style. The mind is thus led in fixed channels to proficiency in every branch of good reading, and the evil results of 'scattering' as practised by most school-book authors, avoided.

The Illustrations, as may be inferred from what has been said, are elegant beyond comparison. They are profuse in every number of the series from the lowest to the highest. This is the only series published of which this is true.

The Type is semi-phonetic, the invention of Prof. Watson. By it every letter having more than one sound is clearly distinguished in all its variations without in any way mutilating or disguising the normal form of the letter.

Elocution is taught by prefatory treatises of constantly advancing grade and completeness in each volume, which are illustrated by wood-cuts in the lower books, and by black-board diagrams in the higher. Prof. Watson is the first to introduce Practical Illustrations and Black-board Diagrams for teaching this branch.

Foot Notes on every page afford all the incidental instruction which the teacher is usually required to impart. Indices of words refer the pupil to the place of their first use and definition. The Biographies of Authors and others are in every sense excellent.

Economy. Although the number of pages in each volume is fixed at the minimum, for the purpose recited above, the utmost amount of matter available without overcrowding is obtained in the space. The pages are much wider and larger than those of any competitor and contain *twenty per cent* more matter than any other series of the same type and number of pages.

All the Great Features. Besides the above all the popular features of the National Readers are retained except the Word-Building system. The latter gives place to an entirely new method of progressive development, based upon some of the best features of the Word System, Phonetics and Object Lessons.

NATIONAL READERS.

ORIGINAL AND "INDEPENDENT" SERIES.

SPECIMEN TESTIMONIALS.

From D. H. Harris, *Supt. Public Schools, Hannibal, Mo.*

The National Series of Readers are now in use in our public schools, and I regard them *the best* that I have ever examined or used.

From Hon. J. K. Jillson, *Supt. of Education, State of South Carolina.*

I have carefully examined your new and beautiful Series of Readers known as "The Independent Readers," and do not hesitate to recommend it as the finest and most excellent ever presented to the public.

From D. N. Rook, *Sec. of School Board, Williamsport, Pa.*

I would say that Parker & Watson's Series of Readers and Spellers give the best satisfaction in our schools of any Series of Readers and Spellers that have ever been used. There is nothing published for which we would exchange them

From Prof. H. Seele, *New Braunfels Academy, Texas.*

I recommend the National Readers for four good reasons: (1.) The printing, engraving, and binding is excellent. (2.) They contain choice selections from English Literature. (3.) They inculcate good morals without any sectarian bias. (4.) They are truly *National*, because they teach pure patriotism and not sectional prejudice.

From S. Findley, *Supt. Akron Schools, Ohio.*

We use no others, and have no desire to. They give entire satisfaction. We like the freshness and excellence of the selections. We like the biographical notes and the definitions at the foot of the page. We also like the white paper and clear and beautiful type. In short, we do not know where to look for books which would be so satisfactory both to teachers and pupils.

From Pres. Robert Allyn, *McKendree College, Ill.*

Since my connection with this college, we have used in our preparatory department the Series of Readers known as the "National Readers," compiled by Parker & Watson, and published by Messrs. A. S. Barnes & Co. They are *excellent;* afford choice selections; contain the right system of elocutionary instruction, and are well printed and bound so as to be serviceable as well as interesting. I can commend them as among the excellent means used by teachers to make their pupils proficient in that noblest of school arts, Good Reading.

From W. T. Harris, *Supt. Public Schools, St. Louis, Mo.*

I have to admire these excellent selections in prose and verse, and the careful arrangement which places first what is easy of comprehension, and proceeds gradually to what is difficult. I find the lessons so arranged as to bring together different treatments of the same topic, thereby throwing much light on the pupil's path, and I doubt not adding greatly to his progress. The proper variety of subjects chosen, the concise treatise on elocution, the beautiful typography and substantial binding—all these I find still more admirable than in the former series of National Readers, which I considered *models* in these respects.

From H. T. Phillips, Esq., *of the Board of Education, Atlanta, Ga.*

The Board of Education of this city have selected for use in the public schools of Atlanta the entire series of your Independent Readers, together with Steele's Chemistry and Philosophy. As a member of the Board, and of the Committee on Text-books, the subject of Readers was referred to me for examination. I gave a pretty thorough examination to ten (10) different series of Readers, and in endeavoring to arrive at a decision upon the sole question of merit, and entirely independent of any extraneous influence, I very cordially recommended the Independent Series. This verdict was approved by the Committee and adopted by the Board.

From Report of Rev. W. T. Brantly, D.D., *late Professor of Belles Lettres, University of Georgia, on "Text-Books in Reading," before the Teachers' Convention of Georgia, May 4, 1870.*

The *National Series*, by Parker & Watson, is deserving of its high reputation. The Primary Books are suited to the weakest capacity; whilst those more advanced supply instructive illustration on all that is needed to be known in connection with the art.

WATSON'S CHILD'S SPELLER.

THE INDEPENDENT CHILD'S SPELLER.

This unique book, published in 1872, is the first to be consistently printed in imitation of writing; that is, it teaches orthography as we use it. It is for the smallest class of learners, who soon become familiarized with words by their forms, and learn to read writing while they spell.

EXTRACT FROM THE PREFACE.

Success in teaching English orthography is still exceptional, and it must so continue until the principles involved are recognized in practice. Form is foremost: the eye and the hand must be trained to the formation of words; and since spelling is a part of writing, the written form only should be used. The laws of mental association, also—especially those of resemblance, contrast, and contiguity in time and place—should receive such recognition in the construction of the text-book as shall insure, whether consciously or not, their appropriate use and legitimate results. Hence, the spelling-book, properly arranged, is a necessity from the first; and, though primers, readers, and dictionaries may serve as aids, it can have no competent substitute.

Consistently with these views, the words used in the Independent Child's Speller have such original classifications and arrangements in columns—in reference to location, number of letters, vowel sounds, alphabetic equivalents, and consonant terminations—as exhibit most effectively their formation and pronunciation. The vocabulary is strictly confined to the simple and significant monosyllables in common use. He who has mastered these may easily learn how to spell and pronounce words of more than one syllable.

The introduction is an illustrated alphabet in script, containing twenty-six pictures of objects, and their names, commencing both with capitals and small letters. Part First embraces the words of one, two, and three letters; Part Second, the words of four letters; and Part Third, other monosyllables. They are divided into short lists and arranged in columns, the vowels usually in line, so as to exhibit individual characteristics and similarity of formation. The division of words into paragraphs is shown by figures in the columns. Each list is immediately followed by sentences for reading and writing, in which the same words are again presented with irregularities of form and sound. Association is thus employed, memory tested, and definition most satisfactorily taught.

Among the novel and valuable features of the lessons and exercises, probably the most prominent are their adaptedness for young children and their being printed in exact imitation of writing. The author believes that hands large enough to spin a top, drive a hoop, or catch a ball, are not too small to use a crayon, or a slate and pencil; that the child's natural desire to draw and write should not be thwarted, but gratified, encouraged, and wisely directed; and that since the written form is the one actually used in connection with spelling in after-life, the eye and the hand of the child should be trained to that form from the first. He hopes that this little work, designed to precede all other spelling-books and conflict with none, may satisfy the need so universally recognized of a fit introduction to orthography, penmanship, and English composition.

The National Readers and Spellers.

THEIR RECORD.

These books have been adopted by the School Boards, or official authority, of the following important States, cities, and towns—in most cases for exclusive use.

The State of Missouri. **The State of Kentucky.**
The State of Alabama.
The State of Florida. **The State of North Carolina.**
The State of Delaware. **The State of Louisiana.**

New York.
New York City.
Brooklyn.
Buffalo.
Albany.
Rochester.
Troy.
Syracuse.
Elmira.
&c., &c.

Pennsylvania.
Reading.
Lancaster.
Erie.
Scranton.
Carlisle.
Carbondale.
Westchester.
Schuylkill Haven.
Williamsport.
Norristown.
Bellefonte.
Wilkesbarre.
&c., &c.

New Jersey.
Newark.
Jersey City.
Paterson.
Trenton.
Camden.
Elizabeth.
New Brunswick.
Phillipsburg.
Orange.
&c., &c.

Delaware.
Wilmington.

D. C.
Washington.

Illinois.
Chicago.
Peoria.
Alton.
Springfield.
Aurora.
Galesburg.
Rockford.
Rock Island.
&c., &c.

Wisconsin.
Milwaukee.
Fond du Lac.
Oshkosh.
Janesville.
Racine.
Watertown.
Sheboygan.
La Crosse.
Waukesha.
Kenosha.
&c., &c.

Michigan.
Grand Rapids.
Kalamazoo.
Adrian.
Jackson.
Monroe.
Lansing.
&c., &c.

Ohio.
Toledo.
Sandusky.
Conneaut.
Chardon.
Hudson.
Canton.
Salem.
&c., &c.

Indiana.
New Albany.
Fort Wayne.
Lafayette.
Madison.
Logansport.
Indianapolis.

Iowa.
Davenport.
Burlington.
Muscatine.
Mount Pleasant.
&c.

Nebraska.
Brownsville.
Lincoln.
&c.

Oregon.
Portland.
Salem.
&c.

Virginia.
Richmond.
Norfolk.
Petersburg.
Lynchburg.
&c.

South Carolina
Columbia.
Charleston.

Georgia.
Savannah.

Louisiana.
New Orleans.

Tennessee
Memphis

The *Educational Bulletin* records periodically all new points gained.

SCHOOL-ROOM CARDS.

Baade's Reading Case,

A frame containing movable cards, with arrangement for showing one sentence at a time, capable of 28,000 transpositions.

Eureka Alphabet Tablet

Presents the alphabet upon the Word Method System, by which the child will learn the alphabet in nine days, and make no small progress in reading and spelling in the same time.

National School Tablets, 10 Nos.

Embrace reading and conversational exercises, object and moral lessons, form, color, &c. A complete set of these large and elegantly illustrated Cards will embellish the school-room more than any other article of furniture.

READING.

Fowle's Bible Reader

The narrative portions of the Bible, chronologically and topically arranged, judiciously combined with selections from the Psalms, Proverbs, and other portions which inculcate important moral lessons or the great truths of Christianity. The embarrassment and difficulty of reading the Bible itself, by course, as a class exercise, are obviated, and its use made feasible, by this means.

North Carolina First Reader
North Carolina Second Reader
North Carolina Third Reader

Prepared expressly for the schools of this State, by C. H. Wiley, Superintendent of Common Schools, and F. M. Hubbard, Professor of Literature in the State University.

Parker's Rhetorical Reader

Designed to familiarize Readers with the pauses and other marks in general use, and lead them to the practice of modulation and inflection of the voice.

Introductory Lessons in Reading and Elocution

Of similar character to the foregoing, for less advanced classes.

High School Literature

Admirable selections from a long list of the world's best writers, for exercise in reading, oratory, and composition. Speeches, dialogues, and model letters represent the latter department.

ORTHOGRAPHY.

SMITH'S SERIES

Supplies a speller for every class in graded schools, and comprises the most complete and excellent treatise on English Orthography and its companion branches extant.

1. Smith's Little Speller .

First Round in the Ladder of Learning.

2. Smith's Juvenile Definer

Lessons composed of familiar words grouped with reference to similar signification or use, and correctly spelled, accented, and defined.

3. Smith's Grammar-School Speller

Familiar words, grouped with reference to the sameness of sound of syllables differently spelled. Also definitions, complete rules for spelling and formation of derivatives, and exercises in false orthography.

4. Smith's Speller and Definer's Manual

A complete *School Dictionary* containing 14,000 words, with various other useful matter in the way of Rules and Exercises.

5. Smith's Etymology—Small, and Complete Ed's.

The first and only Etymology to recognize the *Anglo-Saxon* our *mother tongue;* containing also full lists of derivatives from the Latin, Greek, Gaelic, Swedish, Norman, &c., &c ; being, in fact, a complete etymology of the language for schools.

Sherwood's Writing Speller
Sherwood's Speller and Definer
Sherwood's Speller and Pronouncer

The Writing Speller consists of properly ruled and numbered blanks to receive the words dictated by the teacher, with space for remarks and corrections. The other volumes may be used for the dictation or ordinary class exercises.

Price's English Speller

A complete spelling-book for all grades, containing more matter than "Webster," manufactured in superior style, and sold at a lower price—consequently the cheapest speller extant.

Northend's Dictation Exercises

Embracing valuable information on a thousand topics, communicated in such a manner as at once to relieve the exercise of spelling of its usual tedium, and combine it with instruction of a general character calculated to profit and amuse.

Wright's Analytical Orthography

This standard work is popular, because it teaches the elementary sounds in a plain and philosophical manner, and presents orthography and orthoepy in an easy, uniform system of analysis or parsing.

Fowle's False Orthography

Exercises for correction.

Page's Normal Chart

The elementary sounds of the language for the school-room walls.

ORTHOGRAPHY—Continued.

Barber's Complete Writing Speller

"The Student's Own Hand-Book of Orthography, Definitions, and Sentences, consisting of Written Exercises in the Proper Spelling, Meaning, and Use of Words." (Published 1873.) This differs from Sherwood's and other Writing Spellers in its more comprehensive character. Its blanks are adapted to writing whole sentences instead of detached words, with the proper divisions for numbering, corrections, etc. Such aids as this, like Watson's Child's Speller and Sherwood's Writing Speller, find their *raison d'être* in the postulate that the art of correct spelling is dependent upon written, and not upon spoken language, for its utility, if not for its very existence. Hence the indirectness of purely oral instruction.

Pooler's Test Speller

The best collection of "hard words" yet made. The more uncommon ones are fully defined, and the whole are *arranged alphabetically* for convenient reference. The book is designed for Teachers' Institutes and 'Spelling Schools," and is prepared by an experienced and well-known conductor of Institutes.

ETYMOLOGY.

Smith's Complete Etymology,
Smith's Condensed Etymology,

Containing the Anglo-Saxon, French, Dutch, German, Welsh, Danish, Gothic, Swedish, Gaelic, Italian, Latin, and Greek Roots, and the English words derived therefrom accurately spelled, accented, and defined.

From HON. JNO. G. MCMYNN, *late State Superintendent of Wisconsin.*

I wish every teacher in the country had a copy of this work.

From PRIN. WM. F. PHELPS, *Minn. State Normal.*

The book is superb—just what is needed in the department of etymology and spelling.

From PROF. C. H. VERRILL, *Pa. State Normal School.*

The Etymology (Smith's) which we procured of you we like much. It is the best work for the class-room we have seen.

From HON. EDWARD BALLARD, *Supt. of Common Schools, State of Maine.*

The author has furnished a manual of singular utility for its purpose.

DICTIONARY.

The Topical Lexicon,

This work is a School Dictionary, an Etymology, a compilation of synonyms, and a manual of general information. It differs from the ordinary lexicon in being arranged by topics instead of the letters of the alphabet, thus realizing the apparent paradox of a "Readable Dictionary." An unusually valuable school book.

ENGLISH GRAMMAR.

CLARK'S DIAGRAM SYSTEM.

Clark's Easy Lessons in Language,

Published 1874. Contains illustrated object-lessons of the most attractive charac. ter, and is couched in language freed as much as possible from the dry technicalities of the science.

Clark's Brief English Grammar,

Published 1872. Part I. is adapted to youngest learners, and the whole forms a complete "brief course" in one volume, adequate to the wants of the common school.

Clark's Normal Grammar,

Published 1870, and designed to take the place of Prof. Clark's veteran "Practical" Grammar, though the latter is still furnished upon order. The Normal is an entirely new treatise. It is a full exposition of the system as described below, with all the most recent improvements. Some of its peculiarities are—A happy blending of SYNTHESES with ANALYSES; thorough Criticisms of common errors in the use of our Language; and important improvements in the Syntax of Sentences and of Phrases.

Clark's Key to the Diagrams,

Clark's Analysis of the English Language,

Clark's Grammatical Chart,

The theory and practice of teaching grammar in American schools is meeting with a thorough revolution from the use of this system. While the old methods offer proficiency to the pupil only after much weary plodding and dull memorizing, this affords from the inception the advantage of *practical Object Teaching*, addressing the eye by means of illustrative figures; furnishes association to the memory, its most powerful aid, and diverts the pupil by taxing his ingenuity. Teachers who are using Clark's Grammar uniformly testify that they and their pupils find it the most interesting study of the school course.

Like all great and radical improvements, the system naturally met at first with much unreasonable opposition. It has not only outlived the greater part of this opposition, but finds many of its warmest admirers among those who could not at first tolerate so radical an innovation. All it wants is an impartial trial to convince the most skeptical of its merit. No one who has fairly and intelligently tested it in the school-room has ever been known to go back to the old method. A great success is already established, and it is easy to prophecy that the day is not far distant when it will be the *only system of teaching English Grammar*. As the SYSTEM is copyrighted, no other text-books can appropriate this obvious and great improvement.

Welch's Analysis of the English Sentence,

Remarkable for its new and simple classification, its method of treating connectives, its explanations of the idioms and constructive laws of the language, etc.

Clark's Diagram English Grammar.

TESTIMONIALS.

From J. A. T. DURNIN, *Principal Dubuque R. C. Academy, Iowa.*

In my opinion, it is well calculated by its system of analysis to develop those rational faculties which in the old systems were rather left to develop themselves, while the memory was overtaxed, and the pupils discouraged.

From B. A. COX, *School Commissioner, Warren County, Illinois.*

I have examined 150 teachers in the last year, and those having studied or taught Clark's System have universally stood fifty per cent. better examinations than those having studied other authors.

From M. H. B. BURKET, *Principal Masonic Institute, Georgetown, Tennessee.*

I traveled two years amusing myself in instructing (exclusively) Grammar classes with Clark's system. The first class I instructed fifty days, but found that this was more time than was required to impart a theoretical knowledge of the science. During the two years thereafter I instructed classes only *thirty* days each. Invariably I proposed that unless I prepared my classes for a more thorough, minute, and accurate knowledge of English Grammar than that obtained from the ordinary books and in the ordinary way in from one to two years, I would make no charge. I never failed in a solitary case to far exceed the hopes of my classes, and made money and character rapidly as an instructor.

From A. B. DOUGLASS, *School Commissioner, Delaware County, New York.*

I have never known a class pursue the study of it under a *live* teacher, that has not succeeded; I have never known it to have an opponent in an educated teacher who had *thoroughly* investigated it; I have never known an *ignorant* teacher to examine it; I have never known a teacher who has used it, to try any other.

From J. A. DODGE, *Teacher and Lecturer on English Grammar, Kentucky.*

We are tempted to assert that it foretells the dawn of a brighter age to our mother-tongue. Both pupil and teacher can fare sumptuously upon its contents, however highly they may have prized the manuals into which they may have been initiated, and by which their expressions have been moulded.

From W. T. CHAPMAN, *Superintendent Public Schools, Wellington, Ohio.*

I regard Clark's System of Grammar the best published. For teaching the analysis of the English Language, it surpasses any I ever used.

From F. S. LYON, *Principal South Norwalk Union School, Connecticut.*

During ten years' experience in teaching, I have used six different authors on the subject of English Grammar. I am fully convinced that Clark's Grammar is better calculated to make thorough grammarians than any other that I have seen.

From CATALOGUE OF ROHRER'S COMMERCIAL COLLEGE, *St. Louis, Missouri.*

We do not hesitate to assert, without fear of successful contradiction, that a better knowledge of the English language can be obtained by this system in six weeks than by the old methods in as many months.

From A. PICKETT, *President of the State Teachers' Association, Wisconsin.*

A thorough experiment in the use of many approved authors upon the subject of English Grammar has convinced me of the superiority of Clark. When the pupil has completed the course, he is left upon a foundation of *principle*, and not upon the *dictum* of the author.

From GEO. F. MCFARLAND, *Prin. McAllisterville Academy, Juniata Co., Penn.*

At the first examination of public-school teachers by the county superintendent, when one of our student teachers commenced analyzing a sentence according to Clark, the superintendent listened in mute astonishment until he had finished, then asked what that meant, and finally, with a very knowing look, said such work wouldn't do here, and asked the applicant to parse the sentence right, and gave the lowest certificates to all who barely mentioned Clark. Afterwards, I presented him with a copy, and the next fall he permitted it to be partially used, while the third of last fall, he openly commended the system, and appointed three of my best teachers to explain it at the two Institutes and one County Convention held since September.

☞ For further testimony of equal force, see the **Publishers' Special Circular, or current numbers of the Educational Bulletin.**

GEOGRAPHY.

NATIONAL GEOGRAPHICAL SYSTEM.

THE SERIES.

I. Monteith's First Lessons in Geography,
II. Monteith's New Manual of Geography,
II. McNally's System of Geography,

INTERMEDIATE OR ALTERNATE VOLUMES.

1*. Monteith's Introduction to Geography,
2*. Monteith's Physical and Political Geography,

ACCESSORIES.

Monteith's Wall Maps 2 sets (see page 15),
Monteith's Manual of Map-Drawing (Allen's System)
Monteith's Map-Drawing and Object-Lessons,
Monteith's Map-Drawing Scale,

1. PRACTICAL OBJECT TEACHING. The infant scholar is first introduced to *a picture* whence he may derive notions of the shape of the earth, the phenomena of day and night, the distribution of land and water, and the great natural divisions, which mere words would fail entirely to convey to the untutored mind. Other pictures follow on the same plan, and the child's mind is called upon to grasp no idea without the aid of a pictorial illustration. Carried on to the higher books, this system culminates in Physical Geography, where such matters as climates, ocean currents, the winds, peculiarities of the earth's crust, clouds and rain, are pictorially explained and rendered apparent to the most obtuse. The illustrations used for this purpose belong to the highest grade of art.

2. CLEAR, BEAUTIFUL, AND CORRECT MAPS. In the lower numbers the maps avoid unnecessary detail, while respectively progressive, and affording the pupil new matter for acquisition each time he approaches in the constantly enlarging circle the point of coincidence with previous lessons in the more elementary books. In the Physical and Political Geography the maps embrace many new and striking features. One of the most effective of these is the new plan for displaying on each map the relative sizes of countries not represented, thus obviating much confusion which has arisen from the necessity of presenting maps in the same atlas drawn on different scales. The maps of "McNally" have long been celebrated for their superior beauty and completeness. This is the only school-book in which the attempt to make a *complete* atlas *also clear and distinct*, has been successful. The map *coloring* throughout the series is also noticeable. Delicate and subdued tints take the place of the startling glare of inharmonious colors which too frequently in such treatises dazzle the eyes, distract the attention, and serve to overwhelm the names of towns and the natural features of the landscape.

GEOGRAPHY—Continued.

3. THE VARIETY OF MAP-EXERCISE. Starting each time from a different basis, the pupil in many instances approaches the same fact no less than *six times*, thus indelibly impressing it upon his memory. At the same time, this system is not allowed to become wearisome—the extent of exercise on each subject being graduated by its relative importance or difficulty of acquisition.

4. THE CHARACTER AND ARRANGEMENT OF THE DESCRIPTIVE TEXT. The cream of the science has been carefully culled, unimportant matter rejected, elaboration avoided, and a brief and concise manner of presentation cultivated. The orderly consideration of topics has contributed greatly to simplicity. Due attention is paid to the facts in history and astronomy which are inseparably connected with, and important to the proper understanding of geography—and *such only* are admitted on any terms. In a word, the National System teaches geography as a science, pure, simple, and exhaustive.

5. ALWAYS UP TO THE TIMES. The authors of these books, editorially speaking, never sleep. No change occurs in the boundaries of countries, or of counties, no new discovery is made, or railroad built, that is not at once noted and recorded, and the next edition of each volume carries to every school-room the new order of things.

6. SUPERIOR GRADATION. This is the only series which furnishes an available volume for every possible class in graded schools. It is not contemplated that a pupil must necessarily go through every volume in succession to attain proficiency. On the contrary, *two* will suffice, but *three* are advised; and, if the course will admit, the whole series should be pursued. At all events, the books are at hand for selection, and every teacher, of every grade, can find among them one *exactly suited* to his class. The best combination for those who wish to abridge the course consists of Nos. 1, 2, and 3, or where children are somewhat advanced in other studies when they commence geography, Nos. 1*, 2, and 3. Where but *two* books are admissible, Nos. 1* and 2*, or Nos. 2 and 3, are recommended.

7. FORM OF THE VOLUMES AND MECHANICAL EXECUTION. The maps and text are no longer unnaturally divorced in accordance with the time-honored practice of making text-books on this subject as inconvenient and expensive as possible. On the contrary, all map questions are to be found on the page opposite the map itself, and each book is complete in one volume. The mechanical execution is unrivalled. Paper and printing are everything that could be desired, and the binding is—A. S. Barnes & Company's.

8. MAP-DRAWING. In 1869 the system of Map-Drawing devised by Professor JEROME ALLEN was secured *exclusively* for this series. It derives its claim to originality and usefulness from the introduction of a *fixed unit of measurement* applicable to every Map. The principles being so few, simple and comprehensive, the subject of Map-Drawing is relieved of all practical difficulty. (In Nos. 2, 2*, and 3, and published separately.)

9. ANALOGOUS OUTLINES. At the same time with Map-Drawing was also introduced (in No. 2) a new and ingenious variety of Object Lessons, consisting of a comparison of the outlines of countries with familiar objects pictorially represented.

GEOGRAPHY—Continued.

MONTEITH'S INDEPENDENT COURSE.

Elementary Geography

Comprehensive Geography (with 103 Maps)

☞ These volumes are not revisions of old works—not an addition to any series—but are entirely new productions—each by itself complete, independent, comprehensive, yet simple, brief, cheap, and popular; or, taken together, the most admirable "series" ever offered for a common-school course. They present the following features, skillfully interwoven—the student learning all about one country at a time.

LOCAL GEOGRAPHY, or the Use of Maps. Important features of the Maps are the coloring of States as objects, and the ingenious system for laying down a much larger number of names for reference than are found on any other Maps of same size—and without crowding.

PHYSICAL GEOGRAPHY, or the Natural Features of the Earth, illustrated by the original and striking ***Relief Maps,*** being bird's-eye views or photographic pictures of the Earth's surface.

DESCRIPTIVE GEOGRAPHY, including the Physical; with some account of Governments, and Races, Animals, etc.

HISTORICAL GEOGRAPHY, or a brief summary of the salient points of history, explaining the present distribution of nations, origin of geographical names, etc.

MATHEMATICAL GEOGRAPHY, including ASTRONOMICAL, which describes the Earth's position and character among planets; also the Zones, Parallels, etc.

COMPARATIVE GEOGRAPHY, or a system of analogy, connecting new lessons with the previous ones. Comparative sizes and latitudes are shown on the margin of each Map, and all countries are measured in the "*frame of Kansas.*"

TOPICAL GEOGRAPHY, consisting of questions for review, and testing the student's general and specific knowledge of the subject, with suggestions for *Geographical Compositions.*

ANCIENT GEOGRAPHY. A section devoted to this subject, with Maps, will be appreciated by teachers. It is seldom taught in our common schools, because it has heretofore required the purchase of a separate book.

GRAPHIC GEOGRAPHY, or MAP-DRAWING by Allen's "Unit of Measurement" system (now almost universally recognized as without a rival) is introduced throughout the lessons, and not as an appendix.

CONSTRUCTIVE GEOGRAPHY, or GLOBE-MAKING. With each book a set of Map Segments is furnished, with which each student may make his own Globe by following the directions given.

RAILROAD GEOGRAPHY, with a grand Map illustrating routes of travel in the United States. Also, a "Tour in Europe."

MAP DRAWING.

Monteith's Map-Drawing Made Easy.

A neat little book of outlines and instructions, giving the "corners of States" in suitable blanks, so that Maps can be drawn by unskillful hands from any atlas; with instructions for written exercises or compositions on geographical subjects, and Comparative Geography.

Monteith's Manual of Map-Drawing (Allen's System).

The only consistent plan, by which all Maps are drawn on one scale. By its use much time may be saved, and much interest and accurate knowledge gained.

Monteith's Map-Drawing and Object Lessons.

The last-named treatise, bound with Mr. Monteith's ingenious system for committing outlines to memory by means of pictures of living creatures and familiar objects. Thus, South America resembles a dog's head; Cuba, a lizard; Italy, a boot; France, a coffee-pot; Turkey, a turkey, etc., etc.

Monteith's Map-Drawing Scale.

A ruler of wood, graduated to the "Allen fixed unit of measurement."

WALL MAPS.

Monteith's Pictorial Chart of Geography.

The original drawing for this beautiful and instructive chart was greatly admired in the publisher's "exhibit" at the Centennial Exhibition of 1876. It is *a picture* of the Earth's surface with every natural feature displayed, teaching also physical geography, and especially the mutations of water. The uses to which man puts the earth and its treasures and forces, as Agriculture, Mining, Manufacturing, Commerce, and Transportation are also graphically portrayed so that the young learner gets a realistic idea of "the world we live in," which weeks of book-study might fail to convey.

Monteith's School Maps, 8 Numbers.

The "School Series" includes the Hemispheres (2 Maps), United States, North America, South America, Europe, Asia, Africa.—Price, $2.50 each.

Each map is 28 × 34 inches, beautifully colored, has the names all laid down, and is substantially mounted on canvas with rollers.

Monteith's Grand Maps, 8 Numbers.

The "Grand Series" includes the Hemispheres (1 Map), United States, South America, Europe, Asia, Africa, The World on Mercator's Projection, and Physical Map of the World.—Price, $5.00 each. Size 42 × 52 inches, names laid down, colored, mounted, &c.

Monteith's Sunday School Maps,

Including a Map of Paul's Travels ($5.00), one of Ancient Canaan ($3.00), and Modern Palestine ($3.00), or Palestine and Canaan together ($5.00).

MONTEITH'S GEOGRAPHIES

Have been adopted, by official authority, for the schools of the following States and Cities—in most cases for *exclusive* and uniform use.

CALIFORNIA,	TENNESSEE,	IOWA,	ARKANSAS,	NORTH CAROLINA,
MISSOURI,	TEXAS,	LOUISIANA,	FLORIDA,	KANSAS,
ALABAMA,	VERMONT,	OREGON,	MINNESOTA,	MISSISSIPPI.

CITIES.—New York City, Brooklyn, Chicago, New Orleans, Buffalo, Richmond, Jersey City, Hartford, Worcester, San Francisco, Louisville, Newark, Milwaukee, Charleston, Rochester, Mobile, Syracuse, Memphis, Salt Lake City, Nashville, Utica, Wilmington, Trenton, Norfolk, Norwich, Lockport, Dubuque, Galveston, Portland, Savannah, Indianapolis, Springfield, Wheeling, Toledo, Bridgeport, St. Paul, Vicksburg, &c.

Monteith & McNally's National Geographies.

CRITICAL OPINIONS.

From R. A. ADAMS, *Member of Board of Education, New York.*

I have found, by examination of the Book of Supply of our Board, that considerably the largest number of any series now used in our public schools is the National, by Monteith and McNally.

From BRO. PATRICK, *Chief Provincial of the Vast Educational Society of the* CHRISTIAN BROTHERS *in the United States.*

Having been convinced for some time past that the series of Geographies in use in our schools were not giving satisfaction, and came far short of meeting our most reasonable expectations, I have felt it my imperative duty to examine into this matter, and see if a remedy could not be found.

Copies of the different Geographies published in this country have been placed at our command for examination. On account of other pressing duties we have not been able to give as much time to the investigation of all these different series as we could have desired; yet we have found enough to convince us that there are many others better than those we are now using; but we cheerfully give our most decided preference, above all others, to the National Series, by Monteith & McNally.

Their easy gradation, their thoroughly practical and independent character, their comprehensive completeness as a full and accurate system, the wise discrimination shown in the selection of the subject matter, the beautiful and copious illustrations, the neat cut type, the general execution of the works, and *other excellencies*, will commend them to the friends of education everywhere.

From the "HOME MONTHLY," *Nashville, Tenn.*

MONTEITH'S AND MCNALLY'S GEOGRAPHIES.—Geography is so closely connected with Astronomy, History, Ethnology, and Geology, that it is difficult to define its limits in the construction of a text-book. If the author confines himself strictly to a description of the earth's surface, his book will be dry, meager, and unintelligible to a child. If, on the other hand, he attempts to give information on the cognate sciences, he enters a boundless field, and may wander too far. It seems to us that the authors of the series before us have hit on the happy medium between too much and too little. *The First Lessons*, by applying the system of object-teaching, renders the subject so attractive that a child, just able to read, may become deeply interested in it. The second book of the course enlarges the view, but still keeps to the maps and simple descriptions. Then, in the third book, we have Geography combined with History and Astronomy. A general view of the solar system is presented, so that the pupil may understand the earth's position on the map of the heavens. The first part of the fourth book treats of Physical Geography, and contains a vast amount of knowledge compressed into a small space. It is made bright and attractive by beautiful pictures and suggestive illustrations, on the principle of object-teaching. The maps in the second part of this volume are remarkably clear, and the map exercises are copious and judicious. In the fifth and last volume of the series, the whole subject is reviewed and systematized. This is strictly a Geography. Its maps are beautifully engraved and clearly printed. The map exercises are full and comprehensive. In all these books the maps, questions and descriptions are given in the same volume. In most geographies there are too many details and minute descriptions—more than any child out of purgatory ought to be required to learn. The power of memory is overstrained; there is confusion—no clearly defined idea is formed in the child's mind. But in these books, in brief, pointed descriptions, and constant use of bright, accurate maps, the whole subject is photographed on the mind.

MATHEMATICS.

DAVIES' NATIONAL COURSE.

ARITHMETIC.

1. Davies' Primary Arithmetic,
2. Davies' Intellectual Arithmetic,
3. Davies' Elements of Written Arithmetic, .
4. Davies' Practical Arithmetic,
   Key to Practical Arithmetic,
5. Davies' University Arithmetic,
   Key to University Arithmetic,

ALGEBRA.

1. Davies' New Elementary Algebra,
   Key to Elementary Algebra,
2. Davies' University Algebra,
   Key to University Algebra,
3. Davies' New Bourdon's Algebra,
   Key to Bourdon's Algebra,

GEOMETRY.

1. Davies' Elementary Geometry and Trigonometry,
2. Davies' Legendre's Geometry,
3. Davies' Analytical Geometry and Calculus,
4. Davies' Descriptive Geometry,
5. Davies' New Calculus,

MENSURATION.

1. Davies' Practical Mathematics and Mensuration,
2. Davies' Elements of Surveying,
3. Davies' Shades, Shadows, and Perspective,

MATHEMATICAL SCIENCE.

Davies' Grammar of Arithmetic,
Davies' Outlines of Mathematical Science,
Davies' Nature and Utility of Mathematics,
Davies' Metric System,
Davies & Peck's Dictionary of Mathematics,

DAVIES' NATIONAL COURSE of MATHEMATICS.

ITS RECORD.

In claiming for this series the first place among American text-books, of whatever class, the Publishers appeal to the magnificent record which its volumes have earned during the *thirty-five years* of Dr. Charles Davies' mathematical labors. The unremitting exertions of a life-time have placed *the modern series* on the same proud eminence among competitors that each of its predecessors has successively enjoyed in a course of constantly improved editions, now rounded to their perfect fruition—for it seems almost that this science is susceptible of no further demonstration.

During the period alluded to, many authors and editors in this department have started into public notice, and by borrowing ideas and processes original with Dr. Davies, have enjoyed a brief popularity, but are now almost unknown. Many of the series of to-day, built upon a similar basis, and described as "modern books," are destined to a similar fate; while the most far-seeing eye will find it difficult to fix the time, on the basis of any data afforded by their past history, when these books will cease to increase and prosper, and fix a still firmer hold on the affection of every educated American.

One cause of this unparalleled popularity is found in the fact that the enterprise of the author did not cease with the original completion of his books. Always a practical teacher, he has incorporated in his text-books from time to time the advantages of every improvement in methods of teaching, and every advance in science. During all the years in which he has been laboring, he constantly submitted his own theories and those of others to the practical test of the class-room—approving, rejecting, or modifying them as the experience thus obtained might suggest. In this way he has been able to produce an almost perfect series of class-books, in which every department of mathematics has received minute and exhaustive attention.

Nor has he yet retired from the field. Still in the prime of life, and enjoying a ripe experience which no other living mathematician or teacher can emulate, his pen is ever ready to carry on the good work, as the progress of science may demand. Witness his recent exposition of the "Metric System," which received the official endorsement of Congress, by its Committee on Uniform Weights and Measures.

DAVIES' SYSTEM IS THE ACKNOWLEDGED NATIONAL STANDARD FOR THE UNITED STATES, for the following reasons:—

1st. It is the basis of instruction in the great national schools at West Point and Annapolis.

2d. It has received the *quasi* endorsement of the National Congress.

3d. It is exclusively used in the public schools of the National Capital.

4th. The officials of the Government use it as authority in all cases involving mathematical questions.

5th. Our great soldiers and sailors commanding the national armies and navies were educated in this system. So have been a majority of eminent scientists in this country. All these refer to "Davies" as authority.

6th. A larger number of American citizens have received their education from this than from any other series.

7th. The series has a larger circulation throughout the whole country than any other, being *extensively used in every State in the Union.*

Davies' National Course of Mathematics.

TESTIMONIALS.

From L. VAN BOKKELEN, *State Superintendent Public Instruction, Maryland.*

The series of Arithmetics edited by Prof. Davies, and published by your firm have been used for many years in the schools of several counties, and the city of Baltimore, and have been approved by teachers and commissioners.

Under the law of 1865, establishing a uniform system of Free Public Schools these Arithmetics were unanimously adopted by the State Board of Education after a careful examination, and are now used in all the Public Schools of Maryland.

These facts evidence the high opinion entertained by the School Authorities of the value of the series theoretically and practically.

From HORACE WEBSTER, *President of the College of New York.*

The undersigned has examined, with care and thought, several volumes of Davies' Mathematics, and is of the opinion that, as a whole, it is the most complete and best course for Academic and Collegiate instruction, with which he is acquainted.

From DAVID N. CAMP, *State Superintendent of Common Schools, Connecticut.*

I have examined Davies' Series of Arithmetics with some care. The language is clear and precise; each principle is thoroughly analyzed, and the whole so arranged as to facilitate the work of instruction. Having observed the satisfaction and success with which the different books have been used by eminent teachers, it gives me pleasure to commend them to others.

From J. O. WILSON, *Chairman Committee on Text-Books, Washington, D. C.*

I consider Davies' Arithmetics decidedly superior to any other series, and in this opinion I am sustained, I believe, by the entire Board of Education and Corps of Teachers in this city, where they have been used for several years past.

From JOHN L. CAMPBELL, *Professor of Mathematics, Wabash College, Indiana.*

A proper combination of abstract reasoning and practical illustration is the chief excellence in Prof. Davies' Mathematical works. I prefer his Arithmetics, Algebras, Geometry and Trigonometry to all others now in use, and cordially recommend them to all who desire the advancement of sound learning.

From MAJOR J. H. WHITTLESEY, *Government Inspector of Military Schools.*

Be assured, I regard the works of Prof. Davies, with which I am acquainted, as by far the best text-books in print on the subjects which they treat. I shall certainly encourage their adoption wherever a word from me may be of any avail.

From T. McC. BALLANTINE, *Prof. Mathematics Cumberland College, Kentucky.*

I have long taught Prof. Davies' Course of Mathematics, and I continue to like their working.

From JOHN McLEAN BELL, B. A., *Prin. of Lower Canada College.*

I have used Davies' Arithmetical and Mathematical Series as text-books in the schools under my charge for the last six years. These I have found of great efficacy in exciting, invigorating, and concentrating the intellectual faculties of the young.

Each treatise serves as an introduction to the next higher, by the similarity of its reasonings and methods; and the student is carried forward, by easy and gradual steps, over the whole field of mathematical inquiry, and that, too, in a *shorter* time than is usually occupied in mastering a single department. I sincerely and heartily recommend them to the attention of my fellow-teachers in Canada.

From D. W. STEELE, *Prin. Philekoian Academy, Cold Springs, Texas.*

I have used Davies' Arithmetics till I know them nearly by heart. A better series of school-books never were published. I have recommended them until they are now used in all this region of country.

A large mass of similar "Opinions" may be obtained by addressing the publishers for special circular for Davies' Mathematics. New recommendations are published in current numbers of the *Educational Bulletin.*

MATHEMATICS—Continued.

PECK'S ARITHMETICS.

By the Prof. of Mathematics at Columbia College, New York.

1. Peck's First Lessons in Numbers,

Embracing all that is usually included in what are called Primary and Intellectual Arithmetics; proceeding gradually from object lessons to abstract numbers; developing Addition and Subtraction simultaneously: with other attractive novelties.

2. Peck's Manual of Practical Arithmetic,

An excellent "Brief" course, conveying a sufficient knowledge of Arithmetic for ordinary business purposes.

It is thoroughly "practical," because the author believes the Theory cannot be studied with advantage until the pupil has acquired a certain facility in combining numbers, which can only be had by practice.

3. Peck's Complete Arithmetic,

The whole subject—theory and practice—presented within very moderate limits. This author's most remarkable faculty of mathematical treatment is comprehended in three words: System, Conciseness, Lucidity. The directness and simplicity of this work cannot be better expressed than in the words of a correspondent who adopted the book at once, because, as he said, it is "free from that *juggling with numbers*" practiced by many authors.

From the "Galaxy," New York.

In the "Complete Arithmetic" each part of the subject is logically developed. First are given the necessary definitions; second, the explanations of such signs (if any) as are used; third, the principles on which the operation depends; fourth, an exemplification of the manner in which the operation is performed, which is so conducted that the reason of the rule which is immediately thereafter deduced is made perfectly plain; after which follow numerous graded examples and corresponding practical problems. All the parts taken together are arranged in logical order. The subject is treated as a whole, and not as if made up of segregated parts. It may seem a simple remark to make that (for example) addition is in principle one and the same everywhere, whether employed upon simple or compound numbers, fractions, etc., the only difference being in the *unit* involved; but the number of persons who understand this practically, compared to the number who have studied arithmetic, is not very great. The student of the "Complete Arithmetic" cannot fail to understand it. All the principles of the science are presented within moderate limits. Superfluity of matter—to supplement defective definitions, to make clear faulty demonstrations and rules expressed either inaccurately or obscurely, to make provision for a multiplicity of cases for which no provision is requisite—has been carefully avoided. The definitions are plain and concise; the principles are stated clearly and accurately; the demonstrations are full and complete; the rules are perspicuous and comprehensive; the illustrative examples are abundant and well fitted to familiarize the student with the application of principles to the problems of science and of every-day life.

☞ The Definitions constitute the power of the book. We have never seen them excelled for clearness and exactness.—*Iowa School Journal.*

MATHEMATICS—Continued.

PECK'S HIGHER COURSE.

Peck's Manual of Algebra,

Bringing the methods of Bourdon within the range of the Academic Course.

Peck's Manual of Geometry,

By a method purely practical, and unembarrassed by the details which rather confuse than simplify science.

Peck's Practical Calculus,

Peck's Analytical Geometry,

Peck's Elementary Mechanics,

Peck's Mechanics, with Calculus,

The briefest treatises on these subjects now published. Adopted by the great Universities; Yale, Harvard, Columbia, Princeton, Cornell, &c.

ARITHMETICAL EXAMPLES.

Reuck's Examples in Denominate Numbers,

Reuck's Examples in Arithmetic,

These volumes differ from the ordinary arithmetic in their peculiarly *practical* character. They are composed mainly of examples, and afford the most severe and thorough discipline for the mind. While a book which should contain a complete treatise of theory and practice would be too cumbersome for every-day use, the insufficiency of *practical* examples has been a source of complaint.

HIGHER MATHEMATICS.

Macnie's Algebraical Equations,

Serving as a complement to the more advanced treatises on Algebra, giving special attention to the analysis and solution of equations with numerical coefficients.

Church's Elements of Calculus,

Church's Analytical Geometry,

Church's Descriptive Geometry, 2 vols.,

These volumes constitute the "West Point Course" in their several departments.

Courtenay's Elements of Calculus,

A standard work of the very highest grade.

Hackley's Trigonometry,

With applications to navigation and surveying, nautical and practical geometry and geodesy.

PENMANSHIP.

Beers' System of Progressive Penmanship. Per dozen

This "round hand" system of Penmanship in twelve numbers, commends itself by its simplicity and thoroughness. The first four numbers are primary books. Nos. 5 to 7, advanced books for boys. Nos. 8 to 10, advanced books for girls. Nos. 11 and 12, ornamental penmanship. These books are printed from steel plates (engraved by McLees), and are unexcelled in mechanical execution. Large quantities are annually sold.

Beers' Slated Copy Slips, per set

All beginners should practice, for a few weeks, slate exercises, familiarizing them with the form of the letters, the motions of the hand and arm, &c., &c. These copy slips, 32 in number, supply all the copies found in a complete series of writing-books, at a trifling cost.

Payson, Dunton & Scribner's Copy-B'ks. P. doz.,

The National System of Penmanship, in three distinct series—(1) Common School Series, comprising the first six numbers; (2) Business Series, Nos. 8, 11, and 12; (3) Ladies' Series, Nos. 7, 9, and 10.

Fulton & Eastman's Chirographic Charts,

To embellish the school room walls, and furnish class exercise in the elements of Penmanship.

Payson's Copy-Book Cover, per hundred

Protects every page except the one in use, and furnishes "lines" with proper slope for the penman, under. Patented.

National Steel Pens, Card with all kinds

Pronounced by competent judges the perfection of American-made pens, and superior to any foreign article.

SCHOOL SERIES.	
School Pen, per gross, . .	$ 60
Academic Pen, do . .	63
Fine Pointed Pen, per gross	70
POPULAR SERIES.	
Capitol Pen, per gross, . .	1 00
do do pr. box of 2 doz.	25
Bullion Pen (imit. gold) pr. gr.	75
Ladies' Pen do	63
Index Pen, per gross . . .	75
BUSINESS SERIES.	
Albata Pen, per gross, . .	40
Bank Pen, do . .	70
Empire Pen, do . .	70
Commercial Pen, per gross .	60
Express Pen, do .	75
Falcon Pen, do .	70
Elastic Pen, do .	75

Stimpson's Scientific Steel Pen, per gross $1 50

One forward and two backward arches, ensuring great strength, well-balanced elasticity, evenness of point, and smoothness of execution. One gross in twelve contains a Scientific Gold Pen.

Stimpson's Ink-Retaining Holder, per doz. 1 50

A simple apparatus, which does not get out of order, withholds at a single dip as much ink as the pen would otherwise realize from a dozen trips to the inkstand, which it supplies with moderate and easy flow.

Stimpson's Gold Pen, $3 00; with Ink Retainer 4 50

Stimpson's Penman's Card, $0 25

One dozen Steel Pens (assorted points) and Patent Ink-retaining Pen holder.

HISTORY.

Monteith's Youth's History.

A History of the United States for beginners. It is arranged upon the catechetical plan, with illustrative maps and engravings, review questions, dates in parentheses (that their study may be optional with the younger class of learners), and interesting Biographical Sketches of all persons who have been prominently identified with the history of our country.

Willard's United States, School and University Editions.

The plan of this standard work is chronologically exhibited in front of the title-page; the Maps and Sketches are found useful assistants to the memory, and dates, usually so difficult to remember, are so systematically arranged as in a great degree to obviate the difficulty. Candor, impartiality, and accuracy, are the distinguishing features of the narrative portion.

Willard's Universal History.

The most valuable features of the "United States" are reproduced in this. The peculiarities of the work are its great conciseness and the prominence given to the chronological order of events. The margin marks each successive era with great distinctness, so that the pupil retains not only the event but its time, and thus fixes the order of history firmly and usefully in his mind, Mrs. Willard's books are constantly revised, and at all times written up to embrace important historical events of recent date.

Lancaster's English History,

By the Master of the Stoughton Grammar School, Boston. The most practical of the "brief books." Though short, it is not a bare and uninteresting outline, but contains enough of explanation and detail to make intelligible the *cause and effect* of events. Their relations to the history and development of the American people is made specially prominent.

Willis' Historical Reader,

Being Collier's Great Events of History adapted to American schools. This rare epitome of general history, remarkable for its charming style and judicious selection of events on which the destinies of nations have turned, has been skillfully manipulated by Prof. Willis, with as few changes as would bring the United States into its proper position in the historical perspective. As reader or text-book it has few equals and no superiors.

Berard's History of England,

By an authoress well known for the success of her History of the United States, The social life of the English people is felicitously interwoven, as in fact, with the civil and military transactions of the realm.

Ricord's History of Rome

Possesses the charm of an attractive romance. The Fables with which this history abounds are introduced in such a way as not to deceive the inexperienced, while adding materially to the value of the work as a reliable index to the character and institutions, as well as the history of the Roman people.

Hanna's Bible History.

The only compendium of Bible narrative which affords a connected and chronological view of the important events there recorded, divested of all superfluous detail.

Summary of History; American, French and English.

A well-proportioned outline of leading events, condensing the substance of the more extensive text-book in common use into a series of statements so brief, that every word may be committed to memory, and yet so comprehensive that it presents an accurate though general view of the whole continuous life of nations.

Marsh's Ecclesiastical History.

Affording the History of the Church in all ages, with accounts of the pagan world during Biblical periods, and the character, rise, and progress of all Religions, as well as the various sects of the worshipers of Christ. The work is entirely non-sectarian, though strictly catholic. A separate volume contains carefully prepared QUESTIONS for class use.

HISTORY—Continued.

BARNES' ONE-TERM HISTORY.

A Brief History of the United States,

This is probably the MOST ORIGINAL SCHOOL-BOOK published for many years, in any department. A few of its claims are the following:

1. Brevity.—The text is complete for Grammar School or intermediate classes, in 290 12mo pages, large type. It may readily be completed, if desired, in one term of study.

2. Comprehensiveness.—Though so brief, this book contains the pith of all the wearying contents of the larger manuals, and a great deal more than the memory usually retains from the latter.

3. Interest has been a prime consideration. Small books have heretofore been bare, full of dry statistics, unattractive. This one is charmingly written, replete with anecdote, and brilliant with illustration.

4. Proportion of Events.—It is remarkable for the discrimination with which the different portions of our history are presented according to their importance. Thus the older works being already large books when the civil war took place, give it less space than that accorded to the Revolution.

5. Arrangement.—In six epochs, entitled respectively, Discovery and Settlement, the Colonies, the Revolution, Growth of States, the Civil War, and Current Events.

6. Catch Words.—Each paragraph is preceded by its leading thought in prominent type, standing in the student's mind for the whole paragraph.

7. Key Notes.—Analogous with this is the idea of grouping battles, etc., about some central event, which relieves the sameness so common in such descriptions, and renders each distinct by some striking peculiarity of its own.

8. Foot Notes.—These are crowded with interesting matter that is not strictly a part of history proper. They may be learned or not, at pleasure. They are certain in any event to be read.

9. Biographies of all the leading characters are given in full in foot-notes.

10. Maps.—Elegant and distinct Maps from engravings on copper-plate, and beautifully colored, precede each epoch, and contain all the places named.

11. Questions are at the back of the book, to compel a more independent use of the text. Both text and questions are so worded that the pupil must give intelligent answers IN HIS OWN WORDS. "Yes" and "No" will not do.

12. Historical Recreations.—These are additional questions to test the student's knowledge, in review, as: "What trees are celebrated in our history?" "When did a fog save our army?" "What Presidents died in office?" "When was the Mississippi our western boundary?" "Who said, 'I would rather be right than President?'" etc.

13. The Illustrations, about seventy in number, are the work of our best artists and engravers, produced at great expense. They are vivid and interesting, and mostly upon subjects never before illustrated in a school-book.

14. Dates.—Only the leading dates are given in the text, and these are so associated as to assist the memory, but at the head of each page is the date of the event first mentioned, and at the close of each epoch a summary of events and dates.

15. The Philosophy of History is studiously exhibited—the causes and effects of events being distinctly traced and their interconnection shown.

16. Impartiality. — All sectional, partisan, or denominational views are avoided. Facts are stated after a careful comparison of all authorities without the least prejudice or favor.

17. Index.—A verbal index at the close of the book perfects it as a work of reference.

It will be observed that the above are all particulars in which School Histories have been signally defective, or altogether wanting. Many other claims to favor it shares in common with its predecessors.

BARNES' ONE-TERM HISTORY—Continued.

From PROF. WM. F. ALLEN, *State Univ. of Wisconsin.*

I think the author of the new "Brief History of the United States" has been very successful in combining brevity with sufficient fullness and interest. *Particularly*, he has avoided the excessive number of names and dates that most histories contain. Two features that I like *very much* are the *anecdotes* at the foot of the page and the "*Historical Recreations*" in the Appendix. The latter, I think, is quite a *new* feature, and the other is *very* well executed.

From S. G. WRIGHT, *Assist.-Supt. Pub. Inst., Kansas.*

It is with extreme pleasure we submit our recommendation of the "Brief History of the United States." It meets the needs of young and older children, combining concision with perspicuity, and if "brevity is the soul of wit," this "Brief History" contains not only that well-chosen ingredient, but wisdom sufficient to enlighten those students who are wearily longing for a "new departure" from certain old and uninteresting presentations of fossilized writers. We congratulate a progressive public upon a progressive book.

From HON. NEWTON BATEMAN, *Supt. Pub. Inst., Illinois.*

Barnes' One-Term History of the United States is an exceedingly attractive and spirited little book. Its claim to several new and valuable features seems well founded. Under the form of six well-defined Epochs, the History of the United States is traced tersely, yet pithily, from the earliest times to the present day. A good map precedes each epoch, whereby the history and geography of the period may be studied together, *as they always should be.* The syllabus of each paragraph is made to stand in such bold relief, by the use of large, heavy type, as to be of much *mnemonic* value to the student. The book is written in a sprightly and piquant style, the interest never flagging from beginning to end—a rare and difficult achievement in works of this kind.

From the "Chicago Schoolmaster" (Editorial).

A thorough examination of Barnes' Brief History of the United States brings the examiner to the conclusion that it is a superior book in almost every respect. The book is neat in form, and of good material. The type is clear, large, and distinct. The facts and dates are correct. The arrangement of topics is just the thing needed in a history text-book. By this arrangement the pupil can see at once what he is expected to do. The topics are well selected, embracing the leading ideas or principal events of American history. . . . The book as a whole is much superior to any I have examined. So much do I think this, that I have ordered it for my class, and shall use it in my school. (Signed) B. W. BAKER.

A Brief History of France,

By the author of the "Brief United States," with all the attractive features of that popular work (which see), and new ones of its own.

It is believed that the history of France has never before been presented in such brief compass, and this is effected without sacrificing one particle of interest. The book reads like a romance, and, while drawing the student by an irresistible fascination to his task, impresses the great outlines indelibly upon the memory.

Gilman's First Steps in General History,

A "suggestive outline" of rare compactness. Each country is treated by itself, and the United States receive special attention. Frequent Maps, contemporary events in Tables, References to Standard Works for fuller details, and a minute Index constitute the "Illustrative Apparatus." From no other work that we know of can so succinct a view of the world's history be obtained. Considering the necessary limitation of space, the style is surprisingly vivid, and at times even ornate. In all respects a charming, though not the less practical, text-book.

Gilman's "Seven Historic Ages,"

This book is written in the style used by a father talking with his children on the progress of history. As one Age after another is taken up, the author brings before the young reader the prominent men and characteristic events by which it is to be remembered. The object is to stimulate the pupil in school or the child at home to study history, to think of it as a lively picture of the doings of men, and not as a dead list of uninteresting dates.

Baker's Brief History of Texas,

On the plan of "Barnes' Brief Histories," with Constitution of the State, for schools.

DRAWING.

Chapman's American Drawing Book,

The standard American text-book and authority in all branches of art. A compilation of art principles. A manual for the amateur, and basis of study for the professional artist. Adapted for schools and private instruction.

CONTENTS.—"Any one who can Learn to Write can Learn to Draw."—Primary Instruction in Drawing.—Rudiments of Drawing the Human Head.—Rudiments in Drawing the Human Figure.—Rudiments of Drawing.—The Elements of Geometry.—Perspective.—Of Studying and Sketching from Nature.—Of Painting.—Etching and Engraving.—Of Modeling.—Of Composition —Advice to the American Art-Student. The work is of course magnificently illustrated with all the original designs.

Chapman's Elementary Drawing Book,

A Progressive Course of Practical Exercises, or a text-book for the training of the eye and hand. It contains the elements from the larger work, and a copy should be in the hands of every pupil; while a copy of the "American Drawing Book," named above, should be at hand for reference by the class.

The Little Artist's Portfolio,

25 Drawing Cards (progressive patterns), 25 Blanks, and a fine Artist's Pencil, all in one neat envelope.

Clark's Elements of Drawing,

A complete course in this graceful art, from the first rudiments of outline to the finished sketches of landscape and scenery.

Fowle's Linear and Perspective Drawing,

For the cultivation of the eye and hand, with copious illustrations and directions for the guidance of the unskilled teacher.

Monk's Drawing Books—Six Numbers, per set,

Each book contains *eleven* large patterns, with opposing blanks. No. 1. Elementary Studies. No. 2. Studies of Foliage. No. 3. Landscapes. No. 4. Animals, I. No. 5. Animals, II. No. 6. Marine Views, etc.

Allen's Map-Drawing, Scale,

This method introduces a new era in Map-Drawing, for the following reasons:—1. It is a system. This is its greatest merit.—2. It is easily understood and taught.—3. The eye is trained to exact measurement by the use of a scale.—4. By no special effort of the memory, distance and comparative size are fixed in the mind.—5. It discards useless construction of lines.—6. It can be taught by any teacher, even though there may have been no previous practice in Map-Drawing.—7. Any pupil old enough to study Geography can learn by this System, in a short time, to draw accurate maps.—8. The System is not the result of theory, but comes directly from the school-room. It has been thoroughly and successfully tested there, with all grades of pupils.—9. It is economical, as it requires no mapping plates. It gives the pupil the ability of rapidly drawing accurate maps.

Ripley's Map-Drawing,

Based on the Circle. One of the most efficient aids to the acquirement of a knowledge of Geography is the practice of map-drawing. It is useful for the same reason that the best exercise in orthography is the *writing* of difficult words. Sight comes to the aid of hearing, and a double impression is produced upon the memory. Knowledge becomes less mechanical and more intuitive. The student who has sketched the outlines of a country, and dotted the important places, is little likely to forget either. The impression produced may be compared to that of a traveller who has been over the ground, while more comprehensive and accurate in detail.

BOOK-KEEPING.

Folsom's Logical Book-keeping,
Folsom's Blanks to Book-keeping,

This treatise embraces the interesting and important discoveries of Prof. Folsom (of the Albany "Bryant & Stratton College"), the partial enunciation of which in lectures and otherwise has attracted so much attention in circles interested in commercial education.

After studying business phenomena for many years, he has arrived at the positive laws and principles that underlie the whole subject of Accounts; finds that the science is based in *Value* as a generic term; that value divides into *two classes* with varied species; that all the exchanges of values are reducible to nine equations; and that all the results of all these exchanges are limited to *thirteen* in number.

As accounts have been universally taught hitherto, without setting out from a radical analysis or definition of values, the science has been kept in great obscurity, and been made as difficult to impart as to acquire. On the new theory, however, these obstacles are chiefly removed. In reading over the first part of it, in which the governing laws and principles are discussed, a person with ordinary intelligence will obtain a fair conception of the *double entry* process of accounts. But when he comes to study thoroughly these laws and principles as there enunciated, and works out the examples and memoranda which elucidate the *thirteen results* of business, the student will neither fail in readily acquiring the science as it is, nor in becoming able intelligently to apply it in the interpretation of business.

Smith & Martin's Book-keeping,
Smith & Martin's Blanks,

This work is by a practical teacher and a practical book-keeper. It is of a thoroughly popular class, and will be welcomed by every one who loves to see theory and practice combined in an easy, concise, and methodical form.

The Single Entry portion is well adapted to supply a want felt in nearly all other treatises, which seem to be prepared mainly for the use of wholesale merchants, leaving retailers, mechanics, farmers, etc., who transact the greater portion of the business of the country, without a guide. The work is also commended, on this account, for general use in Young Ladies' Seminaries, where a thorough grounding in the simpler form of accounts will be invaluable to the future housekeepers of the nation.

The treatise on Double Entry Book-keeping combines all the advantages of the most recent methods, with the utmost simplicity of application, thus affording the pupil all the advantages of actual experience in the counting-house, and giving a clear comprehension of the entire subject through a judicious course of mercantile transactions.

The shape of the book is such that the transactions can be presented as in actual practice; and the simplified form of Blanks—three in number—adds greatly to the ease experienced in acquiring the science.

NATURAL SCIENCE.

FAMILIAR SCIENCE.

Norton & Porter's First Book of Science,

By eminent Professors of Yale College. Contains the principles of Natural Philosophy, Astronomy, Chemistry, Physiology, and Geology. Arranged on the Catechetical plan for primary classes and beginners.

Chambers' Treasury of Knowledge,

Progressive lessons upon—*first*, common things which lie most immediately around us, and first attract the attention of the young mind; *second*, common objects from the Mineral, Animal, and Vegetable kingdoms, manufactured articles, and miscellaneous substances; *third*, a systematic view of Nature under the various sciences. May be used as a Reader or Text-book.

NATURAL PHILOSOPHY.

Norton's First Book in Natural Philosophy,

By Prof. NORTON, of Yale College. Designed for beginners. Profusely illustrated and arranged on the Catechetical plan.

Peck's Ganot's Course of Nat. Philosophy,

The standard text-book of France, Americanized and popularized by Prof. PECK, of Columbia College. The most magnificent system of illustration ever adopted in an American school-book is here found. For intermediate classes.

Peck's Elements of Mechanics,

A suitable introduction to Bartlett's higher treatises on Mechanical Philosophy, and adequate in itself for a complete academical course.

Bartlett's SYNTHETIC, AND ANALYTIC, Mechanics,

Bartlett's Acoustics and Optics,

A system of Collegiate Philosophy, by Prof. BARTLETT, of West Point Military Academy.

Steele's 14 Weeks Course in Philos. (see p. 34)

Steele's Philosophical Apparatus,

Adequate to performing the experiments in the ordinary text-books. The articles will be sold separately, if desired. See special circular for details.

GEOLOGY.

Page's Elements of Geology,

A volume of Chambers' Educational Course. Practical, simple, and eminently calculated to make the study interesting.

Emmons' Manual of Geology,

The first Geologist of the country has here produced a work worthy of his reputation.

Steele's 14 Weeks Course (see p. 34)

Steele's Geological Cabinet,

Containing 125 carefully selected specimens. In four parts. Sold separately, if desired. See circular for details.

Peck's Ganot's Popular Physics.

TESTIMONIALS.

From PROF. ALONZO COLLIN, *Cornell College, Iowa.*

I am pleased with it. I have decided to introduce it as a text-book.

From H. F. JOHNSON, *President Madison College, Sharon, Miss.*

I am pleased with Peck's Ganot, and think it a magnificent book.

From PROF. EDWARD BROOKS, *Pennsylvania State Normal School.*

So eminent are its merits, that it will be introduced as the text-book upon elementary physics in this institution.

From H. H. LOCKWOOD, *Professor Natural Philosophy U. S. Naval Academy.*

I am so pleased with it that I will probably add it to a course of lectures given to the midshipmen of this school on physics.

From GEO. S. MACKIE, *Professor Natural History University of Nashville, Tenn.*

I have decided on the introduction of Peck's Ganot's Philosophy, as I am satisfied that it is the best book for the purposes of my pupils that I have seen, combining simplicity of explanation with elegance of illustration.

From W. S. MCRAE, *Superintendent Vevay Public Schools, Indiana.*

Having carefully examined a number of text-books on natural philosophy, I do not hesitate to express my decided opinion in favor of Peck's Ganot. The matter, style, and illustration eminently adapt the work to the popular wants.

From REV. SAMUEL MCKINNEY, D.D., *Pres't Austin College, Huntsville, Texas.*

It gives me pleasure to commend it to teachers. I have taught some classes with it as our text, and must say, for simplicity of style and clearness of illustration, I have found nothing as yet published of equal value to the teacher and pupil.

From C. V. SPEAR, *Principal Maplewood Institute, Pittsfield, Mass.*

I am much pleased with its ample illustrations by plates, and its clearness and simplicity of statement. It covers the ground usually gone over by our higher classes, and contains many fresh illustrations from life or daily occurrences, and new applications of scientific principles to such.

From J. A BANFIELD, *Superintendent Marshall Public Schools, Michigan.*

I have used Peck's Ganot since 1868, and with increasing pleasure and satisfaction each term. I consider it superior to any other work on physics in its adaptation to our high schools and academies. Its illustrations are superb– better than three times their number of pages of fine print.

From A. SCHUYLER, *Prof. of Mathematics in Baldwin University, Berea, Ohio.*

After a careful examination of Peck's Ganot's Natural Philosophy, and an actual test of its merits as a text-book, I can heartily recommend it as admirably adapted to meet the wants of the grade of students for which it is intended. Its diagrams and illustrations are *unrivaled*. We use it in the Baldwin University.

From D. C. VAN NORMAN, *Principal Van Norman Institute, New York.*

The Natural Philosophy of M. Ganot, edited by Prof. Peck, is, in my opinion, the best work of its kind, for the use intended, ever published in this country. Whether regarded in relation to the natural order of the topics, the precision and clearness of its definitions, or the fullness and beauty of its illustrations, it is certainly, I think, an advance.

☞ For many similar testimonials, see current numbers of the Illustrated Educational Bulletin.

NATURAL SCIENCE—Continued.

CHEMISTRY.

Porter's First Book of Chemistry,

Porter's Principles of Chemistry,

The above are widely known as the productions of one of the most eminent scientific men of America. The extreme simplicity in the method of presenting the science, while exhaustively treated, has excited universal commendation.

Darby's Text-Book of Chemistry,

Purely a Chemistry, divesting the subject of matters comparatively foreign to it (such as heat, light, electricity, etc.), but usually allowed to engross too much attention in ordinary school-books.

Gregory's Chemistry, (Organic and Inorganic, each)

The science exhaustively treated. For colleges and medical students.

Steele's Fourteen Weeks Course,

A successful effort to reduce the study to the limits of a *single term.* (See page 34.)

Steele's Chemical Apparatus,

Adequate to the performance of all the important experiments.

BOTANY.

Thinker's First Lessons in Botany,

For children. The technical terms are largely dispensed with in favor of an easy and familiar style adapted to the smallest learner.

Wood's Object-Lessons in Botany,

Wood's American Botanist and Florist,

Wood's New Class-Book of Botany,

The standard text-books of the United States in this department. In style they are simple, popular, and lively; in arrangement, easy and natural; in description, graphic and strictly exact. The Tables for Analysis are reduced to a perfect system. More are annually sold than of all others combined.

Wood's Plant Record,

A simple form of Blanks for recording observations in the field.

Wood's Botanical Apparatus,

A portable Trunk, containing Drying Press, Knife, Trowel, Microscope, and Tweezers, and a copy of Wood's Plant Record—composing a complete outfit for the collector.

Willis's Flora of New Jersey,

"*Catalogus Plantarum in Nova Cæsarea repertarum.*" This remarkable flora is of great interest to all botanists, and the Jersey Pines have been termed "the Mecca to which every young botanist hopes some day to make a pilgrimage." This work is indispensable to those botanizing on the ground, and is the most useful book of reference ever published for collectors in all parts of the country. It contains also a Botanical Directory, with addresses of living American botanists.

Young's Familiar Lessons,

Combining simplicity of diction with some degree of technical and scientific knowledge for intermediate classes. Specially adapted for Texas and the Southwest.

Darby's Southern Botany,

Embracing general Structural and Physiological Botany, with vegetable products, and descriptions of Southern plants, and a complete Flora of the Southern States.

NATURAL SCIENCE—Continued.

WOOD'S BOTANIES.

TESTIMONIALS.

From PROF. RICHARD OWEN, *University of Indiana.*

I am well pleased with the evidence of philosophical method exhibited in the general arrangement, as well as with the clearness of the explanations, the ready intelligibility of the analytical tables, and the illustrative aid furnished by the numerous and excellent wood-cuts. I design using the work as a text-book with my next class.

From PRIN. B. R. ANDERSON, *Columbus Union School, Wisconsin.*

I have examined several works with a view to recommending some good text-book on Botany, but I lay them all aside for "Wood's Botanist and Florist." The arrangement of the book is in my opinion excellent, its style fascinating and attractive, its treatment of the various departments of the science is thorough, and last, but far from unimportant, I like the topical form of the questions to each chapter. It seems to embrace the entire science. In fact, I consider it a complete, attractive, and exhaustive work.

From M. A. MARSHALL, *New Haven High School, Conn.*

It has all the excellencies of the well-known Class-Book of Botany by the same author in a smaller book. By a judicious system of condensation, the size of the Flora is reduced one-half, while no species are omitted, and many new ones are added. The descriptions of species are very brief, yet sufficient to identify the plant, and, when taken in connection with the generic description, form a complete description of the plant. The book as a whole will suit the wants of classes better than anything I have yet seen. The adoption of the Botanist and Florist would not require the exclusion of the Class-Book of Botany, as they are so arranged that both might be used by the same class.

From PROF. G. H. PERKINS, *University of Vermont and State Agricultural College.*

I can truly say that the more I examine Wood's Class-Book, the better pleased I am with it. In its illustrations, especially of particulars not easily observed by the student, and the clearness and compactness of its statements, as well as in the territory its flora embraces, it appears to me to surpass any other work I know of. The whole science, so far as it can be taught in a college course, is well presented, and rendered unusually easy of comprehension. The mode of analysis is excellent, avoiding as it does to a great extent those microscopic characters which puzzle the beginner, and using those that are obvious as far as possible. I regard the work as a most admirable one, and shall adopt it as a text-book another year.

AGRICULTURE.

Pendleton's Scientific Agriculture,

A text-book for colleges and schools; treats of the following topics: Anatomy and Physiology of Plants: Agricultural Meteorology; Soils as related to Physics; Chemistry of the Atmosphere; of Plants; of Soils; Fertilizers and Natural Manures; Animal Nutrition, etc. By E. M. PENDLETON, M. D., Prof. of Agriculture in the University of Georgia.

From President A. D. WHITE, *Cornell University.*

Dear Sir: I have examined your "Text-book of Agricultural Science," and it seems to me excellent in view of the purpose it is intended to serve. Many of your chapters interested me especially, and all parts of the work seem to combine scientific instruction with practical information in proportions dictated by sound common sense.

From President ROBINSON, *of Brown University.*

It is scientific in method as well as in matter, comprehensive in plan, natural and logical in order, compact and lucid in its statements, and must be useful both as a text-book in Agricultural colleges, and as a hand-book for intelligent planters and farmers.

NATURAL SCIENCE—Continued.

PHYSIOLOGY.

Jarvis' Elements of Physiology,

Jarvis' Physiology and Laws of Health,

The only books extant which approach this subject with a proper view of the true object of teaching Physiology in schools, viz., that scholars may know how to take care of their own health. In bold contrast with the abstract *Anatomies*, which children learn as they would Greek or Latin (and forget as soon), to *discipline the mind*, are these text-books, using the *science* as a secondary consideration, and only so far as is necessary for the comprehension of the *laws of health.*

Hamilton's Vegetable and Animal Physiology,

The two branches of the science combined in one volume lead the student to a proper comprehension of the Analogies of Nature.

Steele's Fourteen Weeks Course,

In the popular style, avoiding technical and purely scientific formulas. It contains beautiful and vivid illustrations, some of them colored, and a blackboard analysis of the skeleton. The sections on diseases and accidents, and their prompt home treatment, give the book great practical value (see p. 34).

ASTRONOMY.

Willard's School Astronomy,

By means of clear and attractive illustrations, addressing the eye in many cases by analogies, careful definitions of all necessary technical terms, a careful avoidance of verbiage and unimportant matter, particular attention to analysis, and a general adoption of the simplest methods. Mrs. Willard has made the best and most attractive *elementary* Astronomy extant.

McIntyre's Astronomy and the Globes,

A complete treatise for intermediate classes. Highly approved.

Bartlett's Spherical Astronomy,

The West Point course, for advanced classes, with applications to the current wants of Navigation, Geography, and Chronology.

Steele's Fourteen Weeks Course,

Reduced to a single term, and better adapted to school use than any work heretofore published. Not written for the information of scientific men, but for the inspiration of youth, the pages are not burdened with a multitude of figures which no memory could possibly retain. The whole subject is presented in a clear and concise form. (See p. 34.)

NATURAL HISTORY.

Carll's Child's Book of Natural History,

Illustrating the Animal, Vegetable, and Mineral Kingdoms, with applicatien to the Arts. For beginners. Beautifully and copiously illustrated.

ZOOLOGY.

Chambers' Elements of Zoology,

A complete and comprehensive system of Zoology, adapted for academic instruction, presenting a systematic view of the Animal Kingdom as a portion of external Nature.

Steele's Fourteen Weeks Course,

Notable for its superb and entertaining illustrations, which include every animal named; blackboard tables of classification and tabular review of the whole animal kingdom; interesting and characteristic facts and anecdotes; directions for collecting and preserving specimens, etc., etc. (See p. 34.)

Jarvis' Physiology and Laws of Health.

TESTIMONIALS.

From SAMUEL B. MCLANE, *Superintendent Public Schools, Keokuk, Iowa.*

I am glad to see a really good text-book on this much neglected branch. This is clear, concise, accurate, and eminently adapted to the *class-room.*

From WILLIAM F. WYERS, *Principal of Academy, West Chester, Pennsylvania.*

A thorough examination has satisfied me of its superior claims as a text-book to the attention of teacher and taught. I shall introduce it at once.

From H. R. SANFORD, *Principal of East Genesee Conference Seminary, N. Y.*

"Jarvis' Physiology" is received, and fully met our expectations. We immediately adopted it.

From ISAAC T. GOODNOW, *State Superintendent of Kansas—published in connection with the "School Law."*

"Jarvis' Physiology," a common-sense, practical work, with just enough of anatomy to understand the physiological portions. The last six pages, on Man's Responsibility for his own health, are worth the price of the book.

From D. W. STEVENS, *Superintendent Public Schools, Fall River, Mass.*

I have examined Jarvis' "Physiology and Laws of Health," which you had the kindness to send to me a short time ago. In my judgment it is far the best work of the kind within my knowledge. It has been adopted as a text-book in our public schools.

From HENRY G. DENNY, *Chairman Book Committee, Boston, Mass.*

The very excellent "Physiology" of Dr. Jarvis I had introduced into our High School, where the study had been temporarily dropped, believing it to be by far the best work of the kind that had come under my observation; indeed, the reintroduction of the study was delayed for some months, because Dr. Jarvis' book could not be had, and we were unwilling to take any other.

From PROF. A. P. PEABODY, D.D., LL.D., *Harvard University.*

* * I have been in the habit of examining school-books with great care, and I hesitate not to say that, of all the text-books on Physiology which have been given to the public, Dr. Jarvis' deserves the first place on the score of accuracy, thoroughness, method, simplicity of statement, and constant reference to topics of practical interest and utility.

From JAMES N. TOWNSEND, *Superintendent Public Schools, Hudson, N. Y.*

Every human being is appointed to take charge of his own body; and of all books written upon this subject, I know of none which will so well prepare one to do this as "Jarvis' Physiology"—that is, in so small a compass of matter. It considers the pure, simple *laws of health* paramount to science; and though the work is thoroughly scientific, it is divested of all cumbrous technicalities, and presents the subject of physical life in a manner and style really charming. It is unquestionably the best text-book on physiology I have ever seen. It is giving great satisfaction in the schools of this city, where it has been adopted as the standard.

From L. J. SANFORD, M.D., *Prof. Anatomy and Physiology in Yale College.*

Books on human physiology, designed for the use of schools, are more generally a failure perhaps than are school-books on most other subjects.

The great want in this department is met, we think, in the well-written treatise of Dr. Jarvis, entitled "Physiology and Laws of Health." * * The work is not too detailed nor too expansive in any department, and is clear and concise in all. It is not burdened with an excess of anatomical description, nor rendered discursive by many zoological references. Anatomical statements are made to the extent of qualifying the student to attend, understandingly, to an exposition of those functional processes which, collectively, make up health; thus the laws of health are enunciated, and many suggestions are given which, if heeded, will tend to its preservation.

☞ For further testimony of similar character, see current numbers of the Illustrated Educational Bulletin.

NATURAL SCIENCE.

"FOURTEEN WEEKS" IN EACH BRANCH.

By J. DORMAN STEELE, A. M.

Steele's 14 Weeks Course in Chemistry (New Ed.)
Steele's 14 Weeks Course in Astronomy
Steele's 14 Weeks Course in Philosophy
Steele's 14 Weeks Course in Geology
Steele's 14 Weeks Course in Physiology
Steele's 14 Weeks Course in Zoology

Our Text-Books in these studies are, as a general thing, dull and uninteresting. They contain from 400 to 600 pages of dry facts and unconnected details. They abound in that which the student cannot learn, much less remember. The pupil commences the study, is confused by the fine print and coarse print, and neither knowing exactly what to learn nor what to hasten over, is crowded through the single term generally assigned to each branch, and frequently comes to the close without a definite and exact idea of a single scientific principle.

Steele's Fourteen Weeks Courses contain only that which every well-informed person should know, while all that which concerns only the professional scientist is omitted. The language is clear, simple, and interesting, and the illustrations bring the subject within the range of home life and daily experience. They give such of the general principles and the prominent facts as a pupil can make familiar as household words within a single term. The type is large and open; there is no fine print to annoy; the cuts are copies of genuine experiments or natural phenomena, and are of fine execution.

In fine, by a system of condensation peculiarly his own, the author reduces each branch to the limits of a single term of study, while sacrificing nothing that is essential, and nothing that is usually retained from the study of the larger manuals in common use. Thus the student has rare opportunity to *economize his time*, or rather to employ that which he has to the best advantage.

A notable feature is the author's charming "style," fortified by an enthusiasm over his subject in which the student will not fail to partake. Believing that Natural Science is full of fascination, he has moulded it into a form that attracts the attention and kindles the enthusiasm of the pupil.

The recent editions contain the author's "Practical Questions" on a plan never before attempted in scientific text-books. These are questions as to the nature and cause of common phenomena, and are not directly answered in the text, the design being to test and promote an intelligent use of the student's knowledge of the foregoing principles.

Steele's General Key to his Works.

This work is mainly composed of Answers to the Practical Questions and Solutions of the Problems in the author's celebrated "Fourteen Weeks Courses" in the several sciences, with many hints to teachers, minor Tables, &c. Should be on every teacher's desk.

Steele's 14 Weeks in each Science.

TESTIMONIALS.

From L. A. BIKLE, *President N. C. College.*

I have not been disappointed. Shall take pleasure in introducing this series.

From J. F. COX, *Prest. Southern Female College, Ga.*

I am much pleased with these books, and expect to introduce them.

From J. R. BRANHAM, *Prin. Brownsville Female College, Tenn.*

They are capital little books, and are now in use in our institution.

From W. H. GOODALE, *Professor Readville Seminary, La.*

We are using your 14 Weeks Course, and are much pleased with them.

From W. A. BOLES, *Supt. Shelbyville Graded School, Ind.*

They are as entertaining as a story book, and much more improving to the mind.

From S. A. SNOW, *Principal of High School, Uxbridge, Mass.*

Steele's 14 Weeks Courses in the Sciences are a perfect success.

From JOHN W. DOUGHTY, *Newburg Free Academy, N. Y.*

I was prepared to find Prof. Steele's Course both attractive and instructive. My highest expectations have been fully realized.

From J. S. BLACKWELL, *Prest. Ghent College, Ky.*

Prof. Steele's unexampled success in providing for the wants of academic classes, has led me to look forward with high anticipations to his forthcoming issue.

From J. F. COOK, *Prest. La Grange College, Mo.*

I am pleased with the neatness of these books and the delightful diction. I have been teaching for years, and have never seen a lovelier little volume than the Astronomy.

From M. W. SMITH, *Prin. of High School, Morrison, Ill.*

They seem to me to be admirably adapted to the wants of a public school, containing, as they do, a sufficiently comprehensive arrangement of elementary principles to excite a healthy thirst for a more thorough knowledge of those sciences.

From J. D. BARTLEY, *Prin. of High School, Concord, N. H.*

They are just such books as I have looked for, viz., those of interesting style, not cumbersome and filled up with things to be omitted by the pupil, and yet sufficiently full of facts for the purpose of most scholars in these sciences in our high schools; there is nothing but what a pupil of average ability can thoroughly master.

From ALONZO NORTON LEWIS, *Principal of Parker Academy, Conn.*

I consider Steele's Fourteen Weeks Courses in Philosophy, Chemistry, &c., the *best* school-books that have been issued in this country.

As an introduction to the various branches of which they treat, and especially for that numerous class of pupils who have not the time for a more extended course, I consider them *invaluable.*

From EDWARD BROOKS, *Prin. State Normal School, Millersville, Pa.*

At the meeting of Normal School Principals, I presented the following resolution, which was unanimously adopted: "*Resolved,* That Steele's 14 Weeks Courses in Natural Philosophy and Astronomy, or an amount equivalent to what is contained in them, be adopted for use in the State Normal Schools of Pennsylvania." The works themselves will be adopted by at least three of the schools, and, I presume, by them all.

LITERATURE.

Gilman's First Steps in English Literature,

The character and plan of this exquisite little text-book may be best understood from an analysis of its contents:

INTRODUCTION. Chapter I, Historical; II, Definition of Terms; III, Languages of Europe, with Chart.

PERIOD OF IMMATURE ENGLISH, with Chart. Chapter IV, Original English; V, Broken English; VI, Dead English; VII, Reviving English.

PERIOD OF MATURE ENGLISH, with Chart. Chapter VIII, The Italian Influence; IX, Puritan Influence; X, French Influence; XI, Age of Pope; XII, Age of Johnson; XIII, Age of Poetical Romance; XIV, Age of Prose Romance.

The volume concludes with a Chart of Bible Translations, a Bibliography or Guide to General Reading, and other aids to the student.

Cleveland's Compendiums,

ENGLISH LITERATURE. AMERICAN LITERATURE.
ENGLISH LITERATURE OF THE XIXTH CENTURY.

In these volumes are gathered the cream of the literature of the English-speaking people for the school-room and the general reader. Their reputation is national. More than 125,000 copies have been sold.

Boyd's English Classics,

MILTON'S PARADISE LOST.	THOMSON'S SEASONS.
YOUNG'S NIGHT THOUGHTS.	POLLOK'S COURSE OF TIME.
COWPER'S TASK, TABLE TALK, &c.	LORD BACON'S ESSAYS.

This series of annotated editions of great English writers, in prose and poetry, is designed for critical reading and parsing in schools. Prof. J. R. Boyd proves himself an editor of high capacity, and the works themselves need no encomium. As auxiliary to the study of Belles Lettres, etc., these works have no equal.

Pope's Essay on Man,

Pope's Homer's Iliad,

The metrical translation of the great poet of antiquity, and the matchless "Essay on the Nature and State of Man," by ALEXANDER POPE, afford superior exercise in literature and parsing.

ÆSTHETICS.

Huntington's Manual of the Fine Arts,

A view of the rise and progress of Art in different countries, a brief account of the most eminent masters of Art, and an analysis of the principles of Art. It is complete in itself, or may precede to advantage the critical work of Lord Kames.

Boyd's Kames' Elements of Criticism,

The best edition of this standard work; without the study of which none may be considered proficient in the science of the Perceptions. No other study can be pursued with so marked an effect upon the taste and refinement of the pupil.

CLEVELAND'S COMPENDIUMS.

TESTIMONIALS.

From the New Englander.

This is the very best book of the kind we have ever examined.

From GEORGE B. EMERSON, Esq., *Boston.*

The Biographical Sketches are just and discriminating; the selections are admirable, and I have adopted the work as a text-book for my first class.

From PROF. MOSES COIT TYLER, *of the Michigan University.*

I have given your book a thorough examination, and am greatly delighted with it; and shall have great pleasure in directing the attention of my classes to a work which affords so admirable a bird's-eye view of recent "English Literature."

From the Saturday Review.

It acquaints the reader with the characteristic method, tone, and quality of all the chief notabilities of the period, and will give the careful student a better idea of the recent history of English Literature than nine educated Englishmen in ten possess.

From the Methodist Quarterly Review, New York.

This work is a transcript of the best American mind; a vehicle of the noblest American spirit. No parent who would introduce his child to a knowledge of our country's literature, and at the same time indoctrinate his heart in the purest principles, need fear to put this manual in the youthful hand.

From REV. C. PEIRCE, *Principal, West Newton, Mass.*

I do not believe the work is to be found from which, within the same limits, so much interesting and valuable information in regard to English writers and English literature of every age, can be obtained; and it deserves to find a place in all our high schools and academies, as well as in every private library.

From the Independent.

The work of selection and compilation—requiring a perfect familiarity with the whole range of English literature, a judgment clear and impartial, a taste at once delicate and severe, and a most sensitive regard to purity of thought or feeling—has been better accomplished in this than in any kindred volume with which we are acquainted.

POLITICAL ECONOMY.

Champlin's Lessons on Political Economy,

An improvement on previous treatises, being shorter, yet containing everything essential, with a view of recent questions in finance, etc., which is not elsewhere found.

From J. L. BOTHWELL, *Prin. Public School No. 14, Albany, N. Y.*

I have examined Champlin's Political Economy with much pleasure, and shall be pleased to put it into the hands of my pupils. In quantity and quality I think it superior to anything that I have examined.

From PRES. N. E. COBLEIGH, *East Tennessee Wesleyan University.*

An examination of Champlin's Political Economy has satisfied me that it is the book I want. For brevity and compactness, division of the subject, and clear statement, and for appropriateness of treatment, I consider it a better text-book than any other in the market.

From the Evening Mail, New York.

A new interest has been imparted to the science of political economy since we have been necessitated to raise such vast sums of money for the support of the government. The time, therefore, is favorable for the introduction of works like the above. This little volume of two hundred pages is intended for beginners, for the common school and academy. It is intended as a basis upon which to rear a more elaborate superstructure. There is nothing in the principles of political economy above the comprehension of average scholars, when they are clearly set forth. This seems to have been done by President Champlin in an easy and graceful manner.

ELOCUTION.

Thwing's Vocal Culture.

A Drill-Book for voice and gesture, by Rev. Prof. Thwing, of Brooklyn Tabernacle Lay College. Price 50 cts.

Taverner Graham's Reasonable Elocution,

Based upon the belief that true Elocution is the right interpretation of THOUGHT, and guiding the student to an intelligent appreciation, instead of a merely mechanical knowledge, of its rules.

Zachos' Analytic Elocution.

All departments of elocution—such as the analysis of the voice and the sentence, phonology, rhythm, expression, gesture, etc.—are here arranged for instruction in classes, illustrated by copious examples.

Sherwood's Self Culture.

Self-culture in reading, speaking, and conversation—a very valuable treatise to those who would perfect themselves in these accomplishments.

SPEAKERS.

Northend's Little Orator—Child's Speaker.

Two little works of the same grade but different selections, containing simple and attractive pieces for children under twelve years of age.

Northend's Young Declaimer.

Northend's National Orator.

Two volumes of Prose, Poetry, and Dialogue, adapted to intermediate and grammar classes respectively.

Northend's Entertaining Dialogues.

Extracts eminently adapted to cultivate the dramatic faculties, as well as entertain an audience.

Swett's Common School Speaker.

Selections from recent literature.

Raymond's Patriotic Speaker,

A superb compilation of modern eloquence and poetry, with original dramatic exercises. Nearly every eminent *living* orator is represented, without distinction of place or party.

COMPOSITION AND RHETORIC.

Brookfield's First Book in Composition,

Making the cultivation of this important art feasible for the smallest child. By a new method, to induce and stimulate thought.

Boyd's Composition and Rhetoric.

This work furnishes all the aid that is needful or can be desired in the various departments and styles of composition, both in prose and verse.

Day's Art of Rhetoric,

Noted for exactness of definition, clear limitation, and philosophical development of subject; the large share of attention given to Invention, as a branch of Rhetoric, and the unequalled analysis of style.

MIND AND MORALS.

Mahan's Intellectual Philosophy.

The subject exhaustively considered. The author has evinced learning, candor, and independent thinking.

Mahan's Science of Logic

A profound analysis of the laws of thought. The system possesses the merit being intelligible and self consistent. In addition to the author's carefully elaborated views, it embraces results attained by the ablest minds of Great Britain, Germany, and France, in this department.

Boyd's Elements of Logic

A systematic and philosophic condensation of the subject, fortified with additions from Watts, Abercrombie, Whately, &c.

Watts on the Mind

The Improvement of the Mind, by Isaac Watts, is designed as a guide for the attainment of useful knowledge. As a text-book it is unparalleled; and the discipline it affords cannot be too highly esteemed by the educator.

Peabody's Moral Philosophy

A short course; by the Professor of Christian Morals, Harvard University—for the Freshman Class and for High Schools.

Fletcher's Practical Ethics

A topical analysis of each of the Virtues and Graces, furnishing outlines for the pupil to illustrate from his own experience or reading.

Alden's Text-Book of Ethics

For young pupils. To aid in systematizing the ethical teachings of the Bible, and point out the coincidences between the instructions of the sacred volume and the sound conclusions of reason.

Willard's Morals for the Young

Lessons in conversational style to indicate the elements of moral philosophy. The study is made attractive by narratives and engravings.

GOVERNMENT.

Howe's Young Citizen's Catechism

Explaining the duties of District, Town, City, County, State, and United States Officers, with rules for parliamentary and commercial business.

Young's Lessons in Civil Government

A comprehensive view of Government, and abstract of the laws showing the rights, duties, and responsibilities of citizens.

Mansfield's Political Manual.

This is a complete view of the theory and practice of the General and State Governments, designed as a text-book. The author is an esteemed and able professor of constitutional law, widely known for his sagacious utterances in the public press.

Martin's Civil Government

Emanating from Massachusetts State Normal School. Historical and statistical. Each chapter summarized by a succinct statement of underlying principles on which good government is based.

MODERN LANGUAGE.

Illustrated Language Primers,

FRENCH AND ENGLISH. GERMAN AND ENGLISH.
SPANISH AND ENGLISH.

The names of common objects properly illustrated and arranged in easy lessons.

Ledru's French Fables,

Ledru's French Grammar,

Ledru's French Reader,

The author's long experience has enabled him to present the most thoroughly practical text-books extant, in this branch. The system of pronunciation (by phonetic illustration) is original with this author, and will commend itself to all American teachers, as it enables their pupils to secure an absolutely correct pronunciation without the assistance of a native master. This feature is peculiarly valuable also to "self-taught" students. The directions for ascertaining the gender of French nouns—also a great stumbling-block—are peculiar to this work, and will be found remarkably competent to the end proposed. The criticism of teachers and the test of the school-room is invited to this excellent series, with confidence.

Worman's French Echo,

To teach conversational French by actual practice, on an entirely new plan, which recognizes the importance of the student learning *to think* in the language which he speaks. It furnishes an extensive vocabulary of words and expressions in common use, and suffices to free the learner from the embarrassments which the peculiarities of his own tongue are likely to be to him, and to make him thoroughly familiar with the use of proper idioms.

Worman's German Echo,

On the same plan. See Worman's German Series, page 42.

Pujol's Complete French Class-Book,

Offers, in one volume, methodically arranged, a complete French course—usually embraced in series of from five to twelve books, including the bulky and expensive Lexicon. Here are Grammar, Conversation, and choice Literature—selected from the best French authors. Each branch is thoroughly handled; and the student, having diligently completed the course as prescribed, may consider himself, without further application, *au fait* in the most polite and elegant language of modern times.

Pujol's French Grammar, Exercises, Reader,

These volumes contain Part I, Parts II and III, and Part IV of the Complete Class-Book respectively, for the convenience of scholars and teachers. The Lexicon is bound with each part.

Maurice-Poitevin's Grammaire Francaise,

American schools are at last supplied with an American edition of this famous text-book. Many of our best institutions have for years been procuring it from abroad rather than forego the advantages it offers. The policy of putting students who have acquired some proficiency from the ordinary text-books, into a Grammar written in the vernacular, cannot be too highly commended. It affords an opportunity for finish and review at once; while embodying abundant practice of its own rules.

Joynes' French Pronunciation,

Willard's Historía de los Estados Unidos,

The History of the United States, translated by Professors TOLON and DE TORNOS, will be found a valuable, instructive, and entertaining reading-book for Spanish classes.

Pujol's Complete French Class-Book.

TESTIMONIALS.

From PROF. ELIAS PEISSNER, *Union College.*

I take great pleasure in recommending Pujol and Van Norman's French Class-Book, as there is no French grammar or class-book which can be compared with it in completeness, system, clearness, and general utility.

From EDWARD NORTH, *President of Hamilton College.*

I have carefully examined Pujol and Van Norman's French Class-Book, and am satisfied of its superiority, for college purposes, over any other heretofore used. We shall not fail to use it with our next class in French.

From A. CURTIS, *Pres't of Cincinnati Literary and Scientific Institute.*

I am confident that it may be made an instrument in conveying to the student, in from six months to a year, the art of speaking and writing the French with almost native fluency and propriety.

From HIRAM ORCUTT, A. M., *Prin. Glenwood and Tilden Ladies' Seminaries.*

I have used Pujol's French Grammar in my two seminaries, exclusively, for more than a year, and have no hesitation in saying that I regard it the best text-book in this department extant. And my opinion is confirmed by the testimony of Prof. F. De Launay and Mademoiselle Harindin. They assure me that the book is eminently accurate and practical, as tested in the school-room.

From PROF. THEO. F. DE FUMAT, *Hebrew Educational Institute, Memphis, Tenn.*

M. Pujol's French Grammar is one of the best and most practical works. The French language is chosen and elegant in style—modern and easy. It is far superior to the other French class-books in this country. The selection of the conversational part is very good, and will interest pupils; and being all completed in only one volume, it is especially desirable to have it introduced in our schools.

From PROF. JAMES H. WORMAN, *Bordentown Female College, N. J.*

The work is upon the same plan as the text-books for the study of French and English published in Berlin, for the study of those who have not the aid of a teacher, and these books are considered, by the first authorities, the best books. In most of our institutions, Americans teach the modern languages, and heretofore the trouble has been to give them a text-book that would dispose of the difficulties of the French pronunciation. This difficulty is successfully removed by P. and Van N., and I have every reason to believe it will soon make its way into most of our best schools.

From PROF. CHARLES S. DOD, *Ann Smith Academy, Lexington, Va.*

I cannot do better than to recommend "Pujol and Van Norman." For comprehensive and systematic arrangement, progressive and thorough development of all grammatical principles and idioms, with a due admixture of theoretical knowledge and practical exercise, I regard it as superior to any (other) book of the kind.

From A. A. FORSTER, *Prin. Pinehurst School, Toronto, C. W.*

I have great satisfaction in bearing testimony to M. Pujol's System of French Instruction, as given in his complete class-book. For clearness and comprehensiveness, adapted for all classes of pupils, I have found it superior to any other work of the kind, and have now used it for some years in my establishment with great success.

From PROF. OTTO FEDDER, *Maplewood Institute, Pittsfield, Mass.*

The conversational exercises will prove an immense saving of the hardest kind of labor to teachers. There is scarcely any thing more trying in the way of teaching language, than to rack your brain for short and easily intelligible bits of conversation, and to repeat them time and again with no better result than extorting at long intervals a doubting "oui," or a hesitating "non, monsieur"

☞ For further testimony of a similar character, see special circular, and current numbers of the Educational Bulletin.

GERMAN.

A COMPLETE COURSE IN THE GERMAN.

By JAMES H. WORMAN, A. M.

Worman's Elementary German Grammar
Worman's Complete German Grammar

These volumes are designed for intermediate and advanced classes respectively.

Though following the same general method with "Otto" (that of 'Gaspey'), our author differs essentially in its application. He is more practical, more systematic, more accurate, and besides introduces a number of invaluable features which have never before been combined in a German grammar.

Among other things, it may be claimed for Prof. Worman that he has been *the first* to introduce in an American text-book for learning German, a system of analogy and comparison with other languages. Our best teachers are also enthusiastic about his methods of inculcating the art of speaking, of understanding the spoken language, of correct pronunciation; the sensible and convenient original classification of nouns (in four declensions), and of irregular verbs, also deserves much praise. We also note the use of heavy type to indicate etymological changes in the paradigms and, in the exercises, the parts which specially illustrate preceding rules.

Worman's Elementary German Reader
Worman's Collegiate German Reader

The finest and most judicious compilation of classical and standard German Literature. These works embrace, progressively arranged, selections from the masterpieces of Goethe, Schiller, Korner, Seume, Uhland, Freiligrath, Heine, Schlegel, Holty, Lenau, Wieland, Herder, Lessing, Kant, Fichte, Schelling, Winkelmann, Humboldt, Ranke, Raumer, Menzel, Gervinus, &c., and contains complete Goethe's "Iphigenie," Schiller's "Jungfrau;" also, for instruction in modern conversational German, Benedix's "Eigensinn."

There are besides, Biographical Sketches of each author contributing, Notes, explanatory and philological (after the text), Grammatical References to all leading grammars, as well as the editor's own, and an adequate Vocabulary.

Worman's German Echo

Consists of exercises in colloquial style entirely in the German, with an adequate vocabulary, not only of words but of idioms. The object of the system developed in this work (and its companion volume in the French) is to break up the laborious and tedious habit of *translating the thoughts*, which is the student's most effectual bar to fluent conversation, and to lead him to *think in the language in which he speaks*. As the exercises illustrate scenes in actual life, a considerable knowledge of the manners and customs of the German people is also acquired from the use of this manual.

Worman's German Copy-Books, 3 Numbers,

On the same plan as the most approved systems for English penmanship, with progressive copies.

Worman's German Grammars.

TESTIMONIALS.

From Prof. R. W. JONES, *Petersburg Female College, Va.*

From what I have seen of the work it is almost certain *I shall introduce it* into this institution.

From Prof. G. CAMPBELL, *University of Minnesota.*

A valuable addition to our school-books, and will find many friends, and do great good.

From Prof. O. H P. CORPREW, *Mary Military Inst, Md.*

I am better pleased with them than any I have ever taught. I have already ordered through our booksellers.

From Prof. R. S. KENDALL, *Vernon Academy, Conn.*

I at once put the Elementary Grammar into the hands of a class of beginners, and have used it *with great satisfaction.*

From Prof. D. E. HOLMES, *Berlin Academy, Wis.*

Worman's German works are *superior.* I shall use them hereafter in my German classes.

From Prof. MAGNUS BUCHHOLTZ, *Hiram College, Ohio.*

I have examined the Complete Grammar, and find it *excellent.* You may rely that it will be used here.

From Prin. THOS. W. TOBEY, *Paducah Female Seminary, Ky.*

The Complete German Grammar is worthy of an extensive circulation. It is *admirably adapted* to the class-room. I shall use it.

From Prof. ALEX. ROSENSPITZ, *Houston Academy, Texas.*

Bearer will take and pay for 3 dozen copies. Mr. Worman deserves the approbation and esteem of the teacher and the thanks of the student.

From Prof. G. MALMENE, *Augusta Seminary, Maine.*

The Complete Grammar cannot fail to *give great satisfaction* by the simplicity of its arrangement, and by its completeness.

From Prin. OVAL PIRKEY, *Christian University, Mo.*

Just such a series as is positively necessary. I do hope the author will succeed as well in the French, &c., as he has in the German.

From Prof. S. D. HILLMAN, *Dickinson College, Pa.*

The class have lately commenced, and my examination thus far warrants me in saying that I regard it as *the best* grammar for instruction in the German.

From Prin. SILAS LIVERMORE, *Bloomfield Seminary, Mo.*

I have found a classically and scientifically educated Prussian gentleman whom I propose to make German instructor. I have shown him both your German grammars. He has expressed *his approbation* of them generally.

From Prof. Z. TEST, *Howland School for Young Ladies, N. Y.*

I shall introduce the books. From a cursory examination I have no hesitation in pronouncing the Complete Grammar *a decided improvement* on the text-books at present in use in this country.

From Prof. LEWIS KISTLER, *Northwestern University, Ill.*

Having looked through the Complete Grammar with some care I must say that you have produced *a good book;* you may be awarded with this gratification—that your grammar promotes the facility of learning the German language, and of becoming acquainted with its rich literature.

From Pres. J. P. ROUS, *Stockwell Collegiate Inst., Ind.*

I supplied a class with the Elementary Grammar, and it gives *complete satisfaction.* The conversational and reading exercises are well calculated to illustrate the principles, and lead the student on an easy yet thorough course. I think the Complete Grammar equally attractive.

THE CLASSICS.

LATIN.

Silber's Latin Course,

The book contains an Epitome of Latin Grammar, followed by Reading Exercises, with explanatory Notes and copious References to the leading Latin Grammars, and also to the Epitome which precedes the work. Then follow a Latin-English Vocabulary and Exercises in Latin Prose Composition, being thus complete in itself, and a very suitable work to put in the hands of one about to study the language.

Searing's Virgil's Æneid,

It contains only the first six books of the Æneid. 2. A very carefully constructed Dictionary. 3. Sufficiently copious Notes. 4. Grammatical references to four leading Grammars. 5. Numerous Illustrations of the highest order, 6. A superb Map of the Mediterranean and adjacent countries. 7. Dr. S. H. Taylor's "Questions on the Æneid." 8. A Metrical Index, and an Essay on the Poetical Style. 9. A photographic *fac simile* of an early Latin M.S. 10. The text according to Jahn, but paragraphed according to Ladewig. 11. Superior mechanical execution.

"Have examined it with great pleasure and can safely say it is the best edition of Virgil with which I am acquainted."—PROF. LESLIE WAGGENER, *Bethel College, Ky.*

"Am *very* much pleased. In following points think it surpasses: instructive illustrations, pointed and sensible notes where they are convenient to use, and a vocabulary that gives the *derivation of Latin words.*"—PRIN. E. L. RICHARDSON, *Addison Union School, N. Y.*

"A fine specimen of art, and edited in a *masterly manner.*"—SUPT. W. C ROTE, *Lawrence Public Schools, Kansas.*

"Of Searing's Virgil I cannot speak in too high terms. While as a text-book it contains as many excellences as any I have ever seen, the fineness of the paper and the beauty of typography and exceeding neatness make it an ornament for the centre-table."—PRIN. E. C. SPALDING, *Nunda Academy, N. Y.*

☞ *For further testimonials, see page 45.*

Blair's Latin Pronunciation,

An inquiry into the proper sounds of the Language during the Classical Period. By Prof. Blair, of Hampden Sidney College, Va.

GREEK.

Crosby's Greek Grammar,
Crosby's Xenophon's Anabasis,

MYTHOLOGY.

Dwight's Grecian and Roman Mythology.

School edition, University edition,

A knowledge of the fables of antiquity, thus presented in a systematic form, is as indispensable to the student of general literature as to him who would peruse intelligently the classical authors. The mythological allusions so frequent in literature are readily understood with such a Key as this.

SEARING'S VIRGIL.

SPECIMEN FRAGMENTS OF LETTERS.

"I adopt it gladly."—PRIN. V. DABNEY, *Loudoun School, Va.*

"I like Searing's Virgil."—PROF. BRISTOL, *Ripon College, Wis.*

"Meets my desires very thoroughly."—PROF. CLARK, *Berea College, Ohio.*

"Superior to any other edition of Virgil."—PRES. HALL, *Macon College, Mo.*

"Shall adopt it at once."—PRIN. B. P. BAKER, *Searcy Female Institute, Ark.*

"Your Virgil is a *beauty.*"—PROF. W. H. DE MOTTE, *Illinois Female College.*

"After use, I regard it the best."—PRIN. G. H. BARTON, *Rome Academy, N. Y.*

"We like it better every day."—PRIN. R. K. BUEHRLE, *Allentown Academy, Pa.*

"I am delighted with your Virgil."—PRIN. W. T. LEONARD, *Pierce Academy, Mass.*

"Stands well the test of class-room."—PRIN. F. A. CHASE, *Lyons Col. Inst., Iowa.*

"I do not see how it can be improved."—PRIN. N. F. D. BROWNE, *Charl. Hall, Md.*

"The most complete that I have seen."—PRIN. A. BROWN, *Columbus High School, Ohio.*

"Our Professor of Language very highly approves."—SUPT. J. G. JAMES, *Texas Military Institute.*

"It responds to a want long felt by teachers. It is beautiful and complete."—PROF. BROOKS, *University of Minnesota.*

"The ideal edition. We want a few more classics of the same sort."—PRIN. C. F. P. BANCROFT, *Lookout Mountain Institute, Tenn.*

"I certainly have never seen an edition so complete with important requisites for a student, nor with such fine text and general mechanical execution."—PRES. J. R. PARK, *University of Deseret, Utah.*

"It is charming both in its design and execution. And, on the whole, I think it is the best thing of the kind that I have seen."—PROF. J. DE F. RICHARDS, *Pres. pro tem. of University of Alabama.*

"In beauty of execution, in judicious notes, and in an adequate vocabulary, it merits all praise. I shall recommend its introduction."—PRES. J. K. PATTERSON, *Kentucky Agricultural and Mechanical College.*

"Containing a good vocabulary and judicious notes, it will enable the industrious student to acquire an accurate knowledge of the most interesting part of Virgil's works."—PROF. J. T. DUNKLIN, *East Alabama College.*

"It wants no element of completeness. It is by far the best classical text-book with which I am acquainted. The notes are just right. They help the student when he most needs help."—PRIN. C. A. BUNKER, *Caledonia Grammar School, Vt.*

"I have examined Searing's Virgil with interest, and find that it more nearly meets the wants of students than that of any other edition with which I am acquainted. I am able to introduce it to some extent at once."—PRIN. J. EASTER, *East Genesee Conference Seminary.*

"I have been wishing to get a sight of it, and it exceeds my expectations. It is a beautiful book in every respect, and bears evidence of careful and critical study. The engravings add instruction as well as interest to the work. I shall recommend it to my classes."—PRIN. CHAS. H. CHANDLER, *Glenwood Ladies' Seminary.*

"A. S. Barnes & Co. have published an edition of the first six books of Virgil's Æneid, which is superior to its predecessors in several respects. The publishers have done a good service to the cause of classical education, and the book deserves a large circulation."—PROF. GEORGE W COLLORD, *Brooklyn Polytechnic, N. Y.*

"My attention was called to Searing's Virgil by the fact of its containing a vocabulary which would obviate the necessity of procuring a lexicon. But use in the class-room has impressed me most favorably with the accuracy and just proportion of its notes, and the general excellence of its grammatical suggestions. The general character of the book in its paper, its typography, and its engravings is highly commendable, and the fac-simile manuscript is a valuable feature. I take great pleasure in commending the book to all who do not wish a complete edition of Virgil. It suits our short school courses admirably."—HENRY L. BOLTWOOD, *Master of Princeton High School, Ill.*

RECORDS.

Cole's Self-Reporting Class-Book,

For saving the Teacher's labor in averaging. At each opening are a full set of Tables showing any scholar's standing at a glance and entirely obviating the necessity of computation.

Tracy's School-Record, Pocket edition,

For keeping a simple but exact record of Attendance, Deportment, and Scholarship. The larger edition contains also a Calendar, an extensive list of Topics for Compositions and Colloquies, Themes for Short Lectures, Suggestions to Young Teachers, etc.

Brooks' Teacher's Register,

Presents at one view a record of Attendance, Recitations, and Deportment for the whole term.

Carter's Record and Roll-Book,

This is the most complete and convenient Record offered to the public. Besides the usual spaces for General Scholarship, Deportment, Attendance, etc., for each name and day, there is a space in red lines enclosing six minor spaces in blue for recording Recitations.

National School Diary,

A little book of blank forms for weekly report of the standing of each scholar, from teacher to parent. A great convenience.

REWARDS.

National School Currency,

A little box containing certificates in the form of Money. The most entertaining and stimulating system of school rewards. The scholar is paid for his merits and fined for his shortcomings. Of course the most faithful are the most successful in business. In this way the use and value of money and the method of keeping accounts are also taught. One box of Currency will supply a school of fifty pupils.

TACTICS.

The Boy Soldier,

Complete Infantry Tactics for Schools, with illustrations, for the use of those who would introduce this pleasing relaxation from the confining duties of the desk.

CHARTS.

McKenzie's Elocutionary Chart,

Baade's Reading Case,

This remarkable piece of school-room furniture is a receptacle containing a number of primary cards. By an arrangement of slides on the front, one sentence at a time is shown to the class. Twenty-eight thousand transpositions may be made, affording a variety of progressive exercises which no other piece of apparatus offers. One of its best features is, that it is so exceedingly simple as not to get out of order, while it may be operated with one finger.

Marcy's Eureka Tablet,

A new system for the Alphabet, by which it may be taught without fail in nine lessons.

Scofield's School Tablets,

On Five Cards, exhibiting Ten Surfaces. These Tablets teach Orthography, Reading, Object-Lessons, Color, Form, etc.

Watson's Phonetic Tablets,

Four Cards, and Eight Surfaces; teaching Pronunciation and Elocution phonetically—for class exercises.

Page's Normal Chart,

The whole science of Elementary Sounds tabulated. By the author of Page's Theory and Practice of Teaching.

Clark's Grammatical Chart,

Exhibits the whole Science of Language in one comprehensive diagram.

Davies' Mathematical Chart,

Mathematics made simple to the eye.

Monteith's Reference Maps, School series, Grand series,

Eight Numbers. Mounted on Rollers. Names all laid down in small type, so that to the pupil at a short distance they are Outline Maps, while they serve as *their own key* to the teacher.

Willard's Chronographers,

Historical. Four Numbers. Ancient Chronographer; English Chronographer; American Chronographer; Temple of Time (general). Dates and Events represented to the eye.

APPARATUS.

Harrington's Geometrical Blocks,

These patented blocks are *hinged*, so that each form can be dissected.

Harrington's Fractional Blocks,

Steele's Chemical Apparatus,

Steele's Philosophical Apparatus, (see p.28)

Steele's Geological Cabinet, (see p.28)

Wood's Botanical Apparatus, (see p.30)

Bock's Physiological Apparatus,

MUSIC.

The National School Singer,

Bright, new music for the day school, embracing Song Lessons, Exercise Songs, Songs of Study, Order, Promptness and Obedience, of Industry and Nature, Patriotic and Temperance Songs, Opening and Closing Songs; in fact, everything needed in the school-room. By an eminent Musician and Composer.

Jepson's Music Readers. 3 vols.

These are not books from which children simply learn songs, parrot-like, but teach the subject progressively—the scholar learning to read music by methods similar to those employed in teaching him to read printed language. Any teacher, however ignorant of music, provided he can, upon trial, simply sound the scale, may teach it without assistance, and will end by being a good singer himself. The "Elementary Music Reader," or first volume, fully develops the system. The two companion volumes carry the same method into the higher grades, but their use is not essential.

The First Reader is also published in three parts, at 30 cents each, for those who prefer them in that form.

Bartley's School Hymn and Tune Book.

A selection of appropriate Hymns, of an unsectarian character, carefully classified and set to popular and "singable" Tunes, for opening and closing exercises. The National, Anniversary, and Parting Hymns form a valuable feature.

Nash & Bristow's Cantara,

The first volume is a complete musical text-book for schools of every grade. No. 2 is a choice selection of Solos and Part Songs. The authors are Directors of Music in the public schools of New York City, in which these books are the standard of instruction.

The Polytechnic

Collection of Part Songs for High and Normal Schools and Clubs. This work contains a quantity of exceedingly valuable material, heretofore accessible only in sheet form or scattered in numerous and costly works. The collection of "College Songs" is a very attractive feature.

Curtis' Little Singer,—School Vocalist,

Kingsley's School-Room Choir,—Young Ladies' Harp,

Hager's Echo (A Cantata).

DEVOTION.

Brooks' School Manual of Devotion,

This volume contains daily devotional exercises, consisting of a hymn, selections of Scripture for alternate reading by teacher and pupils, and a prayer. Its value for opening and closing school is apparent.

Brooks' School Harmonist,

Contains appropriate *tunes* for each hymn in the "Manual of Devotion" described above.

A. S. BARNES & CO.'S CATALOGUE.

DEPARTMENT OF GENERAL LITERATURE.

PRICES INCLUDING POSTAGE.

THE TEACHERS' LIBRARY.

Object Lessons—Welch, - - - - - $1 00

This is a complete exposition of the popular modern system of "object-teaching," for teachers of primary classes.

Theory and Practice of Teaching—Page, - - 1 50

This volume has, without doubt, been read by two hundred thousand teachers, and its popularity remains undiminished—large editions being exhausted yearly. It was the pioneer, as it is now the patriarch, of professional works for teachers.

The Graded School—Wells, - - - - - - 1 25

The proper way to organize graded schools is here illustrated. The author has availed himself of the best elements of the several systems prevalent in Boston, New York, Philadelphia, Cincinnati, St. Louis, and other cities.

The Normal—Holbrook, - - - - - - 1 50

Carries a working school on its visit to teachers, showing the most approved methods of teaching all the common branches, including the technicalities, explanations, demonstrations, and definitions introductory and peculiar to each branch.

School Management—Holbrook, - - - - - 1 50

Treating of the Teacher's Qualifications; How to overcome Difficulties in Self and Others; Organization; Discipline; Methods of inciting Diligence and Order; Strategy in Management; Object Teaching.

The Teachers' Institute—Fowle, - - - - - 1 25

This is a volume of suggestions inspired by the author's experience at institutes, in the instruction of young teachers. A thousand points of interest to this class are most satisfactorily dealt with.

Schools and Schoolmasters—Dickens, - - - - 1 25

Appropriate selections from the writings of the great novelist.

The Metric System—Davies, - - - - - 1 50

Considered with reference to its general introduction, and embracing the views of John Quincy Adams and Sir John Herschel.

The Student; The Educator—Phelps, - - each, 1 50

The Discipline of Life—Phelps, - - - - - 1 75

The authoress of these works is one of the most distinguished writers on education; and they cannot fail to prove a valuable addition to the School and Teachers' Libraries, being in a high degree both interesting and instructive.

A Scientific Basis of Education—Hecker, - - 2 50

Adaptation of study and classification by temperaments.

Teachers' Hand-Book — Phelps - - - - - $1 50

By Wm. F. Phelps, Principal of Minnesota State Normal School. Embracing the objects, history, organization and management of Teachers' Institutes, followed by Methods of Teaching, in detail, for all the fundamental branches. Every young teacher, every practical teacher, every experienced teacher even, needs this book.

From the New York Tribune.

"The discipline of the school should prepare the child for the discipline of life. The country schoolmaster, accordingly, holds a position of vital interest to the destiny of the republic, and should neglect no means for the wise and efficient discharge of his significant functions. This is the key-note of the present excellent volume. In view of the supreme importance of the teacher's calling, Mr. Phelps has presented an elaborate system of instruction in the elements of learning, with a complete detail of methods and processes, illustrated with an abundance of practical examples and enforced by judicious counsels, which may serve as an aid to the teacher in the performance of his arduous duties, and in the attainment of the highest excellence in his profession. The author's directions may not always be accepted without challenge by experienced instructors, who, however, are encouraged to think for themselves; but they are always suggestive, and cannot fail to be of signal value to those who are just entering upon their profession and beginning to comprehend its difficulties, as well as to discover its secrets."

American Education — Mansfield - - - - - 1 50

A treatise on the principles and elements of education, as practised in this country, with ideas towards distinctive republican and Christian education.

American Institutions — De Tocqueville - - - - 1 50

A valuable index to the genius of our Government.

Universal Education — Mayhew - - - - - 1 75

The subject is approached with the clear, keen perception of one who has observed its necessity, and realized its feasibility and expediency alike. The redeeming and elevating power of improved common schools constitutes the inspiration of the volume.

Higher Christian Education — Dwight - - - - 1 50

A treatise on the principles and spirit, the modes, directions and results of all true teaching; showing that right education should appeal to every element of enthusiasm in the teacher's nature.

Oral Training Lessons — Barnard - - - - - 1 00

The object of this very useful work is to furnish material for instructors to impart orally to their classes, in branches not usually taught in common schools, embracing all departments of Natural Science and much general knowledge.

Lectures on Natural History — Chadbourne - - 75

Affording many themes for oral instruction in this interesting science—especially in schools where it is not pursued as a class exercise.

Outlines of Mathematical Science — Davies - - 1 00

A manual suggesting the best methods of presenting mathematical instruction on the part of the teacher, with that comprehensive view of the whole which is necessary to the intelligent treatment of a part, in science.

Nature and Utility of Mathematics — Davies - - 1 50

An elaborate and lucid exposition of the principles which lie at the foundation of pure mathematics, with a highly ingenious application of their results to the development of the essential idea of the different branches of the science.

Mathematical Dictionary — Davies and Peck - - 5 00

This cyclopædia of mathematical science defines, with completeness, precision, and accuracy, every technical term; thus constituting a popular treatise on each branch, and a general view of the whole subject.

Liberal Education of Women—Orton . . *$1 50

Treats of "the demand and the method;" being a compilation of the best and most advanced thought on this subject, by the leading writers and educators in England and America. Edited by a Professor in Vassar College.

Education Abroad—Northrop *1 50

A thorough discussion of the advantages and disadvantages of sending American children to Europe to be educated; also, Papers on Legal Prevention of Illiteracy, Study and Health, Labor as an Educator, and other kindred subjects. By the Hon. Secretary of Education for Connecticut.

The Teacher and the Parent—Northend . . *1 50

A treatise upon common-school education, designed to lead teachers to view their calling in its true light, and to stimulate them to fidelity.

The Teachers' Assistant—Northend *1 50

A natural continuation of the author's previous work, more directly calculated for daily use in the administration of school discipline and instruction.

School Government—Jewell *1 50

Full of advanced ideas on the subject which its title indicates. The criticisms upon current theories of punishment and schemes of administration have excited general attention and comment.

Grammatical Diagrams—Jewell *1 00

The diagram system of teaching grammar explained, defended, and improved The curious in literature, the searcher for truth, those interested in new inventions, as well as the disciples of Prof. Clark, who would see their favorite theory fairly treated, all want this book. There are many who would like to be made familiar with this system before risking its use in a class. The opportunity is here afforded.

The Complete Examiner—Stone *1 25

Consists of a series of questions on every English branch of school and academic instruction, with reference to a given page or article of leading text-books where the answer may be found in full. Prepared to aid teachers in securing certificates, pupils in preparing for promotion, and teachers in selecting review questions.

School Amusements—Root *1 50

To assist teachers in making the school interesting, with hints upon the management of the school-room. Rules for military and gymnastic exercises are included. Illustrated by diagrams.

Institute Lectures—Bates *1 50

These lectures, originally delivered before institutes, are based upon various topics in the departments of mental and moral culture. The volume is calculated to prepare the will, awaken the inquiry, and stimulate the thought of the zealous teacher.

Method of Teachers' Institutes—Bates . . . *75

Sets forth the best method of conducting institutes, with a detailed account of the object, organization, plan of instruction, and true theory of education on which such instruction should be based.

History and Progress of Education *1 50

The systems of education prevailing in all nations and ages, the gradual advance to the present time, and the bearing of the past upon the present in this regard, are worthy of the careful investigation of all concerned in education.

THE SCHOOL LIBRARY.

The two elements of instruction and entertainment were never more happily combined than in this collection of standard books. Children and adults alike will here find ample food for the mind, of the sort that is easily *digested*, while not degenerating to the level of modern romance.

LIBRARY OF LITERATURE.

Milton's Paradise Lost. Boyd's Illustrated Ed., $1 60

Young's Night Thoughts . . . . do. . . 1 60

Cowper's Task, Table Talk, &c. . do. . . 1 60

Thomson's Seasons . . . . do. . . 1 60

Pollok's Course of Time . . . . do. . . 1 60

These works, models of the best and purest literature, are beautifully illustrated, and notes explain all doubtful meanings.

Lord Bacon's Essays (Boyd's Edition) . . . 1 60

Another grand English classic, affording the highest example of purity in language and style.

The Iliad of Homer. Translated by POPE. . . 80

Those who are unable to read this greatest of ancient writers in the original, should not fail to avail themselves of this metrical version.

Compendium of Eng. Literature—Cleveland, 2 25

English Literature of XIXth Century do. 2 25

Compendium of American Literature do. 2 25

Nearly one hundred and fifty thousand volumes of Prof. CLEVELAND'S inimitable compendiums have been sold. Taken together they present a complete view of literature. To the man who can afford but a few books these will supply the place of an extensive library. From commendations of the very highest authorities the following extracts will give some idea of the enthusiasm with which the works are regarded by scholars:

With the Bible and your volumes one might leave libraries without very painful regret.—The work cannot be found from which in the same limits so much interesting and valuable information may be obtained.—Good taste, fine scholarship, familiar acquaintance with literature, unwearied industry, tact acquired by practice, an interest in the culture of the young, and regard for truth, purity, philanthropy and religion are united in Mr. Cleveland.—A judgment clear and impartial, a taste at once delicate and severe.—The biographies are just and discriminating.—An admirable bird's-eye view.—Acquaints the reader with the characteristic method, tone, and quality of each writer.—Succinct, carefully written, and wonderfully comprehensive in detail, etc., etc.

Milton's Poetical Works—CLEVELAND . . . 2 25

This is the very best edition of the great Poet. It includes a life of the author, notes, dissertations on each poem, a faultless text, and is *the only* edition of Milton with a complete verbal Index.

LIBRARY OF HISTORY.

Seven Historic Ages—Gilman, - - - - $1 00

Or, Talks about Kings, Queens, and Barbarians. These delightful sketches of notable events stir the imagination of the young reader, and give him a taste for further historical reading. Illustrated.

Outlines of General History—Gilman, - - - 1 25

The number of facts which the author has compressed into these outline sketches is really surprising; the chapters on the Middle Ages and Feudalism afford striking examples of his power of succinct but comprehensive statement. In his choice of representative periods and events in the histories of Nations he shows very sound judgment, and his characterization of conspicuous historical figures is accurate and impartial.

Great Events of History—Collier, - - - - - 1 50

This celebrated work, edited for American readers by Prof. O. R. Willis, gives, in a series of pictures, a pleasantly readable and easily remembered view of the Christian era. Each chapter is headed by its central point of interest to afford association for the mind. Delineations of life and manners at different periods are interwoven. A geographical appendix of great value is added.

History of England—Lancaster, - - - - - 1 50

An arrangement of the essential facts of English History in the briefest manner consistent with clearness. With a fine Map.

History of Liberty—Aiken, - - - - - - 1 00

Explaining the growth of the "fair consummate flower" of freedom in America as the result of centuries of trial and experieuce in the Old World.

Critical History of the Civil War—Mahan, - - 3 00

A logical analysis of campaigns and battles, and the causes of victory and defeat. By Dr. Asa Mahan, first President of Oberlin College. Dr. Mahan never forgets that history is "philosophy teaching by examples," and his work should be a text-book for American youth.

History of Europe—Alison, - - - - - - 2 50

A reliable and standard work, which covers with clear, connected, and complete narrative the eventful occurrences of the years A. D. 1789 to 1815, being mainly a history of the career of Napoleon Bonaparte.

History of Rome—Ricord, - - - - - - 1 75

An entertaining narrative for the young. Illustrated. Embracing successively, The Kings; The Republic; The Empire.

Ecclesiastical History—Marsh, - - - - - - 2 00

A history of the Church in all ages, with a comprehensive review of all forms of religion from the creation of the world. No other source affords, in the same compass, the information here conveyed.

History of the Ancient Hebrews—Mills, - - - 1 75

The record of "God's people" from the call of Abraham to the destruction of Jerusalem; gathered from sources sacred and profane.

The Mexican War—Mansfield, - - - - - 1 50

A history of its origin, and a detailed account of its victories; with official despatches, the treaty of peace, and valuable tables. Illustrated.

Early History of Michigan—Sheldon, - - - 2 50

A work of value and deep interest to the people of the West. Compiled under the supervision of Hon. Lewis Cass. Portraits.

History of Texas—Baker, - - - - - - 1 25

A pithy and interesting resumé. Copiously illustrated. The State constitution and extracts from the speeches and writings of eminent Texans are appended.

NEW LIBRARY OF HISTORY.

Barnes' Centenary History, - - - - - - *$6 00

"*One Hundred Years of American Independence.*" This superbly illustrated work, by the author of "Barnes' Brief Histories" (for schools), is appropriately issued in the "centennial year" (1876). An extended Introduction brings down the history from the earliest times. The leading idea is to make American History *popular* for the masses, and especially with the young. The style is therefore life-like and vivid, carrying the reader along by the sweep of the story as in a novel, so that when he begins an account of an important event he cannot very well lay down the book until he finishes.

☞ *Sold only by subscription.*

Lamb's History of New York City.

One of the most important works ever issued. It opens with a brief outline of the condition of the old world prior to the settlement of the new, and proceeds to give a careful analysis of the two great Dutch Commercial Corporations to which New York owes its origin. It sketches the rise and growth of the little colony on Manhattan Island; describes the Indian Wars with which it was afflicted; gives color and life to its Dutch rulers; paints its subjugation by the English, its after vicissitudes, the Revolution of 1689; in short, it leads the reader through one continuous chain of events down to the American Revolution. Then, gathering up the threads, the author gives an artistic and comprehensive account of the progress of the City, in extent, education, culture, literature, art, and political and commercial importance, during the last century. Prominent persons are introduced in all the different periods, with choice bits of family history, and glimpses of social life. The work contains maps of the City in the different decades, and several rare portraits from original paintings, which have never before been engraved. The illustrations, about 250 in number, are all of an interesting and highly artistic character.

The work is now being published, by subscription only, in about 30 parts, at 50 cents each.

Carrington's Battles of the Revolution, - - - $6 00

A careful description and analysis of every engagement of the War for Independence, with topographical charts prepared from personal surveys by the author, a veteran officer of the U. S. Army, and Professor of Military Science in Wabash College.

Baker's Texas Scrap-Book, - - - - - $5 00

Comprising the History, Biography, Literature, and Miscellany of Texas and its people. A valuable collection of material, anecdotical and statistical, which is not to be found in any other form. The work is handsomely illustrated. (Sheep, $6.00.)

LIBRARY OF REFERENCE.

Home Cyclopædia of Literature and Fine Arts, - $3 00

A complete index to all terms employed in belles lettres, philosophy, theology, law, mythology, painting, music, sculpture, architecture, and all kindred arts.

The Rhyming Dictionary—Walker, - - - 1 25

A serviceable manual to composers, being a complete index of allowable rhymes.

The Topical Lexicon—Williams, - - - - 1 75

The useful terms of the English language *classified by subjects* and arranged according to their affinities of meaning, with etymologies, definitions, and illustrations. A very entertaining and instructive work.

Mathematical Dictionary—Davies and Peck, - - 5 00

A thorough compendium of the science, with illustrations and definitions.

www.ingramcontent.com/pod-product-compliance
Lightning Source LLC
LaVergne TN
LVHW020236110826
845151LV00003B/942